W9-COL-199

If the Irish Ran the World
Montserrat, 1630–1730

What would have happened if the Irish had conquered and controlled a vast empire? Would they have been more humane rulers than the English? Using the Caribbean island of Montserrat as a case study of "Irish" imperialism, Donald Akenson addresses these questions and provides a detailed history of the island during its first century as a European colony.

Montserrat, although part of England's empire, was settled largely by the Irish and provides an opportunity to view the interaction of Irish emigrants with English imperialism in a situation where the Irish were not a small minority among white settlers. Within this context Akenson explores whether Irish imperialism on Montserrat differed from English imperialism in other colonies.

Akenson reveals that the Irish proved to be as effective and as unfeeling colonists as the English and the Scottish, despite the long history of oppression in Ireland. He debunks the myth of the "nice" slave holder and the view that indentured labour prevailed in the West Indies in the seventeenth century. He also shows that the long-held habit of ignoring ethnic strife within the white ruling classes in the West Indies is misconceived.

If the Irish Ran the World provides interesting insights into whether ethnicity was central to the making of the colonial world and the usefulness of studies of seventeenth- and eighteenth-century English imperialism in the Americas.

DONALD HARMAN AKENSON is professor of history, Queen's University. His most recent books include *Conor: A Biography of Conor Cruise O'Brien* (McGill-Queen's), winner of the Trillium Award, and *God's Peoples: Covenant and Land in South Africa, Israel, and Ulster* (McGill-Queen's), winner of the Grawemeyer Award.

If the Irish Ran the World

Montserrat, 1630–1730

DONALD HARMAN AKENSON

Being the Joanne Goodman Lectures of
the University of Western Ontario, 1997

Liverpool University Press

ISBN 0-85323-952-5 (cased)
ISBN 0-85323-962-2 (paper)

Legal deposit third quarter 1997
Bibliothèque nationale du Québec

Published simultaneously

In the Caribbean by
The Press University of the West Indies
Mona Kingston 7 Jamaica WI

In the European Union by Liverpool University Press.

Printed in Canada on acid-free paper

British Library Cataloguing in Publication Data

A British Library CIP record is available

Typeset in Palatino 10/12
by Caractéra inc., Quebec City

The Joanne Goodman Lecture Series has been established by Joanne's family and friends to perpetuate the memory of her blithe spirit, her quest for knowledge, and the rewarding years she spent at the University of Western Ontario

Contents

Maps and Tables

MAPS

TABLES

Acknowledgments

I am particularly grateful to the Goodman family who endowed the lecture series at the University of Western Ontario on which this book is based. At the university, Neville Thompson and Peter Neary were especially kind in arranging my visit and helping with publication arrangements.

It is a pleasure to be able to express my gratitude to my friends at McGill-Queen's University Press, especially Philip Cercone, Joe Cheng, Diane Duttle, Joan Harcourt, Roger Martin, Susanne McAdam, Joan McGilvray, Joanne Pisano, and Roy Ward.

For historical advice and for other items of relevant information and, sometimes, for sharp criticism, I am indebted to Paul Bew, Trevor Burnard, Nancy Cutway, David Eltis, Roy Foster, Carolyn Heald, John V. Kelleher, John Messenger, Hannah Rapport, the late George Rawlyk, and Brian Walker.

If the Irish Ran the World

1 Who's in Charge?

God may rule the universe, if He or She so disposes, but By-god rules the history of the Irish, and, especially, the history of the Irish diaspora. As in: "By god, if the Normans had only lost a few battles, Drogheda would be the centre of the Christian world." The great By-god for generations of the diaspora Irish, tucked snugly into snugs the world around has been, "If we were only in charge here, by-god, things would be different." That sentiment, if not the exact words, has been expressed in an infinitely echoing litany from the tobacco fields of early seventeenth-century Virginia to the building sites of twentieth-century London, and it is based on a perfectly valid historical reasoning, not mere vapouring. Such reasoning is the fundamental working mechanism of all historical scholarship, namely that if, in an historical chain of contingent events, a cause is altered, so is an entire cascade of effects.

Such By-god thinking relates not only to the fundamental rational structure of historical thought, but also to the emotional heart of most historians. For historians, when they are not being starch-collared professionals, are usually persons with a great deal of curiosity in their personal make-up. Finding out what happened in a given historical situation helps to slake their curiosity about the human animal, the obsessive focus of all really good professional historians. But, frequently, usually in their off hours when they think nobody is watching, historians conjecture about the way the world (or, at least *a* world) would be different, if only some basic event in a contingent chain had been different. "Counterfactual history" describes this sort of exercise when it is formalized, and, given modern computer simulations, one can ask and receive answers to some basic questions: how would the economic history of North America differ if the steam train had not been invented? What would the world's population be if smallpox had been conquered 100 years earlier than it was? And so on. The really intriguing counterfactual questions, however, are too complicated to permit examination by any known technique: how would world history have differed without, say, Moses, or Jesus, or Mohammed?

In the medium range, between narrow counter-factual questions of demography and economics, and impossibly broad ones of a cultural and religious character, lie matters that, while they cannot be responded to mechanically (such as through computer simulations) can be responded to by analogy. This occurs when, by fortuitous circumstances, natural historical laboratories are created, wherein we are provided with information that helps us to speculate sensibly in response to a "what if?" question.

So, what if the Irish had controlled more of the world in the modern era, say from the Protestant Reformation onwards? How would they have acted?

The natural place to look for suggestions is, of course, Ireland itself, after the dust of the years 1920–22 had settled. Despite residual imperial mortmains (especially, but not solely, in Northern Ireland), the Irish were in charge of creating their own domestic society. Hence, why not note how they acted once they were in charge of their own worlds, and project the basic characteristics backward in time, and around the globe? Because the plural is operative – worlds. Irish society, partitioned in 1920, became two societies, and each was cruelly amputated. Partition brought out the worst in the culture of the island of Ireland. Two sectarian states emerged, each blind to its own faults, and intolerant of its critics. Each state discriminated against minorities within its borders, all the while pointing either to its own alleged generosity and tolerance, or appealing to the principle of majority-rule. This was an unnatural situation, a function of partition. To then declare the behaviour of the two Irish societies from, say, 1920 to 1972 (when the northern state was effectively abolished by Direct Rule), to be representative would be to invite objections of unfair dealing. Certainly, the Irish were really not like *that*. So, we abandon the homeland, post-1920, as a possible historical laboratory.

Instead, we look abroad, to the lands of the Irish diaspora. There exist two jurisdictions where they were the largest ethnic group and where, although they were not culturally dominant, they were the most powerful group in the civil polity. One of these areas was

Ontario – or, to use its successively earlier titles, Canada West, and Upper Canada. This was the heart of British North America, and its spine was solidly Irish.[1] Shortly after the confederation of British North America in 1867, a good census was taken, and each person's ethnicity was enumerated. Persons of Irish ethnicity were 34.5 percent of Ontario's population, persons of English derivation 27.1 percent and individuals of Scots background 20.3 percent.[2] That was at Confederation, the birth of Canada as a nation. In the decades just before Confederation, the Irish proportion of the population was even higher. (Immigration statistics make that certain; it is only the precise percentages that are in doubt.) The Irish remained the largest ethnic group until roughly the end of Queen Victoria's reign, when the English became predominant.

That the Irish were the primary ethnic group in the heartland of English-speaking Canada in the two or three decades when Canada was a-borning means that they imprinted themselves upon the social equivalent of the nation's genetic code. Their values and attitudes and beliefs programmed Canadian society to move in certain ways, and to do so generations after the Irish had ceased to be a dominant group. That the Irish imprint was deeply encoded (and therefore easily ignored by Canadian historians, who have usually been connoisseurs of the obvious) was made possible by the willingness of the Protestant portion of the Irish cohort to disguise itself as "British" or, in dire circumstances, even as English.

There exists an historical literature on central Canada so extensive as to form a virtual library in itself, and one would not attempt to summarize it even in a score of lectures. However, from a distant perspective, the features that stand out in the historical development of Ontario are items that the Irish directly (and I think primarily) determined: an immense respect for law; a strong and consensual sense of public decorum; loyalty to the state; an historically deep, but no longer deeply divisive sectarianism (until the 1980s, Catholic schools were not fully funded by the state). When, in the twentieth century, Irish influence waned and, more importantly, confronted a series of incoming cultures that worked by different rules, the eventual product was a society that is immensely tolerant of all forms of dissent, save violence and public mischief; is remarkably protective of minority cultures (the Ontario Human Rights Code is quite simply the most advanced in the world); and is still, despite the importation of neo-conservative economics from the United States of America, committed to providing for all of its citizens in such matters as health care. It is, most visitors agree, a bit boring, but nice in the nice sense of the word: a civilized, gentle place, the kind of world that the Irish might have created, the earth around, had they had a bit more power.

Now, as a laboratory specimen, Ontario has one big drawback. It is a sequoia; it is so large a specimen that it requires us to cut a hole in the roof; it is just too big to deal with in our present space.

Instead, we require the equivalent of a bonsai shrub, an evergreen, say, of the same genus as the huge sequoia, but handier; something we can pick up and examine from all angles without either compromising the specimen or giving ourselves a striated disc. This is why the tiny island of Montserrat is so useful. It, like Ontario, was a part of England's empire and, even more than Ontario, its culture was determined by the Irish.

There the structural similarity ends. Size, location, and time of study differ greatly and are not comparable. Montserrat's Irish period was over before there were more than a few thousand persons of Irish origin in central Canada. Montserrat belonged to the first English empire, Canada to the second, and the rules were very different. Still, although we may refuse to compare directly the two cases, Ontario and Montserrat, this does not stop our being aware that in each we have the opportunity to view the interaction of Irish emigrants with English imperialism, and to do so in a context wherein the Irish were not a small, and therefore easily bullied, minority among the white settlers. To continue the analogy of laboratory plants: although the structural characteristics of massive Ontario and minuscule Montserrat are not comparable, their physiology – their basic metabolic processes – indeed are comparable. All living cells have to accomplish the same physiological processes (ingestion, digestion, excretion) and so do all societies (birth, reproduction, and death). Hence, the physiology of these two polar members of the same genus – the sequoia and the bonsai shrub – is comparable. These two cases may show to us the two extremes of normal behaviour that would have existed had Ireland had more than two colonial empires, the giant one in the middle of North America, and the tiny one in the West Indies.

That said, I shall not again mention Ontario. It seems to me an important reference point for a Canadian audience, but for non-Canadians, the following discussion is designed to be free-standing. Its vocabulary and substance derive from Irish and from Caribbean historiography. Those whose intellectual life is not concerned with 49° north latitude need not feel any pressure to draw that, or any other, parallel.

Tiny Montserrat is a nice case. It is so far away in time that few, if any, of us have any great emotional fear of looking at its history with both eyes open. The only problems that we encounter with Montserrat are technical. As Carl and Roberta Bridenbaugh noted, "most West Indian historians stress society as it existed in the second half of the eighteenth century, largely because of more abundant sources."[3] The Bridenbaughs' statement holds true for the first half of the eighteenth century, is doubly applicable to the second half of the seventeenth, and exponentially so to the first half, but with this amendment: that in the first half of the twentieth century, some fine work was done on the West Indies in the earliest period of European conquest by historians of empire, and although their glorification of empire is no longer acceptable, their archival standards were high, and their work therefore useful. What we most want to know about Montserrat concerns its first century as a European colony, roughly 1630 to 1730, the very era for which records are generally weakest in the West Indies. Fortunately – and inexplicably – Montserrat possesses some of the best sources of social information for any of the British colonies in the New World. This includes not only data on the planter elite, but on the poor whites, the indentured servants and, to a lesser degree, the slave population. Montserrat is located historiographically at an important intersection in the history of the first English empire, namely the question of whether or not ethnicity was central to the making of the colonial world.[4] Further, it has a location near to a second historiographic intersection, which is the question of how useful it is to consider sixteenth- and seventeenth-century English imperialism in the Americas.[5] Montserrat, being an English colony, run and peopled mostly by persons from Ireland, who were schooled in early English imperialism (sometimes quite unpleasantly), provides an interesting laboratory case of how true (or how untrue) to type this imperialism ran at a second remove.

One of our sources of information, the 1729 census, is, according to Richard B. Sheridan, "the only one of its kind in the records of the sugar colonies."[6] Robert V. Wells, who has made the most systematic survey of social data available for the British colonies, adjudges that the enumeration of Montserrat in 1729 was one of the most comprehensive studies ever made of a colonial population before the American Revolution.[7] That is good indeed, but there is more. In 1678 a full census was also done of the island. This one was somewhat eccentric, but it is serviceable and can be linked to the 1729 data. Most importantly, this census yielded ethnic information, establishing beyond cavil how Irish the island actually was. And, equally important, in the early 1670s, a cartographically eccentric but extremely informative map of the island was done, one that shows, among other things, settlement patterns that can be tied to matters of ethnicity. Moreover, the English imperial authorities, fearing that they were losing control of the situation on their empire's margin, required of the Montserrat governors in the eighteenth century that they collect and send to London the laws passed by the legislature of Montserrat. These were collated and printed in full in 1790. (An abridgement also was published, in 1790, but this is only a summary of the main statutes and is slightly misleading.) Strangely, these four sources of information have yet to be tied together by historians of the West Indies, although each has been used separately. When put together they let us delineate quite fully the social structure of Montserrat, not completely, but in significant detail. Of course, reasonable inferences are necessary to fill in the blank spaces between known datum points, but that is required in any form of history.

One is also fortunate in having to hand the work of generous guides who have worked on the history of the island. Each has his or her special interest and little tricks that go along with that interest, and if I do not agree entirely with any of my predecessors, that does not mean that I am not grateful for their work. The godfather of historians of Montserrat is the Rev. Aubrey Gwynn, S.J., who in the 1920s and 1930s collected a raft of miscellaneous material about the West Indies and the influence of the Irish and of the Catholic church on the islands. The Bridenbaughs refer somewhat dismissively to Gwynn's having assembled "the obvious printed sources together with Jesuit documents,"[8] but this is unfair. Gwynn's sources are not merely the obvious ones, and his articles form a corpus of primary material that has made the labour of his successors much easier than would otherwise have been the case. The only trouble with Gwynn is that he sometimes gets a bit cute (in the Irish sense of the word) with his sources. So keen was he to assert Hibernian exploration and colonization activities, and so devoted was he to the service of his church, that he occasionally made his Irish colonizers less aggressive and more holy than actually they were. Whenever possible, I have checked Gwynn's usage of primary material against the original documents.

At the same time the Rev. Fr. Gwynn was collecting material in Dublin and London, T. Savage English, a British civil servant on Montserrat, was putting together his own *omnium gatherum* of material that he obtained during his eleven-year residence. English was not aware of the work of Gwynn (which came out in the Jesuit periodical *Studies* in the late 1920s and early 1930s and in *Analecta Hibernica*) and Gwynn was equally unaware of English's researches. English's work was completed in 1930 under the title "Records of Montserrat," and was not published. It circulated in typescript form on the island and a copy found its way to the old West India Library and thence to the Institute of Commonwealth Studies. English's and Gwynn's work rarely duplicate each other and then on matters of general knowledge. English's material is especially useful because he drew upon records and memoirs that were in bad shape when he used them and which now, after sixty years of further neglect and Hurricane Hugo in 1989, are permanently lost. On matters that one can check (such as his copying out of seventeenth-century laws held in government offices on Montserrat in the 1920s, which one can compare to copies sent to London and printed in 1790), English is accurate. Thus, one is predisposed to trust him on things one cannot check. This is crucial, since he does not provide conventional citations, and one has to proceed somewhat on faith. (Mind you, even if he had provided citations, these would now be of little value, for the most important documents he transcribed were in moulding, disintegrating fragments when he had access to them.) The real worry about English (unlike Gwynn) is not his leaving out potentially embarrassing sentences in any given document, but rather that we know only what he chose to take down and have no idea what he considered to be of no value.[9]

The works of Gwynn and of English, based on material collected nearly three-quarters of a century ago, and put together in a basically empirical frame of mind, are by way of being quasi-primary sources. Not so the efforts of the four main scholars who have worked on Montserrat's history during the last three decades. This work, engaged in from the early 1960s to the present day, is entirely different from that of English and of Gwynn, for each piece is engagé. I am mentioning the major figures briefly here, in order to alert the reader to an issue that runs, *sotto voce*, through this entire study and to which we will return explicitly in the final chapter: the nature of the creation of a sense of historical identity among small groups on the periphery of empire and the function of the historical chronicler as a weaver of the cloth (whether synthetic or real) that bedrapes this identity.

The first of these more recent scholars is the anthropologist John Messenger, who spent seven weeks on Montserrat in 1965 and three weeks of library research in Ireland. His basic viewpoint was formed in that period, and, although he revisited the island and kept up on the topic, his published views, repeated into the 1990s, were fixed by that initial period of research. Messenger (a broad-gauged anthropologist who did significant work on African indigenous peoples and an ethnography of an Irish island community) became convinced of the importance of the Irish influence upon present-day Montserrat. In his enthusiasm for things Hibernian he is a lineal descendant intellectually of Aubrey Gwynn. In spite of Messenger's work having taken a fair amount of criticism from his fellow anthropologists (notably Riva Berleant-Schiller, who is discussed below), I must confess to a soft spot for his efforts. This stems in part from his having an affection for the Irish, and also from his having taken a good deal of stick from the Irish themselves for that affection (a not uncommon experience for anyone in Irish studies). Specifically, in 1969 he published a volume about one of the Aran Islands, one he disguises as "Inis Beag." This book, though sympathetic to the culture, raised a howl of primal dimensions among contemporaries and historians of Ireland, for it told the Irish something that was demonstrably true but which they did not wish to know: that rural Ireland in the late nineteenth and the first two-thirds of the twentieth century, pure, god-fearing, and frequently Gaelic as it was, also was the most sexually repressed and biologically ignorant of any western society that has yet been studied in this regard. This was not the way the Irish of the 1960s wanted their virtues described. Messenger, to his credit, took the onslaught with dignity and a wry smile.[10]

Secondly, one encounters Howard A. Fergus, Montserrat resident, and for several decades the island's leading intellectual. Poet, sometime university tutor, and speaker of the legislative council of Montserrat, he has produced a wide variety of political and historical commentaries on the island. His earlier historical volume (1975) was written for a popular audience and unfortunately contains no documentation, although much of it is accurate, coming as it does from English's work (as Fergus freely admits). His later historical work (1994) is a mixture of astute observations about recent time and of less percipient, and only partially documented, assertions about earlier eras. In a more fully documented article in the Dublin ecclesiastical journal *Studies*, he has articulated a theme that is latent in his other work, namely that although there is much of antiquarian interest concerning the Irish in Montserrat's history, the actual twentieth-century influence of this Irish history is virtually nil.[11]

This mildly "Africanist" interpretation (as distinct from the "Hibernicist" views of John Messenger) was articulated more tartly by a third modern scholar, the anthropologist Riva Berleant-Schiller. The author of a short commentary on the economy of seventeenth-century Montserrat, her real influence is through the comprehensive bibliography of the island which she published in 1991. Since each item in it is annotated, there is plenty of opportunity for the etching of sharp commentary under the names of each writer, rather like an old-fashioned engraver doing epitaphs on brass plaques for the walls of the parish church.[12]

A fourth scholar, the historical geographer Lydia Mihelic Pulsipher, has been the least ideological of the scholars. Beginning with her 1977 doctoral thesis, Pulsipher has stayed at the last, working away, publishing her thesis and related research notes, and then initiating a significant project in the industrial archaeology of the island's sugar plantations. If she is as much interested in what the various peoples of Montserrat have done to the ecology and landscape as in what the peoples did to each other, that viewpoint has its virtues. Not least of these is the realization that humans are only one of the species to have occupied Montserrat; not the first, certainly, and probably not the last.[13]

2 Ireland's Neo-Feudal Empire, 1630–1650

Ireland's putative empire in the West Indies, the island of Montserrat, was a fragment kicked loose by the cultural equivalent of a nuclear blast, the so-called "expansion of Europe" of the sixteenth and seventeenth centuries. It was a bizarre, and totally unprecedented time in human history. Europeans, having discovered what to them were new worlds, began to exploit them with a ferocity that challenges description and defies explanation. Having found several Edens, Europeans treated these places instead as Eldorados, sites to be strip-mined for quick, or at least easy, riches. In so doing, the Europeans turned their various new worlds into a new solar system, one whose laws were force and whose forces were fickle.*

The chief power in the seventeenth century expansion of Europe had been Spain, but by the late century, military and monarchical problems seriously weakened the Spanish position as the predominant colonial power in the western hemisphere. Nevertheless, well into the seventeenth century, the Spanish were to be reckoned with. Their interests in Hispaniola (today's Haiti and Dominican Republic) in particular assured their position as a primary party, and, indeed, they had ambitious claims to almost all the Americas, certainly all the Caribbean islands. Portugal from the early 1580s to 1640 was subordinate to the Spanish crown and therefore was not a

* Dates in the discussion which follows are given in Old Style, save that the start of the year is taken to be the first of January.

truly independent agency. France in the first decade of the seventeenth century began to assert itself as an exploring and colonizing power. Simultaneously, the Dutch, who had traded aggressively, if often clandestinely, with the West Indies as early as the 1540s, became, by virtue of a series of truces and arrangements with the other powers, bigtime, open traders.

The English came to the game haphazardly in the 1560s.[1] The key names are the ones once known to every schoolboy – John Hawkins and Francis Drake, and Walter Raleigh. Their activities were a mixture of piracy upon the Spanish fleet, slaving, illegal trade with Spanish colonies, and poorly thought out attempts at planting colonies.[2] Chaotic as these efforts may have been from the viewpoint of public policy, they were immensely attractive to the English entrepreneurial class, a body that was breaking free of the vestigial feudal restraints and discovering the rush of mercantile risk as their drug of choice. "It is probable that English investors – chiefly London merchants – put more money into commerce and piracy in the Caribbean from 1560 to 1630 than into any other mode of long-distance business enterprise, even the East India Company."[3]

This game – high-risk, high-potential profit – was played with very few rules, and it was played outside the regulated fields of European life. The contemporary phrase, well-worn by historians of the period, is that life was "beyond the line." This referred specifically to a secret clause in the 1598 Treaty of Vervains between France and Spain, wherein the principals agreed that despite whatever peace they might have in European waters, there was no truce west of the Azores or south of the Tropic of Cancer. Those vast areas were a free-fire zone, everyone a potential sniper and a potential target. Truces and local arrangements sometimes modified this Darwinian madness, but it was not until the Treaty of Utrecht in 1713 that something approaching order was established among the European powers. For the purposes of the present discussion it is well to keep in mind that from 1618 until the Peace of Westphalia in 1648, the Thirty Years War pitted Catholic against Protestant powers in Europe (with, of course, the exception of moments of truce and occasional instances of diplomatic misalliance).

But being beyond the line was more than a geopolitical term. It was cultural as well. "To live 'beyond the line' meant more than a flouting of European treaty obligations," Richard S. Dunn has noted. "It meant a general flouting of European social convention. The sixteenth and early seventeenth centuries plainly showed that Spaniards, Englishmen, Frenchmen, and Dutchmen who sojourned in the tropics all tended to behave in a far more unbuttoned fashion than at home." His lapidary judgment is that "white men who scrambled for riches in the torrid zone exploited their Indian and black slaves more shamelessly than was possible with the unprivileged labouring class in Western Europe. And they robbed and massacred each other more freely than the rules of civility permitted in Europe."[4]

Although piracy and smuggling remained in the repertoire of English adventurers throughout the seventeenth century, David B. Quinn emphasizes that during the reign of James I (that is, roughly, during the first quarter of the seventeenth century, "planting colonies became big business for Englishmen."[5] He instances the creation of colonies in the Amazon, Newfoundland, Virginia, and the Irish plantations in Wexford and Longford, as well as the plantation of Ulster, as cases in point. The momentum thus established carried right through the civil wars of the mid-seventeenth century. At the time of the Restoration, 1660, charters by the English state had been granted for settlements in fifty-nine separate locations, counting New England as a single entity, and this number does not include the plantations in Ireland.[6]

Most Irish persons of the late sixteenth and early seventeenth centuries were only indirectly affected by the pyrotechnics of the European empires, but a goodly number were directly involved – some as colonizers, some as victims. And a few were both.[7]

The first significant number of Irishmen to serve the European powers in the western hemisphere seem to have been part of the Spanish garrison in Florida in the mid-1560s. In the long war with England, from 1585 onwards, Irish sailors and marines served with the Spanish fleet. This was an extension of the military tradition of thousands of "Wild Geese" who migrated to serve Catholic European countries, from the mid-sixteenth century onwards. Still other Irishmen served on English ships and in early English colonies in the Americas. That said, these individuals have been mostly lost from the historical record and the world they inhabited, much less their mental maps of that world, are beyond our recovering.[8]

When, in the early seventeenth century, the European powers place greater emphasis upon schemes of plantation, our glimpses of the Irish outriders of empire become clearer: still tantalizingly brief, but now recognizable figures can be discerned, if only in outline. They are the hyper-aggressive settlers who take over the new worlds of the west. Three areas of settlement give us an indication of the sort of enterprise that was attractive to Irish adventurers and their retainers:

the Guiana (or Amazon) region, Newfoundland, and Virginia. These cases are particularly useful for they provide a portfolio of pre-1630 behaviour on the part of Irish colonizers and thus the early settlement of Montserrat, which is otherwise an ill-chronicled and partly mysterious event, comes to make a bit more sense.

"Guiana" was a term used loosely by contemporaries and involved a vast area in South America. In this context it is defined on its eastern side by the ocean, on the north by the Orinoco River (Spanish), and on the south and west by the Amazon (Portuguese) and its tributary the Negro River.[9] Irish settlers took part in various Guiana enterprises of English origin, such as the first English colony of 1604–05, and an equally unsuccessful venture of 1609–12.[10]

More directly Irish was the settlement established on the Amazon by Philip and James Purcell, brothers or cousins, who traded out of Dartmouth, England. They began with fourteen Irishmen, and probably a few Englishmen, and developed a tobacco trade. This "Tauregue River settlement" grew through the further importation of Irish settlers. The Purcells were Catholics, of "Old English" stock in Ireland, and most of the colonists were Catholic. The prospering little colony was caught in international politics, however, when, in 1625, the Portuguese cavalier Pedro Teixeira besieged the Tauregue settlement. Captain James Purcell and seventy-plus of his men surrendered. Fifty-four or fifty-six Irish colonists (the reports vary) were killed after they had surrendered and the rest, at least eighteen in number, were taken prisoner, including James Purcell. The latter escaped and returned to England and, in 1628, returned as part of an Anglo-Dutch force in an attempt to revive the Tauregue settlement. In February 1631 this was destroyed a second time by the Portuguese.[11]

A much different experience was that of the early Irish settlers in Newfoundland. Two ventures, both involving Sir George Calvert (created Lord Baltimore, 1625), bear notice. Calvert, a crypto-Catholic (until 1625, when the change of monarchs made Catholicism both permissible and potentially profitable) had obtained land in Ireland in Longford and in Wexford. He was a colonist, if not a colonizer, even before he left the British Isles. In 1623, he and his associates promoted the Irish colony at Renews, Newfoundland. Ostensibly, this was to be a colony composed of Protestants, but that was only a cover. In fact, the project was intended to appeal to Irish Catholic landowners who were being pushed aside by the English plantations in Leinster and Munster. The colony was no great success and was gone by 1627. Another effort by Calvert, however, was more successful. Granted the entire Avalon peninsula soon after receiving his title of nobility in 1625, he sent out agents, and then, in 1627, fifteen Irish Catholics, Old English landholders threatened by English expansion in Ireland. Two Catholic priests accompanied this group. This colony was viable, although at first hardly robust.[12]

If Calvert's Newfoundland colonies were intended to appeal to the Catholics of Old English extraction, the Virginia colony, though certainly not an Irish venture, had an appeal to some Irishmen, especially those of the "New English" (Protestants) who had recently settled in Ireland but had not done as well as they wished. One such individual was Captain William Nuce who acquired several pieces of Munster land, and was involved in creating the Brandon settlement, after the English defeat of the Irish in 1603. He eventually put together an Irish seigneury of his own with, in 1622, twenty-four houses and about 100 settlers. He had bigger plans, however, and in 1621, obtained land in Virginia as part of a grand scheme of bringing over to Virginia 1,000 settlers from Ireland. In the actual event, he brought over fewer than 100 labourers (probably native Irish Catholics) and most of these were killed in an Indian attack in 1622.[13]

A similar, but more successful figure was Daniel Gookin, another Protestant planter, in Munster. He developed a lucrative trade bringing cattle, and a few settlers to Virginia, and taking back tobacco. The settlers he brought, presumably native Irish Catholics, were labourers, and, by 1625, they had all disappeared, victims of Indian attack and disease. The cattle trade, however, had longer term impact, and eventually the Irish cattle trade spread to all the British colonies. Virginia, by 1630, had become heavily Protestant, and was therefore unwelcoming to both the Old English and to the native Irish.[14]

These three examples of Irish colonizing efforts, Guiana, Newfoundland, and Virginia (from a wide array of Irish involvements, some proposed and never assayed,[15] others tried, but lost from the historical record), do not provide a full typology of activities. These three examples, however, define a spectrum of Irish involvement in empire: it could be on the shirttails of the English, or the Dutch, or the Spanish. But, mostly, it would be English. Both Irish men and women could be involved (as was the case with the Newfoundland settlement), but usually it was men. These individuals could be of all sorts, Protestants and Catholics, landowners on the rise, landowners on the way down, merchants, servants and labourers, Old English, New English, native Irish, laymen and the occasional priest or pastor. Anyone.

(It is from this period onwards that the now-standard vocabulary of seventeenth-century Irish historians becomes important. "The Irish" comprised four separate cultural groups: (1) the "native Irish," who were descended from the pre-Norman inhabitants and were almost universally Roman Catholic. (2) The "Old English," whose forebears were Norman and who had taken lands from the native Irish. The Old English were mostly Catholic in religion and royalist in politics. (3) The "New English," Protestant adventurers who began settling in Ireland in the 1580s and came in large numbers in the first half of the seventeenth century. They shouldered aside both native Irish and Old English, but often with less ease than they expected. And (4), in the north of Ireland, the Scottish Presbyterians (today called Ulster-Scots), some of whom were part of the official plantation of Ulster, but most of whom were self-impelled migrants who came across the Irish Sea from the Scottish lowlands, and settled themselves by force among the native Irish of Antrim and Down.)

When we ask what the motives of this broad column of Irish adventurers and colonists were, we find ourselves wrapped in a tautology. We can assume that each individual who chose freely to migrate to the western hemisphere (and at this time, there were few if any Irish prisoners being forcibly transported) did so because he believed that this would improve his lot in life. Usually this was a material matter, but people who chose to migrate for religious reasons are not excluded from this assumption, for a person can define his life in terms either temporal or eternal. Even apparently selfless behaviour (such as migration to a dangerous clime to repair the family fortunes, or serving as a priest to Irish migrants) fits into this framework, for an individual need not define his sense of self solely in terms of himself as a biological entity. Wider definitions (familial, tribal, or spiritual) are possible. So, unless one proposes that the adventurers and colonists were intentionally acting against their own self-interest – a suggestion that, besides being nearly infinitely improbable, introduces massive, virtually insoluble evidentiary problems – we are stuck within our tautology. We assume they intended to make their lives better and, therefore, that individual behaviours were directed towards that end. Given that we can never know actual human motives (the black box that is the human mind and soul being forever sealed), we can only deal with observable behaviours on the part of the colonists and with the context of those behaviours.

The key context of the years 1580–1630 was that, amidst sharp social changes in their own homelands, English and Scottish colonists poured into Ireland. Mostly these were Protestants but, as the case of George Calvert indicates, a Catholic could grab Irish lands if he was willing to disguise his religious convictions. This influx at first directly affected the native Irish and Old English landowners, but ultimately it had a knock-on effect, making vulnerable the position of their tenants lower down the social scale.

The oldest of the invasive settlements in Ireland was the Munster plantation of the late 1580s, of which one of the chief beneficiaries was Walter Raleigh. This plantation continued to grow at least until the Rising of 1641 and the subsequent Irish civil war. An estimated 12,000 to 15,000 settlers were in the province of Munster by 1622.[16] By 1641, the number of English settlers in Munster was probably 22,000.[17] The second major settlement was the plantation of Ulster, which followed the defeat of the native Irish leadership of the north in 1603. By 1622, 25,000 to 30,000 Scots and English settlers were in Ulster,[18] some were part of the Offaly plantation but others, mostly Scots in Antrim and Down, came of their own volition. Though larger in numerical terms than the Munster plantation, this northern subinfeudation was at first more easily achieved than the Munster venture, because of the flight of the native Irish leadership to the Continent. At the close of the first decade of the seventeenth century, the Dublin government began a third plantation, this one in county Wexford. Most of the northern portion of the county was confiscated and parcelled out in large blocks to officials of the Dublin administration, who then brought in settlers. The areas confiscated included all the remaining native Irish lands in Wexford as well as blocks of Old English holdings.[19] The Wexford confiscations have left a telling vignette. Some 200 of the landholders whose property had been confiscated (both native Irish and Old English), came to Dublin to plead their case. The authorities responded by forcibly transporting some of them to Virginia.[20] In addition to these major colonial settlements in Ireland, there were several minor ones: a late sixteenth-century effort in Queen's County that took on new life in the mid-seventeenth century; a plantation in County Longford which came on the heels of the Wexford endeavour; and continual, additive settlement in the port cities by English merchants.[21]

The character of this English and Scottish invasion of Ireland was not everywhere the same, but neither was it random. Running throughout was what W.J. Smyth has called "the method of frontiers,"[22] by which he means a constant harrying move forward, fragmented, uneven, but forever moving, confronting, outflanking, aggressive, unpredictable. Though not as far from central authority as was the world beyond-the-line in the western hemisphere, colonial elites in Ireland were far enough from central discipline that they "acted strictly and often violently in terms of their interests and not that of the wider society."[23] Thus, Ireland became a school for imperialism. Some of those who first settled in Ireland moved on to other colonial ventures. And those who were the colonized – the native Irish and the Old English – learned from experience how successful colonizers behaved, and themselves took up these methods on several new frontiers.

The actual number of migrants into and out of Ireland are necessarily speculative, but informed estimates imply an interesting balance. It is suggested that between 1586 and 1700, a minimum of 150,000 settlers entered Ireland.[24] And, for the somewhat shorter period 1601–1700, an informed estimate of out-migrants is 132,500.[25] In other words, a rough balance prevailed.

That numerical balance, however, masks the social disequilibrium caused by the forcible inflow. The individuals who were discomfited by English and Scottish incursions did not simply pack and leave. Some did, but many stayed and became a part of a social flotsam that drifted slowly in the backwaters of Irish society. This dislocation was heightened by the fact (which contemporaries accurately perceived) that Ireland in the first half of the seventeenth century was experiencing a population explosion: total population rose from somewhere between 1 to 1.4 million in 1600 to approximately 2.1 million in 1641, according to Louis Cullen.[26] The combination of burgeoning population and social displacement was ultimately toxic, as events of 1641 and thereafter were to prove.

In 1623, Sir Henry Bourchier, afterwards fifth earl of Bath, the son of a great Elizabethan adventurer in Ireland, himself with strong connections in County Cork, and also one of the English commissioners who enquired into Irish affairs, summarized the dislocated social structure as follows:[27]

> They that prove to be gentry amongst the mere Irish, of which there be a great number, though they have not sixpence to live on, they disdain to follow any trade, but only some turn footboys and should be compelled to service: for now they press to other men's houses of their acquaintance or alliance, and there spend their days idle to the excessive charge of housekeepers, who there perpetually be pestered with such guests. The inveterate customs and their abuse have strengthened this for a law of hospitality amongst them. This kind of rabble, and many others of the mere Irish, that sometimes were rebels within this twenty years since the peace began [that is, since the Irish defeat of 1603] have been multiplied to an incredible number far more than here [England] for two reasons;[28] because they generally (be they never so poor) affect to marry timely or else keep one unmarried [woman] and cohabit with her as their reputed wife; and they take much felicity and content in their procreation and issue; and because they devote themselves to idleness and rest and do feed altogether on moist meats, they abound with more children than such as take pains to dry their superfluous humours.

Sir Henry believed that the only way to prevent the déclassé gentry and their affines from becoming a threat to the public order was either to put them to work building bridges, walls and the like, or to send them to "Virginia or some other of the newly discovered lands in the West."

Though no friend of the Irish, Sir Henry was no fool. A modern historian has described the matter more dispassionately, but similarly:

> The magnetic pull of Ireland was soon reduced once the effects of the first generation of rapid population growth [post 1603] had worked its way through the system and opportunities were reduced. An apparently faster rate of population growth in Munster than in Ulster suggests that even with internal settler migrations, there was a perceived shortage of local opportunity. As early as the 1620s there is evidence of emigration from Munster to America by recently arrived settlers and by native Irish. In particular, the expanding economy of the Caribbean provided an outlet for surplus Munster population.[29]

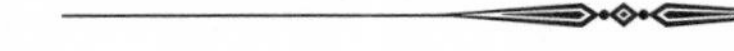

The course from the south of Ireland to Montserrat was not charted in advance and had something of the lottery about it. However, that considerable numbers of Irish persons of all sorts would find their way to the West Indies was virtually inevitable. The settlement of Montserrat is best approached the same way that the people of the time did so: by proceeding from the general area to the specific locale.

The island in which many Munster Irish settled is part of a group that by convention is called the "Leeward Islands." There is no good reason for this, save convention, for these islands are no more in the lee of the prevailing winds than are the "Windward Islands." Early settlers did not use the term "Leeward Islands" in a specific geographic sense and it is not until 1671 that the term appears on official documents as a designation for specific sites. Previous to that, it was simply a navigational term, and whether an island was leeward or windward depended upon where the speaker was when giving directions.[30]

The four Leeward Islands of seventeenth-century "Anglo-Celtic" settlement (to use a useful term which is becoming prevalent among historians of ethnicity to embrace all the populace of the archipelago called the "British Isles") were St Christopher (var: St Christopher's and St Kitts), Nevis, Antigua, and Montserrat. They and their south-eastern neighbour Barbados (with which they were grouped administratively until 1671) are part of the Lesser Antilles, a crescent-shaped chain of islands that runs from present-day Puerto Rico to Trinidad, just off the coast of modern Venezuela.

The Leeward Islands' location in the seventeenth century was effectively very different from what it is today. Prior to the invention of air travel, Great Circle routes – that is, direct travel from one point on the globe to another – were non-existent. To get to the Leeward Islands from, say, Plymouth, or Kinsale, one sailed southwards to the Canary or the Cape Verde Islands and then picked up the trade winds and ran west until sighting one of the Leewards (or, after the discovery of Barbados, that island). This voyage could be expected to take six weeks. To make the homeward trip, a vessel worked northward until it hit the anti-trade winds which drove it eastward to home. This voyage was notoriously unpredictable and in the seventeenth century usually took seven to ten weeks.[31] From the viewpoint of seventeenth-century geopolitics, the convenient characteristic of the Leeward Islands (as indeed, of all the Lesser Antilles) was that the prevailing trade winds made it easier to reach the islands from London or Dublin than from the Spanish strongholds of Cuba or Hispaniola.[32]

And, in socio-political terms, they were different in size from what they are today. Excluding minor atolls and tiny uninhabitable volcanic outcroppings, the Leewards in total comprise only 255 square miles (660 square kilometres) and even if one adds to that number the 166 square miles (430 km^2) of Barbados and Jamaica (the latter taken by the English in 1655), of 4,244 square miles (10,991 km^2), and even if one adds to that every minuscule inhabited item in British hands, one still is dealing with a total area less than that of present-day Northern Ireland.[33] Yet, recent studies suggest that in the years 1630–1700, the Caribbean received 59 percent of all emigrants from the British Isles.[34] In the eighteenth century this dropped to 20 percent of British Isles emigrants, and the North American mainland colonies came to the fore. But in the seventeenth century, in the perspective of potential Irish (and British) migrants, the islands in the Caribbean bulked larger than did all of North America.

The mother-colony of the Leewards was St Christopher. Its founder was Thomas Warner, a Suffolk man who had spent time in one of the Amazon settlements and learned that farming tobacco was potentially highly rewarding, and that being surrounded by Spanish and Portuguese was not. In 1622, he had made his way home from the Amazon and on his way had seen St Christopher and was impressed. It seemed to him a perfect tobacco garden, having deep soil, plenty of fresh water, and a safe anchorage. It also had the advantage of being outside the usual sea lane by which the Spanish fleets returned to Europe, no small asset.[35] According to Captain John Smith, Warner managed to interest fifteen associates in this secluded tobacco garden and in late 1622 or early 1623, these sixteen men bought passage on a ship bound for Virginia. There they stayed for about a year, before finally making for St Christopher, arriving on 28 January 1623. There they ran into three French settlers (the rival parties eventually split the island into English and French sectors), and Carib Indians (who tended to side with the French). Their first crop of tobacco was wiped out by a hurricane. Still, Warner remained enthusiastic and he returned with 100 new settlers.[36]

Thereafter, the St Christopher colony grew quickly, though not gently. Thomas Warner, having done all the hard work, nearly had its fruits stolen from him by his social betters. Warner had occupied non-English territory, without first receiving state authority. Fortunately for him, the new king, Charles I, was intent on putting a thumb in the eye of the Spanish, so on 13 September 1625, Warner and his chief colleague (one Ralph Merrifield) were given a royal commission confirming their authority, at King's pleasure, over St Christopher and also the islands of Nevis, Montserrat and Barbados (the latter, Warner had yet to see). This was not a grant of property rights, however, and it became clear that actual title to the new islands would be granted only to some courtier with a great deal more cachet than Warner possessed. The thought of acquiring a foreign overseas plantation was very attractive to aristocrats at court. Thus, Warner was very fortunate when, following a scrimmage involving the earl of Pembroke, the earl of Marlborough and the earl of Carlisle, the last won. Carlisle, an amiable, hugely entertaining and highly influential Scot, had allied himself with Warner in the great scramble, a shrewd tactic, given Warner's undeniable priority as developer of the colony. The end of all this was that on 2 July 1627, Carlisle was granted, by royal proprietary letters patent, hereditary rights to St Christopher, Nevis, Montserrat, and Barbados and to most of the Caribbean islands lying between 10 degrees and 20 degrees north latitude. Warner was appointed governor of St Christopher by Carlisle and did well out of land grants.[37]

The Carlisle patent, which controlled all the Leeward islands, was a strange device which ran counter to the spirit of an age when merchant capitalism was developing and when chartered companies were the preferred form of imperialism. This quasi-feudal form, stemming from the Crown, and granted to a nobleman, was an attempt to set the clock back. In practical terms, its implications were

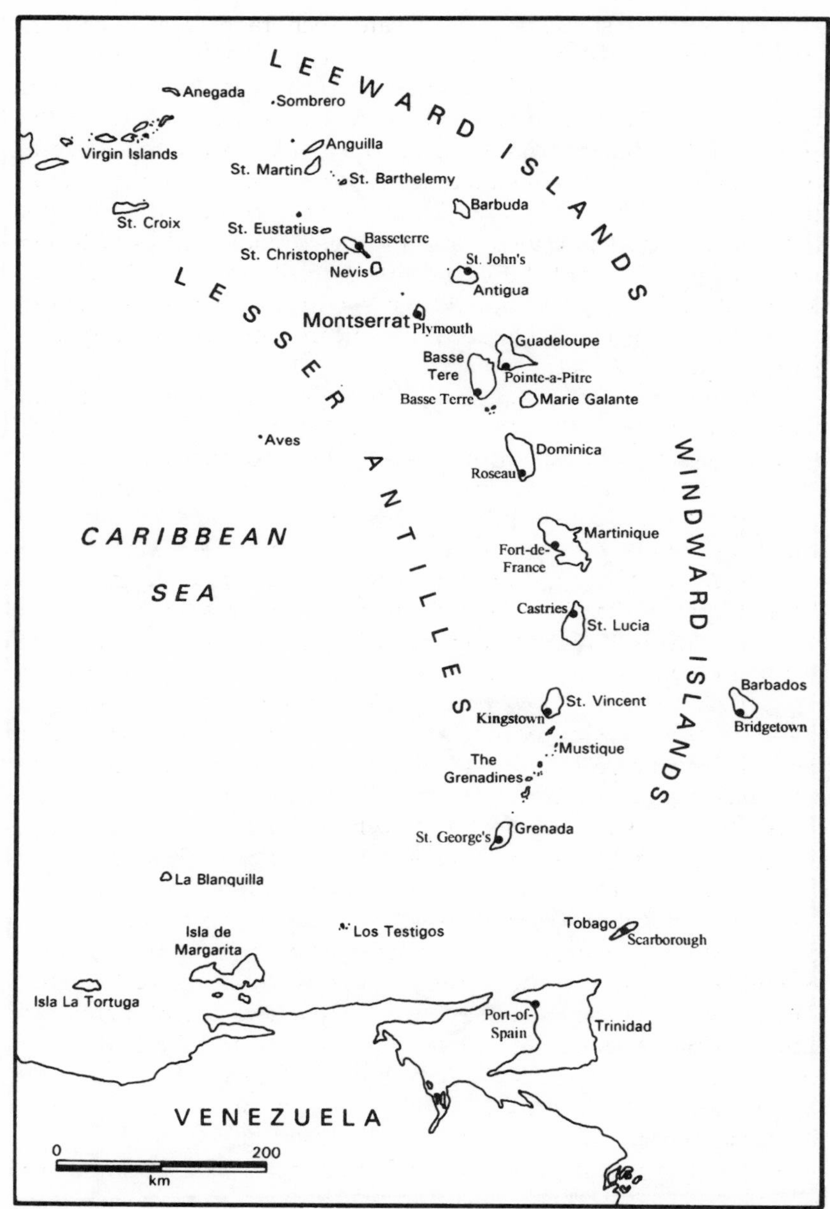

Map 1 The Lesser Antilles, late twentieth century

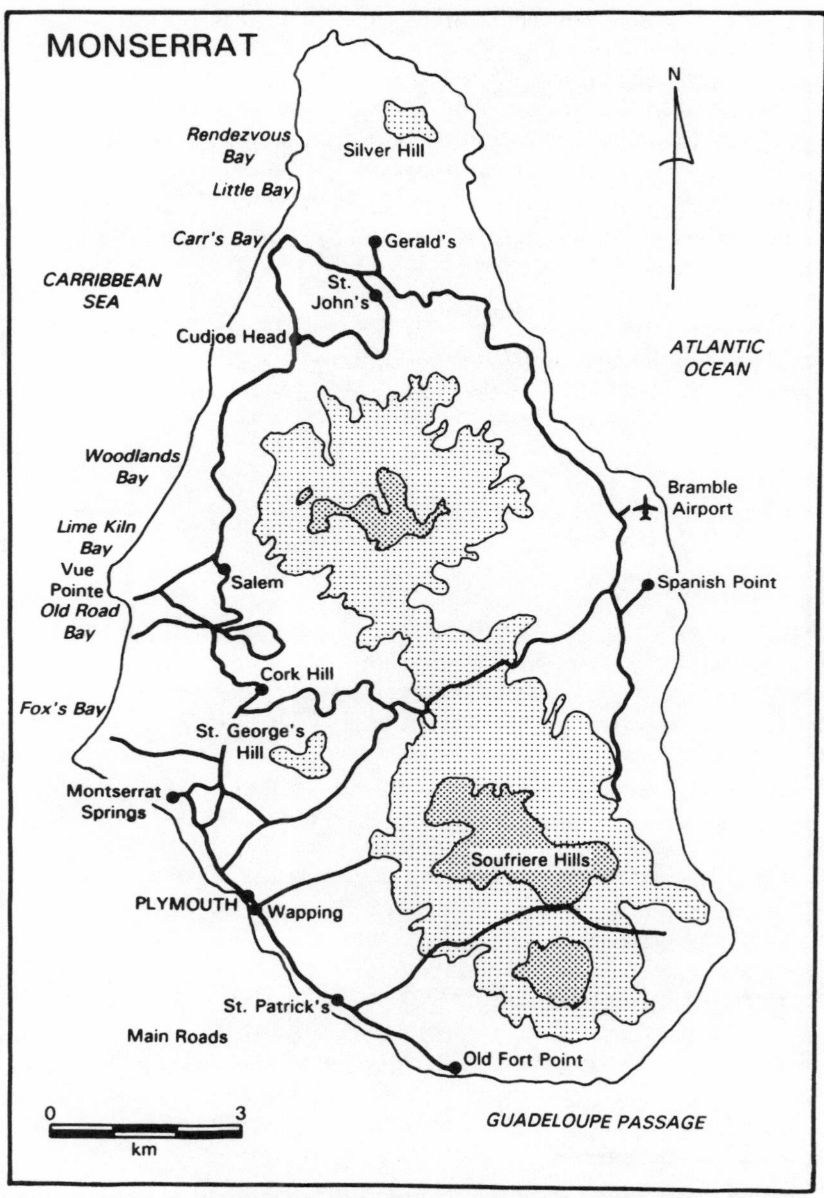

Map 2 Montserrat, late twentieth century

two: first, that the governors of the various islands would be named by a private person (Carlisle and his heirs), rather than by the civil state;[38] and second, that the land titles of the settlers on the several islands would eventually be found to be very muddy indeed. Unlike the case of chartered companies that were granted freehold land on their plantations and which passed land in fee simple on to their chief adventurers, the neo-feudal grant to Carlisle meant that the landholders on the various islands would possess their land in some form of tenancy, rather than in perpetuity.[39] Since most occupiers of land in the British Isles at the time did not hold land in freehold, this was not an immediate problem. (The various forms of tenancies and of non-freehold land-holding were sufficient to fill several legal texts, and did; and this is not to mention the various Celtic forms of joint ownership of property which, though often banned in statute, were honoured in practice). For the moment the neo-feudal complications of the Carlisle grant did not bother the settlers in the Leeward Islands. However, it led to land titles from 1660 onwards being in a state of confusion.[40]

Warner's original company had consisted solely of Englishmen, but Irish refugees from the Amazon arrived before the first year was out.[41] Then, probably in 1626 (the date is uncertain), Anthony Hilton, an adventurer in the employ of some merchants of Barnstaple, England, brought a group of Irish settlers to St Christopher. There they were assigned lands by Thomas Warner on the windward side of the island, which had the dual disadvantage of being open to raids by the Carib Indians and being harsh for good tobacco growing. They moved to the leeward side of the island, and there managed to raise a crop.[42] Hilton, having returned to England to sell his Irish settlers' tobacco, garnered a commission from the earl of Carlisle to settle any of the uninhabited isles in the Carlisle grant. Hilton and some associates "landed att ye Barbados which they did not like, nor of Antegoa [Antigua] nor Mount Serrat." But, surveying Nevis on 22 July 1628, they found what they wanted. So Hilton gathered up his Irish colonists from St Christopher and moved to Nevis.[43] Within a year they, like the mother colony on St Christopher, were run off their island by a Spanish force that swept through the area on its way to attack the Dutch in Brazil, but both settlements soon were reconstituted.[44]

It is a bit surprising that Hilton landed at Barbados to evaluate it as a potential site of settlement, for in February 1627 a colony had already begun on Barbados. Indeed, a nasty feud was beginning between the earl of Carlisle and his supporters, and rival claimants to this part of the Carlisle patent (which had also been granted to the earl of Pembroke, as a result of Crown ignorance of West Indian geography and through bad spelling, which permitted another reading of Barbados on early documents to mean Barbuda, a barren little island, virtually uninhabitable). The earl of Carlisle won. King Charles I decided in his favour in London, and on the island of Barbados, Carlisle's governor took the representatives of the earl of Pembroke captive and chained them to the mainmast of his ship for an entire month.[45]

The other islands surveyed by Anthony Hilton as a potential site for his Irish colonists were Antigua, which was eventually settled in 1632 and Montserrat, which was settled sometime in the early 1630s (of which more in a moment). These colonies, like Nevis, were spill-overs from St Christopher.

Throughout the English portions of the West Indies (which, up to mid-century meant the Leeward Islands and Barbados), one finds large numbers of Irish migrants. The Bridenbaughs state that "despite meager evidence it is difficult not to conclude that in the English West Indies in 1650, the Irish settlers constituted more than half of the entire population."[46] Even if this estimate is somewhat high (as I suspect it is, given the rudimentary enumerations which were begun after mid-century), the number of Irish people and their importance as prosecutors of what was at the time the prime sector of English imperialism, is undeniable. The great pity is that we have only scant records of what sort of Irish they were. There seem to have been all sorts: Catholics (native Irish, and Old English), and Protestants (mostly New English, and a few Ulster-Scots). The well-off adventurers left their individual marks (as we will see in the case of Montserrat), as did members of the merchant class. But the majority of indentured labourers, small farmers, and artisans did not, save when they made trouble for their social betters or for the governors.

It is clear that throughout the Leeward Islands in the first decades of settlement there was a considerable tension between Protestants and Catholics and between Irish and English, these being overlapping, but by no means identical, lines of social fracture. Some of the Irish Catholics were disadvantaged. Thus, Captain Peter Sweetman's proposal to the Portuguese authorities that he transfer 400 Irish settlers from St Christopher to a Portuguese colony. His reason was that, following the Irish rebellion of 1641, the English Protestants harshly oppressed the Irish Catholics.[47] Still, it would be a mistake to misread as ethnic or sectarian, tensions that rose from other causes. For example, in a journal entry for 21 July 1631, Sir Henry Colt, an English adventurer on St Christopher, wrote that the servants on the island desired that the Spaniards might come back, so that they might be freed. Sir Henry believed that they would not fight to defend their masters.[48] In other circumstances, we will see that the Irish Catholics of the poorer classes are frequently accused of disloyalty. Religion and ethnic matters certainly were pivotal, but so too was class resentment. At some important moments, Irish Catholic planters and Irish Catholic servants and small landholders were on the opposite sides of divisive issues.

The early settlement of Montserrat is a mystery. We do not know when white colonists first arrived. Nor when black slaves were first imported. Nor what use the indigenous inhabitants had for the island.

Probably the first European to set eyes on Montserrat was the lookout on Christopher Columbus's fleet in 1493. Columbus named the West Indian island after the monastery of Santa Maria de Monserrate, located in the Catalan mountains. (This was the place where Ignatius Loyola in the next century saw the vision that led him to form the Jesuits.)[49] Honorific as the name may have been, Columbus did not find the West Indian island worth setting foot on.[50] Thereafter, Montserrat must have been sighted now and again by adventurers who were off-course in their passage to bigger and more tempting places. The first recorded post-Columbian sighting was that previously referred to, Anthony Hilton's reconnaissance of July 1628. On that occasion the only impression Hilton left was his judgment that he did not like Montserrat as a place of possible settlement. Sir Henry Colt on 20 July 1631 recorded that it was high, rough, mountainous and full of woods. There were no inhabitants, he reported, but he did find the "footstepps ... of some naked men."[51] (That Colt assumed from the footprints that the men were naked and not merely shoeless is culturally diagnostic.)

Colt had come upon footprints that almost certainly were those of Carib Indians. These were one of three major indigenous groups in the West Indies: the Ciboney, the Arawak and the Carib. The Carib were a forceful group and were on a long-term northward march from the mainland of South America, driving out the Arawak as they progressed.[52] Precisely when the local Arawak had been driven out by the Carib is not known, but both archaeological and anecdotal evidence indicate that it was shortly pre-Columbian: an Indian woman informed Columbus that Montserrat had been depeopled by the Carib.[53] The Arawak left a burial ground and pottery hoards on Montserrat, but nothing else is known of them on the island.[54]

Their successors, the Carib, were highly mobile, being capable of putting two or three thousand men in war canoes and descending upon an enemy with frightening efficiency. They seem to have been organized in the equivalent of metropoles and hinterlands. That is, the islands of Guadeloupe and Dominica had large permanent populations, as did St Christopher in the Leeward Islands. Montserrat and other small islands seem to have been part of the Carib spheres of influence, being either sparsely peopled or temporarily peopled for specific purposes. The best authorities on the Carib culture suggest that they practised a form of slash-and-burn agriculture. Work parties of men cleared a strip of forest, moving ahead like a Spartan phalanx at the rate of up to 100 metres a day. After the brush dried for six weeks or so, it was set on fire and the land was thus cleared. Then the women moved in and planted root crops. Agricultural production was in the hands of the women who, after harvesting their crop, quickly replanted. When the plot became unproductive it went back to bush, the equivalent of a fallow period in European agriculture.[55]

The early white settlers on Montserrat can only have been grateful that their island was not one of the Carib metropoles. St Christopher was, and from its founding, knew constant terror. Indeed, the settlers on St Christopher had made it through their first year only by forging a temporary alliance with the French (who held part of the island) against the Carib.[56] Battles with the Carib were endemic and in later years, the Carib, although dislodged from St Christopher, allied themselves with the French. Operating out of Guadeloupe, St Vincent, and Dominica, they swept down in fearsome raids, not only upon St Christopher, but on the other Leeward Islands as well.

From the existence of a site of a large garden high in the mountains of Montserrat, it is clear that the island was used on occasion by the Carib. (The garden was possibly a fortified site, for the Carib elsewhere are known to have planted fortified gardens as fall-back positions for use in time of war.)[57] However, whether or not there was a permanent Carib settlement on Montserrat at the time of white colonization is unknown.

There is no doubt that the new colonists on Montserrat were in constant fear of the Carib. It seems likely that there were Carib raids on the colony during its first two decades, but we have no documentation.[58] The son of Montserrat's first governor stated in 1669 that his father "at his own great cost, gained from the Indians and planted the Island of Montserat,"[59] which implies both Amerindian inhabitants on the island and considerable strife. However, that is exactly what one would expect in a petition for royal favour (from which the statement comes), and the statement was intended to resonate with

European beliefs concerning the Carib that were in part real, in part xenophobic myth. The real part was that the Carib were fierce warriors and that they had a special antipathy toward the Anglo-Celtic settlers. They were disposed to ally themselves with the French. According to French accounts, this was in part due to early traders from the British Isles having enticed Carib onto their ships and then selling them as slaves.[60] Given the mobility of the Carib war "periagoes," they were not a nice enemy to have.

But the Carib went beyond being a real enemy and became a nightmare monster, terrifying to the colonists and fascinating to those safely at home in the British Isles. In contemporary letters and government documents of the mid-seventeenth century, one frequently comes across the words "barbarous," "villainous," "treacherous" to describe these Amerindians. Indeed, the word "Indian" is infrequently used without an opprobrious adjective to accompany it. The most interesting aspect of this nightmare vision, which turned the Carib into the equivalent of one of those imaginary, but terrifying, sea monsters that surround the West Indies on contemporary maps, is that they were believed to be cannibals. This was accepted as an article of faith among the Leeward Island colonists. To take an example from Montserrat: as late as 1676, it was being stated in official reports to London that during the Anglo-French war of the 1660s, the Carib of St Vincent and Dominica "surprised the inhabitants of Montserrat and Antigua, burned their houses, tormented and killed the men without quarter, eating many of them."[61]

I doubt the accuracy of this account and of all of the other accounts of Carib cannibalism. Although I would not go as far as does William Arens and question if (save for flesh-eating in survival conditions or as a rare individual psychopathology) cannibalism has ever existed, one has to accept his statement that anthropology (and the historiography which anthropologists frequently use in discussing alleged cannibalism) "has not maintained the usual standards of documentation and intellectual rigour expected when other topics are being considered."[62] This is particularly unfortunate, because, as Arens illustrates in scores of case studies, to call one's enemy, or some group one considers strange, a human-eater, is one of the most universal of human slurs. Everybody seems to have done it.[63] Irish scholars would be, therefore, particularly interested in the seemingly authoritative statement of the great geographer Strabo, who in the first century A.D. reported that there was nothing very interesting to say about the island of Ireland, "except that the inhabitants are more savage than the Britons, since they are man-eaters … and they count it an honourable thing, when their fathers die, to devour them."[64]

That, of course, is pure (or rather, impure) invention, and is no more accurate than the belief that the Carib found their enemies digestible. The credulity of historians and anthropologists concerning Carib flesh-eating is best indicated by the word "cannibal." It is a variant of the word "Carib." Is that not proof? Yes, but it is only proof that Christopher Columbus in 1493 encountered not Carib, but Arawak, and his Arawak informants gave him an earful about the vices of their enemies, the Carib.[65] Later European colonists took this as fact, so of course their reports contained this "fact." The settlers of Montserrat, therefore, were not consciously fabricating anything when they talked of Carib cannibalism. They believed. The new settlers lived in a constant state of fear of the indigene.

The reality behind these fears of the military prowess of the Carib (though not the alleged gustatory habits) was confirmed in 1651, when a force of 2,000 Carib caught the Montserrat colonists unaware. They burned a number of houses, killed several people, and took away cattle and provisions.[66]

If the Carib sweep in and out of the picture, resembling the early Vikings in their fearsomeness and in the reputation of barbarism that surrounded them, the early white settlers of Montserrat are hardly more in focus. Recall here that in July 1631, when Henry Colt reconnoitred the island, he reported no white settlers. The next report is from a Jesuit, Father Andrew White, who accompanied the second Lord Baltimore, on his 1633–34 voyage to Maryland. In late January 1634, he recorded that they approached Montserrat, which was a "noble plantation" of "Irish Catholiques."[67] Therefore, the Montserrat colony was established sometime between mid-1631 and the end of 1633. Better than that one cannot do.[68]

Nor can one be precise about who first settled Montserrat. In this case priority of arrival had no implications concerning ownership, that having been decided by the Carlisle grant which preceded Montserrat's colonization. There is no historical merit in speculating about who arrived first and exactly when. Instead, it is more profitable to suggest that between mid-1631 and the end of 1633,[69] a composite white settlement had arisen. This settlement had four elements, none of which had demonstrable chronological priority over the others. The most exotic of these was a party of Irish settlers who had been captured in the Amazon, probably at Tauregue, but possibly from some other settlements. According to one of their group, Bernard O'Brien, they escaped sometime in 1629 or 1630. These men, only eighteen in number, made their way first to Trinidad, where they established friendly relations with the Amerindians and acquired canoes. They then journeyed to an English settlement on the Surinam

River and thence some went to St Christopher, others to Montserrat and others to Barbados. How many stayed on in Montserrat is not known, but it could have been only a handful of persons at most.[70]

Second, the early settlement probably had Irish Catholics in it who had been thrown out of the Virginia Colony. "The inhabitants of Montserrat are Irishmen who were expelled by the English of Virginia for the profession of the Catholic faith," was Father White's report.[71] White was no neophyte in the New World, for he had accompanied the first Lord Baltimore on his reconnaissance of the Chesapeake region, and had been priest to a congregation of "Irish exiles" who came with Baltimore in 1629–30.[72] Hence, one credits both his describing the Montserrat settlers as being Irish Catholics and as being Virginia exiles. (What one cannot do, however, is assume that his one descriptive statement covered the entire population of Montserrat, small as that was.) And what is tricky, is that there is a variant reading of the Latin text of Father White's note which states not, as does the official Jesuit history quoted above, that the Irish were "expelled" from Virginia but that they were Irish Catholics "whom the Virginians would not suffer to live with them because of their religion."[73] This helps, because, in the absence of corroborative evidence concerning an expulsion from among the Virginia settlers of persons of Irish Catholic background, it is best to tie Father White's observations to a group of Irish Catholics of whom we have independent evidence: the group of dispossessed Old English landlords from Waterford who were sent to Virginia by order, but whom that colony turned away.[74] This occurred in 1630, and it would not have been an unnatural reach for men who were in essence exiled to the New World to seek out the more accommodating settlements of St Christopher and Nevis, each with their large Irish component. And from thence to move in a year or two on to Montserrat. That process fits well into our known time boundaries.

A third group enters the picture. These are Irish colonists brought to Montserrat by Anthony Briskett (var: Brisket, Bryskett) who was in a technical sense "New English" in Ireland (that is, Protestant, belonging to the band of outside settlers whose roots in Ireland ran back no further than the last quarter of the seventeenth century: colonizers in Ireland.) But his family background was unusual. It satisfied none of the usual criteria except one: that the people who came to Ireland as colonizers were men on the make. Some were civilized, others near barbarians, but always they had an eye on the main chance.

Anthony Briskett was the grandson of Antonio Bruschetto, an Italian merchant of considerable capital who settled in England in the

1530s and anglicized his name as "Anthony Bryskett."[75] (The spelling "Briskett" later became standard, but variations occur.) He prospered as a London merchant, married and had several children. His third son was named Lodowick, born in 1536, a man of charm, literary ability, and of reasonable, but not overarching ambition. Presumably the Briskett family conformed to English Protestantism, as represented by the Established Church at the Reformation, because young Lodowick matriculated at Trinity College, Cambridge, at a time when religious conformity was required. Through good luck (and probably through his father's having become well known to the Cecil family and others, through business dealings, especially on the European continent), Lodowick was taken on by Sir Henry Sidney as a secretary. Thus, in 1565, he visited Ireland while Sidney was on his second tour as Lord Deputy of Ireland. Moreover, Sir Henry in 1572 chose Lodowick as one of two companions to take young Philip Sidney on a tour of Europe. When Sir Henry was appointed Lord Deputy of Ireland yet again in 1575, Lodowick Briskett again went with him, this time with a royal appointment as Clerk of the Irish Privy Council. From that base, Briskett put together a portfolio of government posts (including, eventually, clerk of the council of Munster). He gained the friendship of fellow colonists in Ireland such as Edmund Spenser and Sir Walter Raleigh, and acquired in 1582 an estate at Macmine, near Enniscorthy, County Wexford. He was expected to maintain twenty men at arms from this estate of roughly 120 acres. These lands, which he rented at £30 sterling per annum, had been seized by the Crown from allegedly contumacious Irish rebels. At first Lodowick thought of his Irish residence as some sort of bucolic experiment. As he told a friend, he wished to test "whether the life of a borderer in this life be alike perilous unto all men, and to see if a just and honest simple life, may not even among the most barbarous people of the world breed security to him that shall live near them or among them."[76] He found out: in the rising of October 1598, he was driven from his estate and thereafter spent several years on the European continent as an agent for the English government and probably for private clients as well. He returned to Ireland in 1609 and died within the next three years.

Who can say whether Lodowick Briskett was Italian, English, New Irish, or, since he probably was all three, in what manner the strands wove round? And how does one characterize his son, Anthony Briskett, the chief colonizer and first governor of Montserrat? Father Aubrey Gwynn strongly implies that he emotionally identified with dispossessed Old English and native Irish who lost their lands, for he was himself "removed" from his family holdings of 120 acres to another of the same size elsewhere in County Wexford.[77] Perhaps: at least he must have understood their response to arbitrary government. Anthony Briskett, however, received another grant of land, quite unlike the truly dispossessed. And Briskett was Protestant and, whatever his frustrations, he had access to people in power in London, because of connections made by his father and even his grandfather. Only those characteristics can explain how he was able to obtain from the first earl of Carlisle the appointment as tenant-in-chief, governor, and colonizer of Montserrat. This he accomplished either in the late 1620s, or at the very beginning of the 1630s. One suspects that in addition to having good connections, he spread a bit of money around (Carlisle was notoriously improvident and forever in financial difficulties), and that he was adjudged to be able to handle the Irish whom he planned to take to the West Indies. The latter is an ugly phrase, ethnically offensive but not unrealistic in the case of a man whose father had thought the Irish the most barbarous people in the world, who had spent his own adult life in keeping Irish servants and tenants, native Irish and Old English, in line. In the actual event, Briskett turned out to be an efficient neo-feudal magnate.

It is very tempting to compress the establishment of Briskett's colony and the rejection of the Irish Catholics by the Virginia colony into a single episode. Father Gwynn attempts this, but it does not work.[78] Briskett's colonizing was a distinct effort and effectively the spine of the Montserrat plantation. Briskett held the legal force of the plantation, in the form of the neo-feudal governorship granted to him by the first earl of Carlisle. Equally important, he had the personal drive to make his will supreme. It was his plantation, his domain, and the hard men from the Amazon, from Munster, along with the smattering of English from other islands and from abroad, played by his rules. We know little of Anthony Briskett as a person, but certainly anyone who could manage a colony that was beyond the line and beyond the agencies of external law enforcement, was no small or soft man.

A fourth group of settlers came from nearby. There is a reasonable probability that settlers from St Christopher (and perhaps from Nevis) moved on to Montserrat. These were apt to be mostly Irish Catholics, but not necessarily entirely so.[79]

Thus, by the time the Rev. Father White saw Montserrat in early 1634, it was a composite community made up mostly of Irish Catholics. That the governor was a Protestant Irishman of Italian background was not something Father White could have been expected to dwell on. He saw what a Catholic priest in the colonies would wish to see. Nor would he have had time to perceive that the Irish Catholics themselves were disparate, Old English and native Irish, men with resources and men without; or that among them were not only a scattering of English settlers but also Irish Protestants of the less privileged sort, former small tenants from Munster who had not done as well in Ireland as they expected.[80] That the main harbour on Montserrat soon was named "Kingsale" (the most common seventeenth-century form of "Kinsale") was an indication of the only thing this diverse collection of Irish colonists had in common: for most of them, Kinsale harbour had been their gateway out of Ireland.

Anthony Briskett was sufficiently confident of his control over the settlers of Montserrat to return to England in 1636, there to pick up another shipload of colonists. The voyage was necessary in part because James Hay, the first earl of Carlisle had died. Briskett successfully negotiated with the second earl a new commission as governor of Montserrat. Then, in a petition to Charles I, Briskett asked for letters of introduction to the Lord Deputy of Ireland "to be admitted contractor for tobacco at the same rate as Captain Warner [of St Christopher] and others."[81] Clearly, what Briskett was developing was a simple and efficient economic loop: he would transport to Ireland tobacco grown on Montserrat and he would take from Ireland colonists who would become part of the island economy and would grow more tobacco for transport to Ireland. This was a potentially profitable business and was not to be entrusted to the wrong sort of Irishman. That is why in his petition to the king, Briskett pointed out that he was erecting on the island "A church of stone and brick, for the glory of God and for your Majesty's honour."[82] This was to indicate his allegiance to the Established Church, and to imply that his colony was loyal to the English state.

Briskett brought over specially recruited colonists, including, one infers, indentured servants, mostly from Munster. Nothing kept either of the larger groups of settlers, the Old English in particular, from doing the same.[83] Aubrey Gwynn noted the presence among Irish emigrants of many clearly Munster names – Collins, Barry, Sullivan, Roche, Cormack, Callaghan, Driscoll, and Ryan[84] – and these were found on Montserrat. Further, recruits joined the settlement from other islands. Of the more exotic origins we have no record, but clearly many came from St Christopher, which was becoming crowded. To those who emigrated voluntarily from St Christopher to Montserrat, must be added a group of Irish Catholics who were shipped there in 1643 in order to reduce the endless squabbling between English Protestants and Irish Catholics.[85] This can only have been done with Anthony Briskett's approval, for his powers on

Montserrat were no less than those of Warner on St Christopher. Presumably, he remained confident of his ability to manage contumacious Catholics. And, probably there continued to be in-migrants who had tried life on the continent of North America and, having found success wanting, tried again elsewhere. If the suggestion that Briskett had a connection with John White of Ballyhea, County Cork, who became "surveyor" of Virginia is true, then this is all the more probable. Virginia in the sense used in White's position, meant the coast of North America from present-day Florida to New York.[86] This included Maryland. So, some of the backwash of North American colonies, especially dissatisfied Irish Catholics, could have been directed to Montserrat.

From whatever mix of sources, by mid-seventeenth century Montserrat was a successful colony. It would last. In 1741, J. Oldmixon stated that the population of Montserrat in 1648 consisted of 1,000 families and that this yielded a militia of 360 men.[87] This undoubtedly is high (for the total white population of Montserrat in 1678 was under 2,700) and, in a context wherein every male between late adolescence and elderly infirmity was needed in the militia, 1,000 families would have produced a militia of well over 1,000 men. Undoubtedly John Messenger is correct to suggest that Oldmixon meant that the population was 1,000 persons, and as a rough estimate that fits well both with the militia figures and with later censuses of the island.[88]

Not all, but most, of these persons were of Irish background, and most (but again, not all) of these were Catholics, either Old English or native Irish. That fits well with a memorial sent to the Sacred Congregation of Propaganda in Rome in December 1639 which estimated that at that time 3,000 Irish persons were living on St Christopher and the neighbouring islands[89] – that is, that as of the start of the 1640s there were 3,000 Irish in the Leewards. Given that most of these would have been on the mother colony, St Christopher, and that Nevis had a strong Irish representation, this would yield a reasonable estimate for 1650 of approximately 1,000 colonists on Montserrat, of whom perhaps three-quarters to four-fifths were Irish of one sort or another.[90]

Notice the one group that has thus far been left out of the discussion – black slaves. T. Savage English thought that no African slaves had been brought to the island before the Restoration,[91] but Howard Fergus points to a list of property confiscated in 1654 in which one of the larger planters on the island had fifty slaves.[92] That is the earliest attested date for an African presence on Montserrat. However, I suspect that some African slaves were on the island virtually from Day One of white colonization (and there may briefly have been some Amerindian slaves as well). Why?

First, because in 1626, Thomas Warner on his way back from England acquired sixty African slaves.[93]

Second, in a tactical move in the tussle between the French and English for control of St Christopher, in 1635 a French governor promised liberation to all the African slaves on the island and this gave the French, with the Africans' aid, temporary victory over Governor Warner and his colonists.[94] Third, consider that the single most valuable chattel, and the most mobile, that any planter possessed was a slave, and one is led to the strong probability that some of the new colonists on Montserrat, specifically those that came from St Christopher, or from other places in the New World, brought with them their most valuable property, their human chattel. This does not mean that there were many slaves on Montserrat in the early years for, in fact, the island's economy in its first two or three decades was based mostly on white labour in tobacco and indigo cultivation. However, there must have been black slaves on the estates of the more substantial colonists. It is difficult, for example, to imagine Anthony Briskett creating an estate of 1,400 acres solely with indentured servants and such free labourers as he could find.[95]

The second (and last) decade of Anthony Briskett's reign as a marcher lord in charge of his own neo-feudal principality, was no less eventful than the first. Indeed Montserrat moved even farther beyond the line of comity and amity than it had previously been.

In some part this was because the Irish Rebellion of October 1641 in the homeland inevitably had long-range reverberations. The massacre of the Protestants, though much less extensive than contemporaries believed, nevertheless was real, and it inevitably increased the Catholic-Protestant rift throughout the English-speaking colonies, most especially where the Catholics were Irish. Further, the set of fissures that appeared between the Irish and the English in British politics from 1641 onwards effected a decline in the status of everyone from Ireland,[96] for, from a distance, all Irishmen looked alike to the English.

More important were direct effects of the civil war within England. From 1642 onwards, the royal chain of authority that backed the proprietary governors (such as Warner on St Christopher and Briskett on Montserrat) ceased to be effective. Yet parliamentary authority did not fill the void. A parliamentary Commission for Plantations under the earl of Warwick was appointed in 1643 and tried to gain control of the Leeward Islands by nominating new governors. The colonists on all four islands, however, refused to accept parliament's authority, and the old governors remained in control.[97] In effect, from 1642 onwards, the Leeward Islands were in reality what they previously had been only in theory: little feudal kingdoms, and now virtually independent.

In 1645 Charles I sent the earl of Marlborough on a mission to the Leeward Islands and to Barbados. For Marlborough, this was a mission both on behalf of royal authority and on behalf of his own financial well-being, because his father had been promised a pension by the first earl of Carlisle and this had run to large arrears. Barbados refused to grant him any authority whatsoever, but both St Christopher and Montserrat accepted his authority. Since, however, the two governors, Warner and Briskett respectively, stayed in power after he left, the mission must have had no effect except to maintain a certain lukewarm royalism on these islands. Meantime, the earl of Warwick kept writing to the Leeward governors asking them to put themselves under parliamentary authority. He had to ask, for there was no way he could make any threats effective.[98]

If, from 1642 onwards, the Leeward Islands were virtually independent principalities, that does not mean life was easy for their governors. Quite the reverse, for without any hope of aid from central authorities in the British Isles, men such as Warner on St Christopher and Briskett on Montserrat had to control a cage full of snarling lions, with only the force of their own personalities. Sir Thomas Warner's notably harsh hand was stayed when a "rebellion" (more a community protest) occurred in December 1641 and a second one in February 1642. On the latter occasion Warner was forced to give up his one-man rule and to create an elected twenty-four member assembly.[99] As mentioned earlier, the next year Warner tried to reduce internal squabbling on St Christopher by shipping off a band of troublesome Irish Catholics to his colleague Anthony Briskett on Montserrat.

Things went somewhat better for Briskett. While Warner was being confronted by 1,500 of his settlers in February 1642, Briskett was able to write with relief, "God be praised, our people here are all quiet."[100] By November 1642, however, he was faced with a partial rent strike. The large planters continued to pay the levies owed to the earl of Carlisle, but the poorer planters did not have the means to pay. Wisely, Briskett forbore to enforce the dues.[101]

How long the Leeward Islands could have gone without falling into chaos and total barbarism is anyone's guess. In 1647, the second earl of Carlisle, in as deep debt as his father had been, leased for twenty-one years his patent of the Caribbean islands to Francis Lord Willoughby: half the revenue from this lease was to go to the payment of Carlisle's creditors. As far as the Leeward Islands were concerned, this was a fictional exercise. Soon after this transaction, Willoughby was forced to flee to Holland, where he took up command of a royalist fleet. A man of plastic loyalties, he previously had been a leader of the Presbyterian interest, and had fought against the king. He now sailed for Barbados to prosecute his own interests as holder of the Carlisle patent. There he installed himself as governor and held power for two years.[102]

Both Thomas Warner and Anthony Briskett hung grimly on, somehow maintaining order, until 1649. Warner, godfather of the Leeward enterprise, died in that year. So too did Anthony Briskett, who left a son, Anthony Briskett II, below the legal age, a wife Elizabeth, an estate of 1,400 acres,[103] and impending chaos.

In the same year, Oliver Cromwell conquered Ireland on his way to establishing personal control over the entire empire, home and abroad.

The neo-feudal domain that Anthony Briskett created and ruled should have been a pleasant little garden. It was easily comprehensible, being roughly pear-shaped, eleven miles (18 km) in length and seven miles (11 km) wide. The total surface area is 39.5 square miles (102 km^2).[104] In the long term, the island may be considered a footnote to volcanic activity. Three mountain ranges, the highest of which reaches to just over 3,000 feet, are the island's central features. Alec Waugh, visiting Montserrat in 1948 just after having been on Dominica, wrote, "the whole thing has a designed architectural effect that Dominica lacks. Moreover, because the mountains are not clustered close, you have a sense of breadth and distance. In Dominica you look down and you look up, but you never look across. In Montserrat you look from one plateau to another, over deep, broad valleys."[105]

Several soufrières produce sulphuric emissions and, in places, a satisfyingly satanic atmosphere. The mountain ranges yield cliffs that provide a barrier to easy landing by ship. In fact there is no natural deep harbour for the island, although on the west coast, sheltered from the winds, there is a stretch of land where the slope is gradual and small craft may land. The cliffs and the mountain ranges are extremely important in making Montserrat livable, for they protect much of the island from the salt-heavy trade winds. The north and east of the island, therefore, is relatively dry and, further, desiccated from the salty trade winds, but the rest of the island receives a fair degree of orographic rainfall.[106]

Rain, of course, is the key to most West Indian islands, for artesian water is virtually non-existent and whether or not fresh water falls determines habitability. On Montserrat the distribution of the rain is very uneven. It ranges from thirty-five to forty inches a year in the northern and eastern dry parts to about sixty inches on the western and southern portions and seventy inches on a few mountainous areas in the centre of the island. The best testimony to the presence of frequent rainfall is the island's volcanic mountains being serrated by over 100 watercourses which drain into the sea. The larger of these are locally termed "ghauts" – pronounced guts – and this means the same as cuts or ravines, stemming as the word does from the same root that gives us the modern architectural term "gutter." The larger of these ravines are several hundred feet deep in places.[107]

Montserrat's climate is remarkably even. The mean maximum temperature is 79 degrees Fahrenheit (26° Celsius) and the mean minimum is 73 degrees.[108] In the hot season the mean maximum is only a few degrees higher. The point here is that despite frequent complaints by people from the British Isles about the soul- and health-destroying nature of the boiling Caribbean climate, a place such as Montserrat was more than merely habitable. There is none of the 100° heat and near-100 percent humidity that settlers in the area that is now Mississippi, Alabama and Louisiana experienced. In fact, the maximum summer temperatures of places as far north as Minneapolis, Minnesota and Winnipeg, Manitoba considerably exceed the maximums for Montserrat (and, one should add, in those places winter temperatures of 30 below Fahrenheit [–34°C] are an annual occurrence.)

It would require a good deal of imagination and a lot of hard work to turn such a place into the valley of Gehenna, but the Anglo-Celtic settlers had both qualities in abundance. They attacked the island foot by foot, soldiers on the march against the natural environment. In so doing they ultimately degraded the island physically, and degraded themselves even more. In watching this European campaign, one is reminded of the march of the crusaders against Saladin. They marched in full European armour, throughout the daylight hours, moving across the Holy Land with no heed for the sun that beat down on them nor the baked land beneath their feet. Saladin let them come, day after day, until finally he and his men, wearing little or no armour and having rested in the shade and filled themselves with water, fell on the crusaders who, being desiccated and exhausted, died, victims of their own hubris.

Montserrat before the arrival of Anthony Briskett and his crusaders was covered down to the shoreline with heavy bush. This was particularly dense in the south and west, where rainfall was heaviest. Aside from the poisonous manchineel tree, and some of the sulphurous pools, there was nothing natural of danger to the colonists (save, perhaps, improperly washed cassava roots). In the absence of any direct descriptions of Montserrat on the eve of European colonization, the best surrogate is the descriptions of St Christopher on the eve of its European invasion, collected by Captain John Smith from the earliest settlers of that island. According to these reports, natural foods grew freely: cassava, maize (New World corn), pineapple, potatoes, cabbage and radishes. Wild sugarcane was found, as were various melons (the modern cantaloupe for example), edible gourds, lettuce and parsley. Those were for the taking. For the shooting were pigeon, turtle doves and flamingoes. Large tortoises provided a meat dish for forty or fifty men, each capture. And there were fish and prawns in abundance.[109] Had the Europeans been interested in practising a restrained form of hunting and gathering economy, supplemented by small gardens, this would have been an ideal place.

Of course they were not. Instead, the settlers of Montserrat were dedicated to making money through the cultivation of what was then Europe's newest and most fashionable drug: nicotine as found in tobacco plants. In fact, drug cultivation was one of the primary ways that most of the New World colonies were financed in their early years, and this by governmental decision. Before the beginning of West Indian colonization, the cultivation of tobacco had been prohibited in England and in Ireland. This was primarily an attempt to help the Virginia colony (as well as to aid the exchequer through duties on imported tobacco),[110] and it virtually pre-ordained the early course of agriculture on Montserrat.

Tobacco was a good start-up crop from a micro-economic point of view. Twenty- to twenty-five thousand adult plants can be grown from half an ounce of seed, and the plants are ready for harvest four to six months after planting.[111] Even taking into account drying time and time required to transport the leaf to the British Isles, a financial turn-around was possible in a year to eighteen months after first planting. In actuality, by the time Montserrat was settled, the new colonists did not have to wait for some British vessel to call for their product. Opportunistic Dutch traders, having gained experience earlier in the Amazon trade, became the middlemen of the tobacco business. Thus, small planters could deliver their leaf to one of the Dutch-built warehouses on Montserrat, and the product would soon be on the way to the Old World on one of the Dutch vessels that were collecting in the region. For small growers this willingness of the Dutch to take their leaf as part of larger consignments was a boon, for it did away with the inequality of bargaining power between buyer and seller. (In effect, the Dutch middlemen provided the tobacco farmers with some of the same advantages that a modern-day producers' marketing cooperative provides.)[112]

Tobacco growing was labour intensive. Obviously, land had first to be cleared. In the pioneer generation, the technique employed was the same as used by the Amerindians. Large trees were cut down and allowed to dry out and then the plot was burned. In the burned-over ground, with large stumps still standing, like carbonized megaliths, food crops and tobacco were planted. Only in the next generation were the fields completely cleared.[113] Pulsipher shrewdly suggests that once the land was cleared, the domestic goat probably was the chief constable of the margins of each field:[114] a tethered goat browsing, as do all members of the deer family, on its hind legs, is able to bring down saplings ten or fifteen feet high. On sloping ground (as most of it is on Montserrat), the goat is especially effective.

The actual growing of tobacco was not easy and it required considerable skill to produce a first-class product. The young plants were germinated from seeds and then were separated and set after a rain, when the ground was soft and moist. They had to be constantly protected against weeds, insects, and grubs. It took some judgment to know when to cut the leaves, which were allowed to lie in the sun for a day and then were hung in drying houses, designed to provide constant ventilation. Thereafter, the leaves were stripped out and the harsh veins removed.[115] Tobacco from Montserrat acquired a reputation as being superior to that of the other islands.[116] To preserve that reputation, an act was passed by the Montserrat assembly in 1669 stopping the practice of selling tobacco in rolls (which permitted the passing off of bad leaf) and requiring that any tobacco which was used in commercial transactions be tendered only in leaf form, which could be easily inspected for quality.[117]

Of significance, but of much less importance than tobacco was another plant which also was looked upon as "a small man's crop" – indigo.[118] The production of indigo dye, however, required several hands and some modest capital. When the plants were in mature form, indigo was harvested four times a year. A system of soaking vats was used to remove the dye from the plants, and it was then fermented until, finally, a reagent was added so that the dye precipitated out in a solid form.[119] Thus, even though a small man's crop, because of the labour and capital requirements, indigo production was beyond the reach of the operators of one- and two-person farms.

A third form of small-time agriculture undoubtedly flourished, namely provision growing. This went untabulated, however, even in the later part of the century because when small farmers grew provisions for their neighbours on large plantations, or for the Sunday market or even for shipment in small boats to St Christopher, the activity was not recorded. It was not part of the imperial system, which was concerned only with items that went back and forth to the British Isles. For borderline farmers, however, growing maize or root crops for barter or sale must have been the difference between surviving or not.

Under any circumstances, clearing the land and planting, tending, and harvesting the tobacco or indigo or root crops was hard manual labour. But there are ways to make this easier and they involve, simply, not fighting the natural world any more than is really necessary. However, as Lydia Pulsipher argues, the Anglo-Celtic settlers (and especially their leaders) were driven by certain cultural determinants which led them to make life much more difficult than it needed to be. Among these was an irrational, but very deep, demand that agricultural spaces be neatly cleared and made as clean (that is, as unnatural) and open as possible.[120] It was as if the island of Montserrat was supposed to look like the modern Curragh of Kildare, an impossibility. And, in the organization of their work methods, they were surpassing strange. The life of the manual labourers and of the small farmers who worked alongside them was remarkably hellish and not least because few adaptations were made to the tropics. Instead of working from early morning to midday and then resting until mid afternoon, and then working until sundown (the pattern adopted in southern Europe and in Latin and South America), the Irish and English worked straight through the middle of the day, just as they would have done in Sussex or Wexford. And this they did in thick, rough clothes that would have served them well after a frosty night in the home islands.[121]

Two historical questions run through the period 1630–50 and neither can be directly answered. Still, they must here be posed, and then posed again in later eras, for they are central to Montserrat's position as Ireland's only seventeenth- and eighteenth-century colony: what was the actual position of the Roman Catholic religion? and how bad were conditions for the poorer white settlers?

The first question requires a certain critical distance, because the presuppositions of church historians, from Aubrey Gwynn onward, has been to view the Irish on Montserrat as demi-martyrs for the Catholic faith. Simultaneously, it has been the assumption of these writers (a presupposition never examined) that the church was seriously and deeply concerned about providing for the spiritual welfare of these Irish colonizers.

As mentioned earlier, the first church on the island was constructed by Governor Anthony Briskett in the 1630s. This stone and brick structure in Plymouth, dedicated to St Anthony, was, according to its builder, intended for the glory of God and the honour of his majesty, Charles I.[122] This is a sure indicator that it was an edifice of the Established Church (which we will frequently denominate "Anglican" in the discussion that follows; it is a useful term, even if not used at the time). The building itself was known for its beauty and must have been one of the most impressive buildings in the West Indies in its day. Not only was it of stone and brick construction (at a time when masonry construction was rare in the islands), but the pews and pulpit were a showplace for some of the West Indies' best carpentry and joinery work. The interior had a sweet savour, for the joinery was done with scented wood from local forests.[123] A second Anglican church (whose date and location are unknown) was built somewhat later. These two buildings were levelled by the French invasion of 1667. They were quickly rebuilt, but were then demolished by a major earthquake on Christmas Day 1672. Both of these Established Church houses of worship were again rebuilt. Each time the rebuilding was at the instruction of the then-governor of the island.[124]

In informing Charles I that he was constructing a church to the glory of God and to his majesty's honour, Anthony Briskett was strictly truthful both in what he said and did not say: he did not suggest that a clergyman was to be appointed (and indeed one was not appointed until the 1670s). To the extent that the island was served, it was by clerics who came from elsewhere, making short visits from the other Leeward Islands or Barbados. Divine service must have been a rare occurrence. As late as 1671, the governor of the Leeward Islands wrote that in the islands there were at least forty parishes of the Established Church, yet he was able to point to only "one drunken orthodox priest, one drunken sectary priest, and one drunken parson who had noe orders."[125] From the viewpoint of the Anglican religious Establishment, Montserrat in the first half of the seventeenth century was virtually forgotten.

The Catholic church did no better, although after the rebellion began in Ireland in 1641, it had an excuse: Irish Catholicism was associated with active disloyalty in the home countries and therefore operated under difficulties abroad. In 1637, two priests from the ecclesiastical province of Tuam went out with a shipload of emigrants to the West Indies. The priests operated out of St Christopher and may have made a visit to Montserrat, although this is by no means certain. In any event, their mission was short: one of them died soon after arrival and the other died less than two years later.[126]

Next, the Irish Jesuits mooted a mission. Father Matthew O'Hartegan proposed that he be allowed to serve the Irish on St Christopher and the neighbouring islands. He had command of the three relevant languages, he noted: French (which presumably would be useful to serve the French Catholics on their half of St Christopher, if he were permitted to do so by French authorities), English, and Irish.[127] However, the mission was not to be, for the Jesuits and the Capuchin Fathers of Normandy became involved in an argument over whose mission this should be. The Capuchins won and the Sacred Congregation of Propaganda forbade any Jesuit to set out on this mission. The Capuchins, French-speaking, had a mission on the French portion of St Christopher.[128]

Only at mid-century is there any certainty that the Catholics of Montserrat actually saw a priest on their island. In 1650, the Jesuits were finally permitted to send a priest to the Leeward Islands and they despatched a Limerick Jesuit, Father John Stritch. He arrived on St Christopher before the end of the year 1650, and built a chapel on the French side of that island, but close to the plantations on the English side. The Irish Catholics were overjoyed, and slipped across the line without hesitation. Father Stritch reported having to hear confession from dawn until one o'clock in the afternoon for three straight months. He gave communion and baptized children, of which there must have been a considerable backlog. (One suspects that he also performed a large number of what contemporary clerics called "subsequent marriages.")

Having engaged in the cure of souls on St Christopher, Father Stritch went on to Montserrat. There he did not erect a chapel, but served mass in the woods. The scene must have resembled the eighteenth-century Penal Era masses in Ireland, but in a tropical setting. He set up an altar, and day after day, he served mass, heard confessions, and performed baptisms and marriages. In order to do so, he disguised himself as a wood cutter, and he and the faithful cut down a few trees every day and made it appear as if a lumbering camp was in operation.[129] Father Stritch stayed in the Leeward Islands, centring his work on St Christopher, but he visited Montserrat at intervals until his recall to Ireland in 1660.[130]

One should take Father Stritch's meeting his flock on Montserrat in the woods, not as an indication of actual secrecy (and certainly not a secret successfully guarded for a full decade), but as part of a tacit

Geneva Convention with the authorities. In actual fact, the Protestant Irishman who served as governor of Montserrat in the 1650s, Roger Osborne, knew about the actions of the visiting priest. This becomes clear in a set of depositions in an unrelated criminal matter Osborne was involved with in 1654. The governor was said to permit a "Romish priest" to come and go on the island and to say mass and perform marriages. Osborne was also said to have permitted crosses to be carried before the coffin at funerals.[131] Yet, though the priest came and went and said mass, even the governor's worst enemy could not say that "publique mass" was said in the island.[132] Notice that fine point: mass yes, but public mass no; sacraments in the woods, yes, in a chapel, no. The governor, being an Irishman, had worked out the same sort of compromise that emerged in Ireland in the mid-eighteenth century Penal Era. The Roman Catholic church was inhibited by the authorities but not seriously prohibited. As long as the priests did not become "cheeky" (to use a South African term applied to assertive non-whites that fits all too perfectly), they would be permitted to serve their flocks. This was a compromise, confirmed by a set of rituals, that both sides understood full well.

After Father Stritch returned home to Ireland in 1660, there was a brief hiatus and then he was replaced on St Christopher by Father John Grace of the diocese of Cashel,[133] the heart of the region from which most of the Irish colonists came. Thereafter, Montserrat was served sporadically by priests from St Christopher or, when wars were not in train, from Martinique or Guadeloupe. Only in 1756 was the first resident priest, Dominic Lynch, settled on the island.[134] At that time, mass was being celebrated in the house of the Hamilton family, wealthy Catholics.[135] The first unmistakeable evidence of there being a Catholic church building on the island is in 1852.[136]

Because religious provision during the neo-feudal era was so very sparse – we have no absolutely firm evidence of any cleric of any sort visiting Montserrat before 1651, although probably both Catholic and Anglican priests made one or two visits before then – this is a good place to make three suggestions that will be relevant to the later period, when we know a bit more about the social and economic position (if not the pastoral care) of the inhabitants.

The first of these is that despite the claims of the ecclesiastical literature (especially Father Aubrey Gwynn's work), the Catholic church did not evince much concern with the faithful. In the seventeenth century, the church authorities had a good deal more on their minds than a few Irish colonists on the far edge of the earth, and the church had severe demands on its resources and little to spare for the separated brethren.

Secondly, despite the implication of most church history of the period, we cannot equate the official religion of the churches with the religious beliefs of the people. The beliefs of the colonists were much more plastic, much less determined by official dogma, than it might appear. Thus, we will see after 1650, a phenomenon that almost certainly existed before then. This has been well described by Brian McGinn: "The religious status of the early settlers was in fact flexible and equivocal. Rather than professing either a Catholic or a Protestant faith, many Irish planters adhered to both – either at separate times or, in some cases, simultaneously."[137] McGinn continues:

> The religious ambiguity was hardly surprising, given the conflicting loyalties the planters had juggled back at home. Many of them were Old English – families of Norman origin who had settled in Ireland as far back as the twelfth or thirteenth century. Some had become hibernicized, and almost all had retained their pre-Reformation Catholic Faith. But the Old English were also loyal to the English Crown, relying on its protections against possible dispossession by the native Irish, whose lands their ancestors had occupied.[138]

Further, as we shall see later, some of the New English – Protestants who had settled in Ireland in the sixteenth and early seventeenth centuries and had displaced both native Irish Catholics and Old English Catholics – maintained ties that imply crypto-Catholicism on the part of some of their number.

As for the native Irish, they had been universally Catholic, and for the most part stayed so. However, I would speculate that if we had detailed information on the religious practices of the native Irish settlers and their descendants on Montserrat for the entire seventeenth century, and for the first half of the eighteenth century, we would find that many of them had recourse to the Anglican church for baptisms, marriages, and burials, and that some of them moved quietly into an ambiguous Establishment Protestantism. I suggest this because it is a pattern that existed on other frontiers, and had little to do with Irish Catholicism or Anglican Protestantism, and everything to do with the fact that simple people desired religious services: call it superstition, call it devotion, call it primitive Christianity, it matters not. When placed in a New World, without their own form of Christianity conveniently to hand, simple people in hard circumstances turned for comfort to the next closest thing. Certainly this happened to many of the Irish Catholics in colonial America, where, by the time of the first census of 1790, probably more than 30,000

Irish Catholics had turned Protestant, largely as a response to frontier conditions.[139] Emphatically, this situation was generic, not simply a matter of Catholics apostatizing into Protestants. It easily could work in the other direction. To provide another frontier example: one observes the lament of the Rev. James MacGregor, a Presbyterian clergyman, who in the early nineteenth century surveyed the religious situation on the Celtic fringe of Nova Scotia. He reported to his synod that "they need not imagine that all Presbyterian emigrants continue Presbyterians. Multitudes of them settle among every other religious denomination, and in a few years become members of their churches." Many, he said, became Roman Catholics.[140]

On Montserrat, most of the conversions must have been towards Protestantism, for two obvious reasons. One is that in the later seventeenth century, the Established Church started to provide full-time religious professionals on the island, while the Roman Catholic church did not until the second half of the eighteenth century. Second, there was a material advantage to becoming Protestant. Even though penal legislation was not (as we shall see) nearly as strict on Montserrat as in the Irish homeland, it made life easier if one were a Protestant, at least part of the time.

To return to the matter of how tough things were for the poorer Irish settlers, this revolves in large part in this period around the issue of what the status of indentured servant actually entailed. This is a wider question in the history of the New World, because it is estimated that between 1630 and 1780 50 to 60 percent of the "labour flow" to the British colonies were servants, who were either formally indentured or whose status was virtually the same as that of indentured servants.[141] For the Leeward Islands and Barbados there exists a strong historiographic tradition which virtually equates white indentured servitude with slavery. One says "virtually" because this is one of those areas where the denotative sense of words and their connotations war with each other. Not many writers go as far as does John C. Messenger, who talks of the "conditions of servitude experienced by Irish slaves in Montserrat."[142] However, it is hard not to read a sentence such as the following – "wherever slavery ultimately developed, indentured servitude had earlier been in use"[143] – and not slide into the inference that the two were overlapping, if not identical, conditions. I mention that particular example, because in fact it is by an author who is opposed to any equation of black slavery and white indentured servitude.

A primary communicator of the idea that white indentured servitude is not merely continuous historically with black slavery, but substantively the same as it, was Eric Williams, who through a vigorous political and intellectual life preached an economic equivalent of Liberation Theology. Williams in his political life tried to escape from the racialism that potentially bedevils most anti-colonial movements by developing in his intellectual life the idea that slavery, while having a good deal to do with race, at heart was the product of something else: it was a logical and inevitable stage in the development of capitalism. In his version of Marxism's canonical stages of development, white servitude was replaced by black slavery, as a footnote to the post-1650 "suppression of the small farm by the large plantation, with its consequent demand for a large and steady supply of labour."[144] Although he does not completely equate the two sorts of labour, Williams' rhetoric bears a strong subtext. When he quotes the declaration of the council of Montserrat of 1680 "that not one of these colonies ever was or ever can be brought to any considerable improvement without a supply of white servants and negroes,"[145] he is implying an overlap, even while rejecting an equation.[146] All this is very slippery rhetorically, and it has the further disadvantage of tripping over the explanatory concept it is designed to escape: race. As David Eltis has recently demonstrated, it is impossible to understand the rise of slavery in the New World unless one notes a characteristic so central as usually to go unremarked: that only non-Europeans were enslaved.[147] Therefore seventeenth-century slavery in the West Indies was in some basic sense racial. And the transition from economies based on white servitude to those based on black slavery was not merely an economic transition, but one that involved giving in to that most dangerous of all human temptations: allocating human beings to positions in life (or, indeed, death) according to the genetic pool from which they stem.

Despite considerable work on labour in Montserrat during the seventeenth century (by Riva Berleant-Schiller whose work focuses, shrewdly, on free labour, the most common form, despite all the talk of indentured servants),[148] a melodramatic miasma still beclouds any discussion of the poorer members of the Irish colony on Montserrat. This floats in from the historiography of Barbados. Were its origins elsewhere, it could easily be ignored, but among historians of the West Indies, Barbados is considered a leading sector and whatever occurs there is frequently used to describe or explain what occurred in the Leeward Islands a bit later. During the 1970s and 1980s two able scholars, Hilary Beckles and Jill Sheppard, completed works on indentured servants in Barbados. Unhappily, Barbados in the twentieth century possessed an ethclass of poor whites – sometimes called "Redlegs" – and the existence of this group implicitly set one of the foundations for both studies. The other parameter was the call by Eric Williams, in *Capitalism and Slavery* (1944), for a full study of West Indian indentured servants. The trouble with these parameters is that the first was unique to Barbados (poor whites were not trapped in amber on the Leeward Islands), and the second is that it assumed (per Williams) an overlap of indentureship and slavery as the basis of interpretation. The validity of that assumption was not questioned. Beckles's work, a PhD dissertation at the University of Hull in 1980, was turned into a book, published in 1989. Beckles writes: "Much of the analysis present in this book is consistent with Williams's contention that in Barbados 'indentured servants were temporary chattels'; though we do not argue that they were 'slaves' in the sense that blacks were."[149] However, when one reads that "many servants nonetheless experienced their plantation service as a form of enslavement and they responded much as black slaves did," the line blurs.[150] Terms such as "white proto-slavery,"[151] or employment of the phrase "Black Men in White Skins" to summarize the position of white indentured labourers[152] exacerbate the confusion. At minimum, they lead to the inference that indentured labourers were passive victims and were caught up in a set of economic and social relationships out of which they would inevitably emerge as losers.

However accurate this may (or may not) be concerning the history of Barbados, it is crucial that it not be imported into the history of Montserrat. There (as elsewhere), white indentured servitude was so very different from black slavery as to be from another galaxy of human experience. As elsewhere, white indentured servants had fixed terms – black slaves were owned for life. As elsewhere, white indentured servants could have their contracts sold, but not their lifetime existence; blacks ceased to exist, outside their chattel status. As elsewhere, white indentured servants entered their contracts freely (if not always wisely) in most cases; black slaves were coerced. And, as elsewhere, the children of black slaves were owned by the slave owner; this never occurred with white indentured servants. Therefore, so different are these two arrangements, white indentured service and African slavery, that to present them as overlapping constructs, is dangerous. And particularly so, if one is trying to understand the position of the poorer Irish on Montserrat.

One reason that the idea of the Irish-as-slave, or as proto-slaves, or as black men in white skins, must be resisted is that it conjoins with a stream in Irish historical writing that presents Irish settlers in various New Worlds as being passive emigrants, victims, and therefore blameless in their furtherance of the several imperialisms in which they participated. The overwhelming majority of Irish indentured servants who went to Montserrat did so by personal choice, with information in hand, and, in fact, made reasonable decisions as between two alternatives: remain in Ireland or emigrate. That neither of these alternatives may have been very attractive does not detract either from the self-preserving agency of the individuals involved, nor obfuscate the impact on other cultures which the exercise of that agency involved.

To return briefly to Barbados, Jill Sheppard's work, in its use of the concept of "Redlegs," is metonymic of the danger of seizing upon the memorable, and the dramatic. Her book of 1981, *The "Redlegs" of Barbados. Their Origin and History,*[153] is an earnest attempt to explain the origins of the "Redlegs," the poor whites who comprised about 4 percent of the population of Barbados in 1970 (approximately 9,000 people). These poor whites are traced to Irish and Scottish indentured servants of the seventeenth century. Neither the original Redlegs nor their descendants escaped from some undefined poverty trap. The interesting point, however, is the term "Redlegs" and its mythology. This is arresting. Sheppard reasonably suggests that the term comes from "Redshanks" and that this term was imported with the Scottish and Irish incomers of the seventeenth century. She believes that it was first used of Highland and other prisoners sent to Barbados by Cromwell in the late 1640s and early 1650s.[154] Actually the word was in common usage in the sixteenth century in both Scotland and Ireland. In fact, "Redshanks" was used to refer to the Scottish heavy infantry that served with the Macdonnells of Antrim and later with Shane O'Neill in Ulster at mid-century.[155] The phrase would have been known, in both English and Gaelic versions, to most Irish and Scottish soldiers and adventurers. Now, Sheppard knows that the term comes from abroad, and she is aware that the usual explanation, that it comes from "the indentured servants from Scotland wearing kilts in the fields and thus getting their legs sunburnt seems, therefore, to be rather less than the truth."[156] But she, like her readers, is trapped in the image of the sun "beating down on the bare-legged labourer in the field"[157] and this is just the sort of thing that is likely to be imported to Montserrat. It should not be, because the image of the Scot or Irishman bare-legged and therefore sunburned because he is wearing a kilt, is fictional. The Scottish short kilt, which Sheppard and almost everyone else has in mind when hearing of the Redshanks or the Redlegs, was an invention of the mid-eighteenth century. Prior to that time (and certainly in the first two-thirds of the seventeenth century), Irish and Scots of the class who were sent to Barbados wore traditional Irish gear: a long shirt that went well past crotch level, a tunic over that, a long cloak, and a primitive form of shoes. This covered them down to mid-shin level at least and, given the flowing character of the garments, did not leave them much exposure to the sun. In actual fact, "Redshanks" had nothing at all to do with weather exposure, but instead almost certainly referred to the simple fact that a lot of the Irish and Scottish men had red hair on their shins, this being one of the two major Celtic phenotypes. Thus, by historians' transposition, a false, but alas memorable, mythic image of the indentured servant was created.[158]

Now it is true that merchants frequently spoke of "buying" and "selling" indentured servants,[159] but it is our own fault if we misread this to mean that the servants were bought and sold in the same way as were African slaves. This is a case of one set of words having two sets of meanings. When people talked of selling servants to a Montserrat planter, or of buying a white servant, they were using a shortened version of what might otherwise be termed buying a labour contract (and today would be termed a "labour future"). Unlike the situation in the home island, colonial indentures were transferrable.[160] This stemmed from their containing different terms of obligation than at home, which was reasonable, given that, unlike the situation at home, an individual farmer or merchant could not make a face-to-face contract with a potential labourer. They were, after all, on opposite sides of a fairly large stretch of water. When talking about buying and selling servants, West Indian farmers and merchants were employing the same kind of verbal shorthand (and the same sort of self-vaunting vocabulary) that, for example, a modern-day publisher uses when talking about "my authors." (Vulgar yes – evidence of oppression, not necessarily.) Because the contracts of indentured servants could be passed on in testamentary arrangements, as could slaves, it is possible to misread the situation grossly: "The inclusion of servants as chattel to be alienated in property transactions illustrates how Barbadian planters imposed market functions on indentured servants as they did on their African slaves. The government of the colony also recognized the market functions of indentured servants as alienable property."[161] As Orlando Patterson comments, the concept of ownership of work-time through a labour contract is specious to the definition of slavery. The labour contract implies reciprocal obligations from the employer, and severe limits on the employer's powers, especially in terms of the duration any powers can be exercised.[162] So, even if contemporaries spoke of "buying" or "selling" servants, instead of buying and selling labour contracts, we should not, for it is historically misleading.

In fact, I suspect that for the male offspring of native Irish undertenants, living in precarious conditions in war-threatened Munster, the decision to enter into an indenture contract with a middleman who was shipping manpower to Montserrat was a sensible attempt at improving their future. What would today be called unemployment was pervasive in Ireland just at the time Montserrat was being settled. "Idleness is the very national disease of this country," was the earl of Cork's description in 1631[163] and, considering the catastrophic upheavals in Ireland in the period, it scarcely could have been otherwise. Irish beggars became a nuisance in several parts of England during the late 1620s and early 1630s,[164] a clear sign that a body of unemployed Irish persons was willing to leave their homes for any chance of improving their lives. It is their obvious sense of desperation, combined with a willingness to be mobile, that makes irrelevant any Cliometric debate about whether average wages were higher in England than in Ireland (as they certainly were) or higher on Montserrat than they were in England (which they may or may not have been). Individuals do not make life-choices according to national averages (even were they known) but according to the specific conditions and the limited opportunities that confront them. Thus, in the early 1630s, the port of Kinsale became a nodal point for middlemen who were contracted to bring indentured servants to the West Indies and for young Irish men and women who wanted out.

A frequently told story of the activities of one of these servant-transporters, Captain Thomas Anthony, who picked up a load of Irish men and women in Kinsale in 1636 is instructive. Anthony was supposed to fill his ship with servants for Virginia. However, when he arrived in April 1636, he found that a Dutch merchant ship had shortly before taken off 120 to 140 young servants and another one was in port filling up. Not only was there strong competition for the Irish servants, Anthony discovered, but the potential servants had considerable knowledge of the various colonies. (This is an important point sometimes left out of Irish emigrant history: namely the impressive degree of information that potential migrants had, for, from the very first, a feed-back system relayed data to friends and family of those who went abroad.) The Irish labourers were well-informed about comparative wage rates and knew that they would be better paid in the West Indies than in Virginia. So Captain Anthony was forced to change his plans and to make St Christopher his destination: that is where most of them wanted to go. (Notice the implied freedom of contract here implied and, further, the bargaining power of the prospective indentured servants.) Finally, Captain Anthony was able to obtain sixty-one servants, of which fifty-three survived to St Christopher, where their contracts were sold for between 450 and 500 pounds of tobacco apiece.[165]

In exchange for putting up with a hard and risky ocean journey[166] and a period of brutal manual labour, they obtained freedom in the New World. Hilary Beckles calculated that for voluntary servants in Barbados between 1635 and 1680, 6.75 years was the average term.[167] This can be taken as a maximum upper boundary for Montserrat, where conditions were better, and were therefore probably closer to the four years as the duration of normal adult servitude found by David W. Galenson in his analysis of late seventeenth-century servants indentured in the English Home Counties for West India and mainland destinations.[168] When done with their term, the servants were discharged with roughly £10–12 sterling (or, more often its equivalent in local currency or tobacco or sugar).[169] They had their freedom and money to hand. It is frequently remarked that the "freedom dues" of servants who had served out their indenture were inadequate because by the 1650s most of the decent land in the Leeward Islands and Barbados was taken. "At no time after 1640 in either Barbados or St Christopher, and probably Nevis was there any land cheap enough for a man to purchase with his freedom dues of £10."[170] Yet, it is important to realize that Montserrat stayed open much later. If one takes as a guide the estimate of the settlement pattern on the island in 1678 (the first census), and merges these data with the modern survey data of the actual size of the island (24,000 acres, or 10,900 hectares), the situation was as follows:[171]

Uncultivatable land	12,000 acres
Arable and already allocated	8,000 acres
Arable and still available	4,000 acres

And, as will be established in chapter 3, the amount of £10–12 sterling would have bought enough land on which to base a living.

However, that is beside the point for the moment, for the entire teleology implied by the notion of a drive-to-acquire fee-simple land is misguided. It is an anachronistic projection from later colonial history back into the first two-thirds of the seventeenth century. Instead of being driven to acquire land in fee simple,[172] the colonist was impelled to obtain a licence of occupation, which is something very different indeed. Very few, if any, of the indentured servants would have had any acquaintance with fee simple property in the Old World. There, the occupancy of, and use of, land was in the usual case separated from final ownership. Further, in the native Irish case, the acquaintance with fee simple ownership of property was further reduced by Irish forms of joint ownership which the Dublin government had unsuccessfully tried to stamp out. What Irish former indentured servants on Montserrat acquired when their time of service on Montserrat was completed was the opportunity either to rent land for money (or its local equivalent in tobacco or sugar) or to sharecrop it. In the latter case, the freedom dues could cover the start-up costs of seed and tools if they were not provided by the person renting out the land.

Further, when an indentured servant completed his (or, less frequently, her) time, the big bonus he acquired was not his £10 or £12 dues, but two economic powers. The first of these was that, once done with indenture, he became the "owner" of an economic value of whatever his transport cost to the colonies had been. One can think of this as the equivalent of a capital endowment (for anyone on the far side of the ocean would have to spend that amount as an entrance fee into the New World labour market). If the auction price of a servant's contract in 1636–60 averaged roughly £10 sterling, as Beckles suggests,[173] then, allowing for mortality and for a profit for the middleman, the post-indentured servant had acquired a transport endowment worth, say, £5 to £6 sterling.[174]

Secondly, the former indentured servant was now free to sell his services in a labour market that was chronically, indeed desperately, short of human labour. He did not have to sell his services to his old employer, or sell them on the same island, or even in the West Indies. Thus, in 1652, one finds a proposal being forwarded to the Council of State for the creation of a settlement in Maine. Great numbers "out of their time" from Barbados, St Christopher, Nevis, and Montserrat will go, it is proposed.[175]

By any set of reasonable demographic assumptions, from the early 1640s onwards, most of the labour force on Montserrat consisted of free men (and, I suspect, the same held true almost everywhere else in the Americas). On Montserrat, they were Irish for the most part. Some few may have been transported against their will[176] but, given the situation in the province of Munster, that usually was not necessary: they volunteered. Indeed, so far were some authorities – notably those in Barbados – from wanting to coerce labourers from Ireland to come to their island, that they went so far in 1644 as to try to ban them: in August 1644, the assembly of Barbados prohibited the landing of Irish persons. The law failed completely; the Irish just kept coming.[177]

That they chose to leave a very unpleasant situation does not mean that we should turn them into passive victims: they maintained their own personal agency. Of course, one should not idealize the state of the native Irish who became indentured servants. Their actual time in service on Montserrat may have been slightly better than it would have been on Barbados by virtue of their being in a predominantly Irish environment (and, one suspects, in many cases, among acquaintances or members of their own extended kin networks), but it still was hard time. Just how hard depended on the luck of the draw, on whether the indentured labourer was allocated to a responsible master or to a brute. In either case, the way the servants were housed was the same. According to a French chevalier who visited the Antilles in the mid-1650s, the servants there lived in little huts, made of four to six forks stuck into the ground, with side walls of reeds and a roof of palms or other leaves.[178] (These forks were usually called "crucks" by the Irish and in fact what was being seen here was a basic Irish building technique that later evolved into the more substantial cruck-trussed cottages of post-Restoration era.) According to observations of Barbados in the 1650s, the standard work day for field servants (which most of the young men would have been) was from six in the morning to eleven and then from one in the afternoon to six: a ten-hour day. The work was hard: clearing land, planting, weeding, harvesting. Yet a ten-hour day is not all that long, even six days a week: frontier agriculture in North America in the nineteenth century demanded a great deal more than sixty hours a week. The diet was boring, consisting of potatoes or dishes made from maize or cassava. The real problem, however, was the arbitrariness of the system. There was little to prevent a master from maltreating his servants. Richard Ligon witnessed a Barbadian overseer beating a labourer with a cane for a minor mistake.[179] Barbados is the source of the best-documented observations of indentured servitude, but unfortunately, it was also in all probability the worst place for a servant to have been, especially if one were Irish. So transference to Montserrat should be done a bit tentatively.[180]

Carl and Roberta Bridenbaugh speculated that by 1650 at least half of the white population that had migrated to the West Indies had died, from plague, war, overwork. They had died, the Bridenbaughs said, "in loneliness, misery and despair."[181] Perhaps the mortality was that high (an annual death rate in the 1630s and 1640s of perhaps as high as 5 percent per year), but it probably was spread across all social classes, and affected masters almost as much as their servants. Life expectancy in the British West Indies was low for everyone. One study of Jamaican and Barbadian tombstones for the years 1650–1750 (a period when life was not as rough as before 1650), showed that of white males who reached age twenty (about the age when indentured servants would arrive), the median age of death was forty-five. For women who reached age twenty, the median death age was thirty-six.[182] As a memorial stone indicated a person whose family was of some substance, these data seem to mean that everybody, masters and servants alike, had a short life expectancy in the islands.

On Barbados (again the extreme case), in 1649 a conspiracy of the indentured servants to slit the throats of their masters and to take over control of the island was given away by one of the servants and suppressed.[183] Although labourers of all national origins were involved, and despite the majority of the indentured servants being British, this failed rebellion nevertheless reinforced the belief by the authorities that the Irish were contumacious, potentially traitorous, capable of supporting slave rebellions, and quite willing to back the French or any other Catholic force in time of trouble.[184]

But were they? Not on Montserrat and not in the 1640s, certainly. In part this was because Governor Anthony Briskett had eased up on the lower orders. As mentioned earlier, he had allowed the smaller planters to stop paying their dues to the earl of Carlisle and this took the pressure off the sort of planter who was most apt to cause a rebellion – those small planters who had three or four servants and who acted as their own overseers, pushing the men very hard.

Still, the aborted servants' rising of 1649 on Barbados is useful, because it reminds us that the dynamic reported by Sir Henry Colt on St Christopher in 1631 (the fear that servants of all sorts would back the Spanish) was operative. That is, there were grievances that were socio-economic in origin and ran through the entire servant class, whatever their religious and ethnic affiliations. Surely Hilary Beckles is right to suggest that "most servants experienced servitude as a structured, organized system of planter tyranny."[185] Not unending tyranny, but tyranny for what many must have thought was an eternity, a period so long that for some the concept of freedom-dues had no meaning.

This is crucial, because when, in 1667, one sees a certain set of Irish Catholics on Montserrat being treasonous – they join the French and then, the French gone, seize control of the island for half a year – it should not be interpreted in a simple way. They revolted, in part, because they were Irish and had national grievances; in part because they were Catholic and had religious grievances; but also, in part because they were mostly former indentured servants who saw the system as slow to benefit them. This last characteristic is a product of the curious neo-feudalism which evolved on Montserrat before mid-seventeenth century. Genuine feudalism was a two-way system.

It implied not only rights on the part of the upper echelons, but also that they had responsibilities to those lower down. Real feudalism had social restraints built into it. Neo-feudalism was one-way feudalism and had very few inherent constraints. This characteristic affected small planters and free labourers, not just indentured labourers.

Actually, the West Indies authorities of the mid-seventeenth century were right to fear those of the Irish group who were Catholic and those of the Irish-Catholic cohort who were lower class. That was not because these people were, in some unexplained way, predestined by their cultural background to be social trouble. Rather, it was because in certain places and at certain brief moments, they formed an ethclass that had a critical mass of population and an ability to mobilize communally. They were the only social group that had any chance of either overthrowing the system or forcing its radical reform.

3 From Neo-Feudalism to Crown Rule, 1650–1680

For most of Montserrat's settlers, the 1650s must have been years of sheer terror, a time when anarchy and arbitrary power alternated. A redoubtable adventurer, Francis Lord Willoughby obtained a twenty-one-year licence of the Carlisle patent in 1647, upon which the governorship of the Leeward Islands and Barbados depended.[1] Though Willoughby tried to enforce his rights by going to Barbados and assuming the governorship, he lasted only two years. His extreme royalism did not commend him to the local settlers and he was turned out, not to return until 1663.[2] Willoughby in 1650 appointed an Irish Protestant, one Roger Osborne (var: Osborn; Osburn) to succeed Anthony Briskett, who had died in 1649, as governor of Montserrat.[3]

Given that the English Crown, the source of power behind the neo-feudal grants, was in the years 1649 to 1660 no longer in control of the English and Irish governments, and given, further, that during the era of Puritan empire, the proprietary grants were in abeyance,[4] the law that Governor Roger Osborne administered on Montserrat was essentially jungle law: the tyranny of the strong, limited only by fear of the coalescence of the weak. (It is well to remember that in 1652–54 matters were even more turbulent by virtue of the First Anglo-Dutch War.)[5]

The society of Montserrat was probably most "civilized" at the top of the social pyramid. That is why a charge of murder brought against Governor Osborne in 1654 is so revealing, for in its gothic quality it reminds us what "analytic" historical discussions too often ignore: the bent and beastly personalities behind society's formal institutions. The affray has all the complications and sanguinary qualities of an Elizabethan drama. The players require identification:

ANTHONY BRISKETT II, not to be confused with his father, the first governor of Montserrat. In this drama he is a cipher, for he is a Protestant minor. His estate counts.

SAMUEL WAAD JR, of Dutch Protestant extraction, he hails from Topsham in Devon. About thirty-two years of age, Waad has a substantial Montserrat estate of his own, but has also married the widow of Anthony Briskett, late governor of the island.

ELIZABETH BRISKETT, wife of Samuel Waad, Jr, widow of Governor Anthony Briskett and mother of Anthony Briskett II. She is fairly young, closer to the age of Samuel Waad Jr than to that of her late husband. Crucially, she is the sister of Roger Osborne (now governor).

ROGER OSBORNE, Irish Protestant, governor of Montserrat. In 1649, he briefly became the trustee of the estate of Anthony Briskett II (his nephew). However, when his sister, Elizabeth Briskett, remarried in 1650, his new brother-in-law (and step-father of young Briskett) became guardian of that plum estate.[6]

NATHANIEL READ, an island apparatchik and major in the militia. He makes a lifelong career of being on the winning side in local power struggles. Though not Irish, he has an Irish wife. He previously had been banished from Barbados.

VARIOUS WITNESSES to the murder and also members of Samuel Waad's family, in England.

The family tableau began in December 1653 when Elizabeth Briskett Waad, mother of the minor Anthony Briskett II, died. This removed the one inhibition that had prevented Governor Roger Osborne from acting simultaneously against Samuel Waad (who lived in better estate than did the governor) and against the property held by the minor Briskett. Osborne began by using all sorts of harassment to force Samuel Waad Jr to go off-side legally: insults, and the like. Waad stayed cool for several months, but finally, in early April 1654, Osborne forced Waad over the edge. An English gentleman, a Thomas Hurst, was a guest in Waad's house, and Osborne had Hurst arrested and committed to prison, allegedly for striking a tailor with a cane. Samuel Waad could keep his temper during moments of personal insult, but this was a calculated affront to his honour: a gentleman who had been under his roof had been roughed up and imprisoned. (That this could have been done by Osborne for any other reason than to enrage Waad is inconceivable; in that society, a colonial governor did not give a fig for the physical safety of some hump-backed, myopic, mendicant tailor.)[7]

Waad responded verbally (the words are not recorded, and, if that was all, could have been denied). However, he also wrote a letter to Osborne that was his undoing. In it, he not only protested against the treatment of his house guest, but charged that Osborne had an "Irish Murderer" in his service. (This was a reference to a Lieutenant Dabram), and a "late acquitted fellon" as well (a reference, almost certainly, to Nathaniel Read). Further, Waad claimed that Osborne kept "the barbarous Irish [meaning Irish Catholics] and their abettors in arms." And, finally, he brought up the matter of Osborne's sexual conduct, something that must have been universally known on the island, so therefore its details are lost. "We are to be regulated by laws, not by your exorbitant will, nor your satisfaction of a Ladies fancy," Waad wrote, unwisely, and added, "I should be loath to hazard my estate upon a frolick."

That letter was written on the second of April. A cloud of further intimidation by Osborne and insult by Waad must have covered the island in the next two or three weeks. Then, Waad was called to appear before the island's general court on the twenty-sixth of April. Usually such a court held open session and was a civilian matter. However, Governor Osborne sprang a trap: the session would be held in secret and it would be a military court martial (quite legal because everyone involved was in the militia and any matter affecting the powers of the governor could be seen as being a matter of military security, particularly since this was wartime). Waad protested vigorously, and so too did a friend of his, a captain in the military, Matthew Ffoyer. For his troubles, Captain Ffoyer was put in prison and held in irons for several days.

This was on Saturday afternoon. Waad was held over to the next Monday forenoon for a court martial. This was a secret inquiry, from which outsiders were barred. A "strong guard of Irish" surrounded the six buildings in Plymouth where the trial was held. The officers of the court consisted of Governor Osborne, his employees, Nathaniel Read, William Bentley (a Catholic), the "Irish Murderer" Lieutenant Dabram, and a Lieutenant Stevens. The verdict was quickly given and at two o'clock Waad, manacled, was taken to the nearby yard of St Anthony's church and a firing squad of "five Irish and one Englishman" prepared to execute him. He was unbound, and having been kept in solitary confinement since his arrest, made the only public pronouncement that he was permitted. He called for a cup of water and drank to the health of the people who were gathered around the churchyard. He said that he died with good conscience and that he died for (meaning to protect) his country's laws. Then he was shot to death.

Immediately, Governor Osborne grabbed everything of Waad's he could, including three estates, one of which had a stone house on it that was the best on the island, plus 70 cows, 500 sheep, 4 horses, 50 slaves, 30 "Christian servants" (presumably indentured), 20,000 pounds of sugar, and 350 rolls of tobacco. (The last item he sent to his brother Robert Osborne who was a Protestant clergyman in Cornwall.)

Roger Osborne's actions were brought to the attention of the Lord Protector (Oliver Cromwell) in December 1654 and the matter was referred by him to the Council of State. That council appointed a three-man commission to collect depositions, and they advised that the whole matter be investigated "at the most speedy opportunity" by the governor of Barbados. There it all ended. The governor of Barbados, now the moderate parliamentarian, Daniel Searle, had little inclination and less military ability. Starting a small war with Montserrat was not to his taste.

So, Osborne got away with everything. He stayed in control of the island until 1668, and if, after the Restoration of 1660, he had to watch his step, he already had done well enough. Eventually he retired to Ireland, where he settled on land owned by his wife in Ballycrenane, County Cork.[8] In 1678, now settled in Ireland, he sold through his agent and attorney eighty-seven acres to another Irishman, Garrett Misset.[9] Presumably he did the same over time with his other properties.

Impressive: but for sheer brass, it is hard to surpass a petition that Osborne sent to Oliver Cromwell in December 1655, slightly over a year and a half after he had judicially murdered the guardian of Anthony Briskett II. I am, Osborne tells Cromwell, now the guardian of the minor Briskett and I would like the cause of Waad's death to be looked into and "the orphan continued in his father's estate"![10] How much Governor Osborne was able to slice off the Briskett estate is not known, given the absence of land records, but he at least left the lad with a part of his rightful inheritance.[11]

If the 1650s were a mixture of anarchy tempered by absolutism for the upper classes, what must life have been like for the lower? (And here we are talking about white society, never mind the horrors of the now-growing slave culture.)

The very bottom of white society were prisoners who were shipped to the West Indies during the civil wars. There had always been prisoners in the flow of indentured servants from the British Isles to the West Indies.[12] This, however, had been overwhelmingly an English matter and, further, had primarily been directed to the Chesapeake region and secondarily to Barbados.[13] The voluntary flows of indentured servants from Munster and Wexford to the West Indies in general, and the strong attraction Montserrat had for freemen, meant that up to 1650 the question of prisoners for Montserrat was not a real issue.[14] Cromwell changed all that, albeit briefly.

After the battle of Drogheda in September 1649, Cromwell sent some common soldiers to Barbados where they served out their time as indentured servants. They were not prisoners, but were banished from ever returning to Ireland. And their numbers were small: although legend talks of hundreds, only thirty were shipped.[15] A problem arose because Barbados was a Royalist stronghold, as indeed were, in some degree, the Leeward Islands, so sending able-bodied soldiers to the enemy did not make any sense to Cromwell's party. There were in 1650 and 1651, therefore, no recorded instances of Irish prisoners being transported to the West Indies.[16] After the Barbadians came to terms with the Commonwealth in 1652, Barbados became a useful place to get rid of Irish undesirables. In the autumn of that year three separate merchants were allocated a total of 700 Irish rebels to carry to Barbados and the other islands.[17]

From then until 1657, a general warrant permitted the taking of Irish military prisoners overseas without legislative sanction being required.[18] Additionally, special arrangements were made for non-military rebels, such as the Irish, Scottish, and English pirates held in Dorchester gaol in England: in 1654 they were ordered sent to Barbados, Bermuda, or to the North American colonies.[19] A mixed bunch of 1,200 men held in Carrickfergus in Ireland and in Port Patrick in Scotland were ordered sent to the only-just-conquered colony of Jamaica in 1656.[20] From May 1653 onwards[21] Irish authorities were instructed to round up able-bodied vagrants and "idle persons" (the unemployed, in other words) and send them to the colonies: New England, Virginia, and the West Indies. Women as well as men were to be sent. "Irish Tories" (by which was meant social bandits) were transported, and in a particularly notorious case, the Council of State ordered that facilities be provided for the removal of 1,000 Irish girls and a like number of Irish boys, all under the age of fourteen, to Jamaica.[22] This, however, was not done.[23] Finally, on 4 March 1657, the Council of State put an end to the transporting of the idle and vagrant to the West Indies,[24] not for humanitarian reasons, but because the colonial authorities objected strongly to the sort of people they were receiving. This change occurred, however, after the forced transportation to Barbados of several Catholic priests,[25] at least four of whom the Barbadian authorities subsequently banished from their island.[26] The Barbados authorities, who always had been afraid of Irish servants and black slaves making common rebellion,[27] now had their fears turned into nightmares, with the addition of Popish priests to the witches' brew. Scant wonder, they pressed for the end to involuntary transportation.

Since most of the non-military transportees were on short indenture and, because almost everyone became free at the time of the Restoration in 1660 (the exception being the very few non-military felons who still had time to serve on their sentences), the general result of the Cromwellian transportations was to introduce into Barbados and the Leeward Islands a significant number of Irish free men and women. These were free individuals who were not entirely happy with their lot in life. After 1660 they constituted a portion of a large mobile labour force, free to circulate throughout the West Indies or to go off to North America.

How many Irish Catholics actually were transported? Nobody knows. One Catholic martyrology claims that in one year Cromwell transported 60,000 Irish Catholics to the West Indies.[28] Aubrey Gwynn, while adjudging that to be a wild exaggeration, concluded that 50,000 might be a fair estimate for the entire period from 1649–60.[29] That, however, has to be grossly high, because, even assuming that only one-fifth of the exiled persons went to the Continent, the remaining number would have nearly doubled the population of the combined white population of Barbados and the Leeward Islands as of 1650.[30] Rather more relevant is the 1655 estimate by the planters of Barbados that they were employing 12,000 prisoners of war. This included Scots and English as well as Irish (while excluding mere vagrants) and is thought by scholars to be an exaggeration.[31] I suspect that a total of 10,000 shipped against their will to all of the West Indies during the Cromwellian era is a reasonable maximum, but that is only a guess.[32]

By the early 1660s, these Irishmen and women must have had a direct impact on Montserrat, the white population of which kept growing until 1665. The island picked up, one infers, a fair number of able-bodied former soldiers, and a number of the formerly workless who had been taught how to labour in a very tough Barbadian school. Thus almost all the new arrivals were Catholics. And, I suspect, most were deeply alienated from authority.

Cromwell did more, however; in its audacity, his attempt to reorder Ireland was as great as Josef Stalin's rearrangement of the ethnic groups of the Soviet Union. Cromwell divided the country into a patchwork of three categories of land: those where the existing arrangements were to be retained (held by people who had either by luck or conviction ended up on the winning side in the multi-sided Irish civil war); those where lands were confiscated, either in whole or part, and reserved for Puritan adventurers and for their army, or by the government for future allocation; and those counties beyond the Shannon to which Catholics were to be transported and required to settle. It was nothing less than a reconfiguring of the map of Ireland.

Even though much of this megalomaniacal plan was never completed, enough of it was effected to dislodge significant numbers of the Irish Catholic population, both native Irish and Old English, and to make almost all Catholics fear for their dispossession. All social levels were affected, landlords down to churls. Sometimes, the younger sons and daughters of displaced native Irish and Old English, instead of marching into dark and unknown Connaught, chose to take their chances as indentured servants in America or the West Indies. And, similarly, the young of Connaught, whose family lands frequently were sharply reduced by the forced inflow of those who, having been given the choice of Hell or Connaught, chose the latter, were thereby pressured to consider migration for themselves. Given the desirability of indentured servants as carriage on merchant ships that sailed from the British Isles to the West Indies, thousands must have left.[33]

That Montserrat should have acted as a lodestone for some of these young people is obvious. The planters on Montserrat, more than any place else in the West Indies, were experienced with Irish servants and, moreover, most of the planters had family links with Ireland. One imagines that the Irish branch of some families helped to round up young people to serve as indentured servants to the overseas branch. Lines of communications, sometimes written, more often word-of-mouth, went back to the potential labourers. (Recall the knowledge the youth of Kinsale had in the 1630s concerning which overseas locations paid the highest wages.)

Whether or not the young servants were directly indentured to Montserrat planters, that island must have served as a powerful magnet for any Irish indentured servant whose time was served, as well as for the former prisoners who were freed after the Commonwealth collapsed. Montserrat's attraction is indicated by the fact that in 1672 (the date of the first accurate census), Montserrat had a white population of 1,171 adult males,[34] and an inferred total white population of 2,836 white men, women, and children.[35] That is a big increase from the roughly 1,000 white persons believed to be on the island in 1650. If anything, however, it understates the great influx of the 1650s and 1660s, the era of the great Irish displacement in the homeland: in 1666–67 the island was temporarily depopulated as a result of the then-war with France, and not all those who left returned. I suspect that the peak of Montserrat's white population occurred just before that war, say in 1665, and that it exceeded 3,000 persons. From that date onwards, it declined.[36]

Of course, not all the incomers of the 1650s and 1660s were Irish. Montserrat's being one of the few places where empty land was still available made it attractive to the English (and, despite the 1651 Navigation Act, a very few Scots) as well. For the Irish, Montserrat was especially attractive, because it was the only place in the empire where they were not a minority. Thus one finds Thomas Gookin (of a Protestant Irish family that had a long history in imperial adventures) operating as a servant collector in Kinsale. He sent young Irish men and women from Munster all over the New World – Carolina, the West Indies, he served them all[37] – and once having done their time, those in the West Indies must certainly have thought of Montserrat. The point to remember is that, unless one makes an outlandish set of demographic assumptions – such as an annual death rate, year after year, equal to that in most parts of Europe during the Black Death – at every single moment in the Cromwellian era, and during the succeeding 1660s, the white population on Montserrat was mostly comprised of free men and women. At no time after the 1630s can indentured labourers have been a majority (again, unless one makes extremely outré assumptions: for example, a 20 percent adult death rate, year-in, year-out) and, indeed, labour among whites on the island was therefore a "product" owned by the labourer him- or herself. That is why, when it became advantageous for them to clear off, they were able to do so with great speed and little trace.

The economy in which these mostly free labourers operated was, in 1650 on Montserrat, almost wholly a tobacco economy (a little indigo and sugar was grown). By 1680, sugar had invaded strongly and Montserrat was on the edge of becoming a typical Caribbean sugar colony. Montserrat was somewhat later in making the transition from tobacco and indigo to sugar than were most of the other islands of the West Indies, and that is the key to one of the island's values in New World historiography. Montserrat was a lag-sector. Therefore, it acts like an historical museum. One can observe on Montserrat certain social processes and structures that must have existed earlier (or in some cases, contemporaneously) on the other islands. On Montserrat these are recorded in some detail. Specifically, we can see what the West Indies must have been like when it still had room for the little man, the small proprietor who himself performed some (or in cases, all) of the manual labour on his own holding. This was before large plantations and black labour took over. Fortunately, the sort of record-keeping that was introduced to keep track of the world of industrial sugar farming (such as the late seventeenth-century censuses) also caught in its lens the places where sugar still was not king. One of the things that we have already learned from this museum is that the frequent tying of "slave-and-indentured-labour" (the phrase is used so often that it almost becomes one word) in describing labour systems in the West Indies is something of which we should be sceptical.[38]

Even though it was a museum, Montserrat operated in the contemporary economy of the Commonwealth and Restoration and that world had some new rules. The Navigation Act of 1651, had it been honoured by the islanders, would have destroyed the tobacco economy. The act, limiting West Indian shipping into Ireland or England to English vessels, marked the end of an era of maritime free trade, wherein, subject to the limitations of frequent wars and the predations of buccaneers, anyone could trade with anyone. This 1651 act was effectively aimed at the Dutch and led eventually to Anglo-Dutch wars in 1652–54, 1665–67, and 1672–74. Those conflicts were for the home governments and their admiralty fleets to engage in. On Montserrat, the locals just kept trading with the Dutch. The trade was clandestine only in the sense that it was illegal. The governor, Roger Osborne, certainly knew about it, tacitly condoned it, and participated in it himself.[39]

An account book of one of the Dutch traders on the island has been preserved for the year 1654. Trade flowed clear; neither war between Holland and England, nor the Navigation Act stood in the way.[40] The Dutch merchant ran at least one warehouse on Montserrat and traded with Amsterdam. He advanced credit to the planters and they paid in leaf. Interestingly, one of the merchants, Jacob Clause, kept his records according to the nationality of the grower, a fair indication that everyone on the island was identified as to national origin: he kept one separate account ledger for eighteen Irish suppliers. Other accountings, of money owed to Messrs Van-gagell-dounce and Van-dekenderth of Amsterdam, mixed the groups. If one assumes that the amount owed to the Amsterdam merchants was a good indication of what each planter could deliver (and these were Dutch businessmen after all), then it is clear that the average English planter on Montserrat was delivering over three times as much tobacco to the Amsterdam merchants as was the average Irish planter.[41] While this may somewhat overstate the difference (there is reason to think that some of the Irish planters dealt directly with Ireland), nevertheless, the picture is clear: even in the early 1650s, before sugar replaced tobacco, the English planters had, on average, larger farming operations than did the Irish, and this despite there being some very substantial Irish planters at the top end of the scale.

A second Navigation Act, of 1660, required that certain specified colonial goods – tobacco, indigo, sugar – not only be carried in English or Irish bottoms but that these vessels must pass through an English or Irish port on their way to Europe (if England or Ireland were not their point of sale of the goods). Then, in 1663, a further Navigation Act dealt with trade in the reverse direction. Ships outward bound to the colonies had to touch an English port, except for vessels taking provisions directly to the colonies from Irish ports. These two measures cut out the Dutch from the tobacco trade, or at least attempted to do so.

The Montserratians petitioned the governor of the Leeward Islands to bring back open trade so, as they phrased it, that it "be restored to their pristine happiness."[42] The new colonial policy, of which the Navigation Acts were the stake-poles, has been well described as follows. "In this policy there were four main elements: the assertion of the sovereignty of the metropolitan governments; the fostering of staple crops for shipment to the United Kingdom [sic] and subsequent sale in the markets of Europe; the direction of trade into English ships bound for English ports; and the concentration of this system on the West Indies."[43] As far as tobacco was concerned, the Montserratians evaded the new rules. They continued to trade their tobacco with whomever gave them the best price and the most liberal credit. This was vitally necessary in the 1660s, because a glut of tobacco on the English market forced the price sharply downward.[44] The tobacco farmers needed the Dutch market if they were not to go under. Into the 1670s, the Dutch were still the main carrier of produce from Montserrat,[45] an especially important arrangement for tobacco growers, for the growers were able to participate in what was effectively an auction mechanism: Dutch versus English buyers bidding for their goods. So widespread was Dutch illegal trade that a slang term, "Stacia sugar" developed, to cover any smuggled commodity. (The Dutch used their island of St Eustacius as a transshipment point for goods coming to and from Holland.)[46] For the moment Britannia ruled the waves, but the Montserratian planters waived the rules.

An indication of how the Cromwellian stirring of Ireland and the development of the post-Restoration economy of Montserrat could interact is found in the case of the Blake family of County Galway.[47] The *paterfamilias* of the clan was John Blake, Sr, a Catholic of Old-English antecedents. He was the direct descendant of Richard Caddle who was sheriff of Connaught in 1306.[48] (This John Blake sometimes employed the name John Blake Fitz Nicholas, meaning John Blake, son of Nicholas Blake.) He possessed substantial resources, being both a merchant in the city of Galway and a large landowner in the countryside. In 1639, he had been elected a member of the Irish parliament for the borough of Athenry, and he also served for a time as mayor of Galway City. He was exactly the sort of substantial Catholic whom the Protestants wanted to break. In 1640, he escaped the attempts of Sir Thomas Wentworth, lord deputy of Ireland, to seize Catholic lands in the province of Connaught. Blake did this by documenting that his family was pure English in descent, having for the preceding eleven generations stayed ethnically pure. "The petitioner and his ancestors did plant thereabout [in various locations in County Galway], being an ancient English family and there continued without change of language, manner or habit and without once matching with any Irish families since the ninth year of King Edward the Second."[49] He survived this attempt, but in 1655, the Cromwellians got him: he had his ancestral lands, rural and urban, confiscated. The best bits went to the New English, the rest being awarded to the hordes of Catholic refugees from the other side of the Shannon, who were being herded into Connaught with the intention of creating a vast rural slum. In return for the confiscated lands, John Blake Sr received a much smaller estate (the usual formula was that Catholic landowners received new estates worth approximately one-third of their confiscated ancestral lands). He ended up with 668 acres of waste land in Mullaghmore, County Galway. He never recovered financially from this confiscation. During his later life he was hounded by creditors (many of them cousins, which is the Irish way of it), and eventually he depended on remittances from his sons to make ends meet.

John Blake Sr had four sons on whom he relied to remake the family fortune. The eldest, Thomas, became a Galway merchant and the financial nodal point for the entire family.[50] In 1668, John Blake's second son, Henry, and his third, John (we shall call him John Jr for convenience) went to the West Indies to recoup the family fortune. A fourth son, Nicholas, stayed at home. (There were also four daughters in the family, but they do not come into the West Indian dealings.)

John Jr in 1668 went to Barbados and there seems to have been a merchant in trade with the Dutch, and the Dutch seem to have done better out of the business than did he. Henry Blake in the same year went directly to Montserrat. It was a good year to do so, because the recently concluded war with the French had scared away many of the planters, so land was available cheaply. Although he had left Ireland with a big backlog of debts (again, mostly to people who were cousins of one description or another), he did very well, both on his plantation and as a merchant. He hired vessels that sailed directly to Ireland and he sold there indigo and tobacco. By 1676 he had cleared his debts at home and had acquired sufficient assets so that he could sell up and return home in good financial condition. Some of the credit for his success has to go to his brothers Nicholas and Thomas who acted on his behalf in several dealings. Returning home in September 1676, he bought an estate in the townland of Lehinch, County Mayo in 1678 and a second estate in the vicinity of the village of Renvyle, County Galway, in 1680. He died, prosperous, and with issue in 1704.

Having himself made a small fortune, Henry in 1676 sold his Montserrat estate to his brother John Jr, who was not doing well in Barbados.[51] Now John was a much less disciplined man than Henry, who was severe indeed. Henry had left his wife and children at home when he went to the West Indies. Although he left his children at home, John not only brought along his wife, but a servant woman whom Henry called "that whore," adding "as I am credibly informed." Henry confided his worries about John Jr to Thomas, the elder brother. "I am afraid she may be the occasion of his confusion by her seducement. I pray God preserve him … I will advise him to throw her away, which I pray God he may do for his own future content."[52] Thomas, playing the elder brother role to the hilt, scolded John Jr about the whore and received in return a self-pitying explanation:

The wench came over along with my wife; I am most sensible what my brother Henry hath writte me of her, likewise what you intimated per your letter. To which I say that though I find her most vicousless here, perhaps deterred through the most severe correcting I keep her under yet because of the said bad report I would not at all abide her under my roof but therunto I am as yet inevitably compelled.

Compelled?

By reason my wife being, as I find her, of very weak constitution, cannot discharge all herself for washing, starching, making of drink, and keeping the house in good order is no small task to undergo here. If I would dismiss her, another [servant] I must have which may prove ten times worse than her – for until a "neger" wench I have, be brought to knowledge, I cannot, considering my present charge, be without a white maid.[53]

In that letter is caught an entire moral, or immoral, universe.

In May 1676, John delivered the plantation and "negers" to Edward Bodkine, yet another cousin, to whom John owed money. Once John had cleared this account, he was able to take possession of the Montserrat estate and he seems to have done so in 1677, for in the census of 1678 he was living on his Montserrat plantation and had thirty-eight black slaves, and was one of the largest slave owners on the island. Unlike his brother, John never returned home. When he died in 1692, John Jr's estate went to his daughter Catherine, who had married Nicholas Lynch, an Irish planter from Antigua.[54]

There is no profit in trying to say too precisely when Montserrat went over the watershed and became more of a sugar economy than a tobacco-indigo economy. The trade statistics of the period are not much help, because of the degree of smuggling that occurred and, especially, because of the island's clandestine trade with the Dutch. Further, certain products – such as provisions grown for local sale or for sale on other islands – were totally invisible as far as trade accounts were concerned. And even if we could know the market value of the various commodities, that would beg a fundamental question: in describing social structure, is the relative market value of the products more accurate as an indicator than are the labour inputs of the economy? Is it not possible (indeed, probable) that at some moment, the Montserrat economy became a sugar economy in the sense that sugar produced most of the market value crop for the island, but that Montserrat remained a tobacco-indigo-provision growing economy in the sense that most of the labour on the island went into producing those items? That, I think, is the picture which the 1678 census implies and this is discussed later in the chapter.

Rather than engage in precise chronology, it is best to think of the years 1667 (the end of the French war) to roughly 1680 as a broad watershed. Before 1667 the economy was mostly tobacco: after 1680 it moved swiftly into being a sugar island, although other crops remained important.[55]

This is of great moment, because a seventeenth-century island changing from growing tobacco to growing sugar was not like a modern farm switching from oats to barley. Sugar was not just another crop; it involved another technology, another economic organization, a new social structure, and a radically different set of moral values. Although it could be produced on any size plot, two to three acres even, if one had a field without hedges – a clear-cut field, as in European agriculture – of ten acres or more, it became increasingly profitable. Part of the reason this was so was that sugar was not just an agricultural crop, but an industrial one. After harvesting, the cane had to be crushed, the juice extracted, the extract boiled and then crystallized. Various kinds of sugar were the end result and molasses and rum were the major by-products. To run one's own sugar factory required perhaps thirty acres or so, although small farmers could club together. However, even if the individual farmer could avoid the full capital expense of building his own sugar processing operation, by sharing it with others or by purchasing access to one of the mills operated by large landowners, he had to be able to invest in a crop that, unlike tobacco which provided two pay-offs in a single year, required a year to fifteen months to grow. On Montserrat one finds (according to the 1678 census) that most sugar plantations were roughly fifty acres in size: not the great open vistas that were found, for example, on Jamaica in its high sugar days, but still not the sort of thing a recently released indentured labourer could reasonably aspire to. Such enterprises required either outside capital or personal savings, the bit by bit working upwards over a lifetime of a young man who, indentured at eighteen, released at twenty-four, saved enough through his labouring on the free market to buy a small farm at age thirty. Thus did indentured labourers become small planters on Montserrat. Land was still available.

One of the problems with sugar was that, unlike tobacco, it required time-synchronized planting and harvesting. There was no reason why an entire tobacco field had to be planted (and therefore harvested) at the same time. But sugar was a modern crop wherein the industrial requirements of the venture (in this case, crushing, boiling, extracting, and crystallizing the sugar) had to be done in a continuous process, not in drips and drops. Firing up a sugar boiler for a few gallons of extract was not economical; one needed a lot to be going on with. Also, speed was important. Therefore, a good deal of very well disciplined, very dependable labour was required, particularly at planting and harvesting time.

Eric Williams once proposed a Wildean epigram, namely that "tobacco was a free white industry intensively cultivated on small farms; sugar was a black slave industry extensively cultivated on large plantations."[56] Like the prototypes set down by dear Oscar, this formulation is a paradox, whose rhetorical strength lies in its being immediately wrong and ultimately right. Thus, ultimately, by the mid-1750s, sugar was produced on large plantations, throughout the West Indies, the labour being done by African slaves. But in the short run, Williams's equations were all wrong. There is not a necessary or exclusive tie in actual historical experience between tobacco and free white and between sugar and slavery – one can find numerous evidences of tobacco farming being conducted at least in part by slave labour (not least as indicated by the 1678 Montserrat census), and one can find equally easily instances of sugar being grown by free labourers. (Indeed, I have seen "East Indian" labourers in Fiji produce sugar by methods only slightly more advanced technically than those of the seventeenth-century West Indian plantations.) Nevertheless, in the long run, and over the entire range of historical cases, Eric Williams was right: everything else being equal, the sugar process worked best with slave labour, for one simple reason: free labour could not be counted on not to skive off just at the point it was most needed. Indeed, free labourers were most apt to become difficult – to demand an increase in pay or a reduction in hours, or more perquisites – just at the point the process was most vulnerable, at planting or boiling time. Dependable gang labour was required. For someone in the seventeenth century who was establishing a proto-industrial process, it was crucial to know that the parts of one's machine were all there when needed. Labour was part of that machine and, in the short run, slavery was the most dependable form of labour.

Briefly, to take the long-view: in pre-Norman Irish history, slavery was an everyday form. One of the few things we know about Saint Patrick, after all, is that he was a slave. John V. Kelleher, the doyen of Irish historians in North America, told me of working through the Irish annals and related records and noticing the effect that the Vikings, who were slavers, had on Ireland. This was indicated by the fact that suddenly in the various battles of *tuatha*, in Leinster and Munster, petty kings started taking hundreds, sometimes 1,000 or more captives, something that they were not recorded as doing previously. This behaviour peters out after 100 years or so. What they probably were doing was capturing and selling their fellow Irish to the Vikings. (The thought of what it might mean for someone who was raised in south Munster to wind up in the neighbourhood of present-day Moscow makes one shudder.) However, by the mid-seventeenth century, as David Eltis argues, the rules of western society were different: it was no longer permissible to enslave permanently one's own sort (punish for crimes, yes, but enslave forever, no).[57] The Irish on Montserrat could not conceive of enslaving their own, but there were no inhibitions on the enslavement of what the Blake family called "Negers."

One of the things that will become clear when we look at the 1678 census is that owning slaves was not a big man's prerogative. The small men, former indentured servants, with a few acres, perhaps rented land, perhaps purchased, used slaves whenever they could, and they used them in all forms of agriculture: tobacco, indigo, provision growing, and, of course, sugar production. Working for the small plantation owner (which was what most of the Irish were by the 1670s) must have been the worst fate of all. Granted, there was little separation between the master and the slave: little more than between the master's cruck-trussed wooden home and the nearby daub and wattle dwelling of the slave, but propinquity increased, not reduced, exploitation. In his monumental trilogy on the European conquest of the western hemisphere, Eduardo Galeano said: "The white servants dream of becoming owners of land and blacks. When they recover their freedom, after years of hard penitence and unpaid toil, the first thing they do is buy a Negro to fan them in the siesta hour."[58] I suspect he is only half right: they bought blacks, indeed, but they worked alongside them, or at least directly supervised the slaves' work. "Nobody could have been a more vicious taskmaster than a recently freed small planter trying desperately to get established by endeavouring to get every penny out of his investment in labour."[59]

The first indication on the historical record of sugar planting on Montserrat occurs in 1659, when one of the large landowners imported twenty geldings for use in his sugar works.[60] These animals were to drive a cane-crushing mill. (Later, windmills were to replace horse-driven machinery, these being very efficient on wind-swept Montserrat.) That this planter was far enough advanced in his production design to need horses (the crushing can be done by hand-driven machines) means that sugar probably had been seriously grown on the island since the mid 1640s. From the documents produced after the judicial murder of the ill-fated Samuel Waad, one learns that he had fifty slaves "young and old" and was involved in both tobacco and sugar production on a large scale.[61] Waad, being the largest settler on the island, was hardly typical: he was more a predictor of the future. The salient point, however, is how slowly slaves came into Montserrat. There were only 523 of all ages in 1671.[62] The number had grown to an estimated 1,894 in 1678, an indication of fast-increasing sugar production, but also still only about 40 percent of the island's total population.[63] Montserrat in 1680 was not by any strength of the imagination a "sugar island."

The Montserrat planters had a terrible time acquiring slaves and they were constantly complaining about this to the imperial authorities. Governor William Stapleton, who was nothing if not well informed (he was the best conductor of enumerations and compiler of records that the Leeward Islands had in the seventeenth century), stated in July 1672 that in the previous seven years Montserrat and Antigua between them had received only a total of 300 slaves from the English slaving monopoly, the Royal African Company.[64] In 1680 the Council of Montserrat wrote to the London authorities complaining that since 1666 only two slave ships of the Royal African Company had called at the island, "with little more than three hundred negroes, half of whom are already dead."[65] He continued, "And, as your Lordships desire our opinion how the island may be improved, we not only think but are ready to prove, that not one of these colonies ever was or ever can be brought to any considerable improvement without a supply of white servants and negroes. The want of them compels the inhabitant to plant a little tobacco and indigo … The result is that the people are kept so poor that they can bring little service to the King nor profit to his kingdoms."[66] They wanted more slaves from the Royal African Company and better. (Most of the slaves were disembarked at Nevis, and the Montserrat planters received only the worst.)[67] Therefore, the Montserrat planters were forced for the most part to acquire their slaves either from the other Leeward Islands and Barbados or illegally, through trade with slavers of the European countries.

Because of the shortage of slave labour, and because therefore the black population was smaller than the white, one finds little of either the pervasive fear of slave revolts (which was constant on Barbados, for example) or little of the savage slave-control laws that already were in existence on other islands and that later were enacted on Montserrat. Granted, there were laws against Africans running away from their masters. A law of 1668, for example, provided for sixty lashes for anyone (black or white) who received or "entertained" any runaway slave. Interestingly, however, this same act provided that any negroes who at the time of the passage of the act were on the run "out in the woods" should be free of all punishment for all their crimes if, within sixteen days of passage of the act, they returned to their masters.[68] The inference that one draws from this general amnesty of 1668 is confirmed by an arrangement of 1675, which permitted the slaves who had been abducted in 1667 during the

French war (meaning virtually the entire slave population of that time) "to make a free choice of their masters."[69] This is not to say that there were not strong penalties for striking an overseer or for major thefts or for incitement to rebellion. There were. The Council of Montserrat had a major item in its budget for bounty for the heads of felonious and runaway slaves. During the 1670s, the council paid £16.5.0 for slaves' heads (out of a total public expenditure of a bit over £3,250.[70]

These operations are hard to glimpse individually and their specific social context is lost. There is one nice case, however (admittedly an unusual one), of an Irish settler whose plantation can be traced in some detail. This settler is the eponymous David Gallway (var: Gallwey, Galway, Galloway, Gallaway) from County Cork. It is from him (rather than for the city or county in Ireland) that the place name of "Galway" on Montserrat stems. Sometime in the 1660s David Gallway came from Ireland, with some resources in hand. He stemmed from a Catholic family from County Cork of gentry standing. He, and (almost certainly) his father Sir Jeffrey Gallway and his brother William Gallway, "gent," were outlawed as a result of their position in the October 1641 Catholic rebellion.[71] However, by the time he fetched up on Montserrat, David Gallway ("gent") was willing publicly to affirm loyalty to the Established Church. This can be inferred from his willingness to become a justice of the peace, a post that assumed both property and Anglicanism.[72] He was, in 1668, prominent amongst a group of substantial landowners (many of them Irish), who petitioned the governor of the Leeward Islands against Irish rebels on Montserrat.[73] Gallway became a major in the militia and served on the island's legislative council, a sure sign that he was willing to take one or more oaths that were repugnant to strict Catholics. Gallway's plantation was carved out of the St Patrick's district, on the southern portion of the island, where most persons of Irish background lived. At 1,100 feet above sea level, it was not easily accessible, but it was in an area that received a good deal of orographic rainfall, sometimes several times a day. How much land Gallway controlled and how many slaves he had at the time of the 1678 census is unknown, because, being the enumerator for the district, he cannily kept his own name out of the census. Gallway's son and then his grandson succeeded him on the estate, so that by 1729 the family estate was the largest on the island, 1,400 acres. However, it was not at that time a conventional plantation. Only about 100 acres were in sugar and this was processed by an antiquated ox-driven crushing mill. Instead, the estate, which had sixty-two slaves and no white servants, was given over to cattle farming. What the Gallways had done, from 1660 onwards, was to buy up land from Irish smallholders who gave up farming their own land. This creation of a ranch may seem strange, but it was very shrewd. From the end of the French war, 1667 onwards, Montserrat was importing provisions and, with each passing year, it imported more, for as more land went into sugar growing, less was available for provisions production. Particularly high in demand was Irish beef. The Blake family had done some beef importing and, in the eighteenth century, several Irish merchant families (the Skerretts, the Goolds, the Husseys, the Frenches, the Lynches, and the Dalys) were exporting and importing a variety of articles, beef being the island's biggest import from Ireland.[74] So the Gallways, by setting up a cattle ranch, were providing locally an item for which there was heavy demand. Only after mid-eighteenth century did the next generation of the family put up a windmill, build a stone sugar boiling house, and finally get into sugar production in a serious manner.[75]

The other noteworthy fact about the Gallways is that despite their being outwardly Anglican, they were probably religious switch-hitters. (One avoids the tendentious "converso" and the opprobrious "marrano.") This can be inferred from the fact that Nicholas Galway of St Christopher (a grandson of the original David Gallway and a brother of the David Gallway who owned the estate in 1729) was a co-donor of a chalice that still is in service in the Catholic parish church of Castletown-Kilpatrick, in County Meath. In Latin was inscribed the donors' wish: "Pray for them." The year was 1735. A year earlier, David Gallway, Montserrat plantation owner, had left in his will £20 "under injunction of my mother to some Roman Catholic Church in Ireland."[76]

Montserrat was a very complicated place: a tiny satrap, controlled on the ground by the Irish – some outright Catholics, some Protestants, others crypto-Catholics – within a massive empire controlled by the English. The ambivalences of being Irish in such a world were pervasive.

And the rules were constantly changing. In the era of empire, nothing was more unsettling to settlers than land questions. Yet, when one enters the historiography of the various New World plantations, one finds that the modern literature takes land for granted and worries almost entirely about labour. An historically anachronistic set of assumptions seems to be built into the literature; unstated, but pervasive. The first of these is that freehold tenure by the occupier of land ("fee simple" is another term) is the natural arrangement. In fact, there is never anything natural about land ownership, for it is a social construct and, crucially, the societies from which the settlers of the New World stemmed viewed freehold ownership by the occupier as distinctly unnatural. Most of the settlers on Montserrat up to 1680 would have not held freehold land in the Old World. Some few of the native Irish aristocracy and some of the more powerful of the Old English may have done so, but most of the migrants to Montserrat were much lower on the social scale. To the extent that they had held land, it had been in some form of tenancy. Sometimes these tenancies were for specific terms of years, sometimes for "lives." (That is: having the duration of the lives of one or more persons specified in the tenancy agreement, thus making the length of the lease a very unpredictable matter.) For larger holdings, leases were written out; for smaller ones they were oral agreements and the rights of both sides were in part determined both by the accuracy (or inaccuracy) of individual memory, and also by practices that frequently were termed the "immemorial custom" of the locale. In the case of individuals from the Celtic parts of the British Isles, joint (or familial, or group) tenancies were common. In 1635, the Irish parliament had initiated a comprehensive set of land law reforms, bringing in the English concepts of private property and of contingent tenancies. This set of reforms was not completed until 1695, by which time the native Irish system of land ownership was largely abandoned.[77]

In some ways, the English-derived system of property ownership was even less secure than the old Irish. Rents bounced about, for in addition to the annual rental, there usually were "fines" to be paid upon renewal of leases or upon the passage of a "life" in the agreements for lives. And, to make matters even more complicated, often there were several layers of middlemen between the owners of the freehold and the person who occupied the land and held the soil for tilling. (In Ireland it was only the 1903 land act that made the occupier into freeholder in the usual case. In the case of agricultural lands in England even at the present day, most agricultural occupiers are not the land owners – that is, the freeholders.) The one thing that the New World settlers were not accustomed to was a situation in which they as occupiers held the land in perpetuity, and held it outright, without fluctuating tenancy changes. In this regard, the New World really was new.[78]

Given our own concern with labour issues (which is really a reflection of the necessary concern of North American society in the second half of the twentieth century with problems of race which stem from African slavery), we are prone to forget that land acquisition was the first priority of New World settlers, and labour matters very much second. Labour availability was irrelevant if land rights were not first sorted out: whether by Old World custom or New World fiat is immaterial, but they had to be agreed. Recognizing this, we thus encounter the second unstated assumption of modern historiography, namely that the natural solution to questions of how land should be organized, was to introduce fee-simple ownership. Actually, this was far from automatic (as reference to the era of neo-feudalism indicates), and it is a major turning point in western European history. Thirdly, one finds that this change not only bears little comment in the historical literature of recent years, but is taken as being swift and apparently painless. As the case of Montserrat will show, the entire business was messy indeed, and fraught with disorder.

To review the situation on Montserrat prior to the Restoration of 1660: the settlers had gone through a period of neo-feudalism, tempered by moments of anarchy and absolutism. The oldest settlers had lived through the first neo-feudal regime of the first earl of Carlisle (1632–36), that of the second earl (1636–47), then that of Francis Lord Willoughby, who leased the Carlisle patent in 1647 and effectively lost control in 1652, and, finally, a period from 1652 to 1660, wherein the Carlisle patent was in abeyance, but in which the chaos was contained by the ruthless reign of Roger Osborne as governor.

How did landholding work in the neo-feudal era? We can make some educated guesses, but the details are forever lost (as, indeed, are almost all of Montserrat's records before the twentieth century). The Crown of course owned all land. In this self-consciously neo-feudal situation, the earl of Carlisle held the land in theory in some form of knight's service, but that in reality meant that he was obliged to be a charming courtier (which he was), to pay the crown £300 annually[79] in dues for Barbados and the Leeward Islands, and to open new lands that would in one way or another turn some profit for the Crown. The tenants on the island owed annual dues to Carlisle. These were collected by the governor, Anthony Briskett, and forwarded to England. These dues (think of them as feudal rents) were the annual reminder that this was not freehold land. Unlike the classic feudal system, the power of the feudal "lord" was distinctly limited by virtue of Carlisle's being far away and virtually without powers of enforcement. As mentioned earlier, in the early 1640s, Anthony Briskett ceased collecting the dues owed by the poorer settlers, and I suspect that from 1647 (when the second earl of Carlisle leased out the patent to Francis Lord Willoughby), neo-feudal dues ceased altogether. (I am also suggesting that Willoughby's "appointment" of Roger Osborne as governor of Montserrat in 1650 was merely his making the best of the fact that the hardest man on the island had taken control of the government.)

Thus, on the ground, the really important person was the governor, first Anthony Briskett and then Roger Osborne. The powers of the governor were threefold (assuming that he had a strong enough right arm and both these Irishmen did): first, to allocate the tenancies on the island. How this was done is unrecorded, but obviously money changed hands, either as up-front payments or as liens on crops as yet to be planted. In a sense, the governors were keepers of a land bank of finite size. They wanted their island to fill up with prosperous settlers, but they wanted it to do so at a rate which did not extinguish too quickly their stock of saleable tenancies. Secondly, the governors, if they collected the feudal dues (which I think was done at least for some tenancies, up to 1647), took something for their efforts. In essence, this was an additional rent. And, thirdly, the governors had the power to assume lands and properties for themselves, which both Briskett and Osborne did with vigour.

Missing in this is the neo-feudal filigree. Neo-feudalism required retainers. Indentured labourers existed and were important in the early days to the settlement, but they soon became free labourers. Therefore, the former indentured servants either had to be kept on as wage labourers or, as they preferred, to be rented small tenancies of their own. Such tenancies could come either directly from the governor (from his bank of unsettled lands) or from earlier planters who had acquired tenancies larger than they could farm themselves. Thus, I suspect, there was an idiosyncratic range of landholding arrangements, tenancies of varying types, not quite as complex in their variety as in the Old Country, but far from simple or standardized.

Suddenly, this changed.

Soon after his Restoration, Charles II wrote to Francis Lord Willoughby, "directing him instantly to apply himself to undertake the government of Barbados, St Christopher, Nevis, Antigua and Montserrat." He was to do this either by going himself or by appointing a governor in his place.[80] (The royal command was very firm, because Willoughby, an adventurer of amazing imagination and ambition, was just then working on becoming the proprietor of Surinam, a nice little property, 1,200 miles in length and 600 wide.[81] Willoughby accepted the King's commission and went to Barbados himself, as head of the government of the various islands. Since Willoughby's lease of the Carlisle patent was not due to run out until 1668, on the surface it appeared that neo-feudalism was back. However, in fact, the Restoration brought with it a determination upon the part of both parliament and the king to manage the colonies in a much more professional manner. This professionalism implied that instead of the unicorns rampant of neo-feudal foppery, both parliament and monarch wanted predictable, and continually increasing, revenues from the colonies.

In the case of the Leeward Islands and of Barbados, this meant getting rid of the Carlisle patent by buying out Willoughby's interest in that patent. For this buy-out to work, however, there would have to be something in the deal both for the planters on the islands and for the Crown. Even so, buying out Willoughby was not very expensive. While it may have been true in the early days of the Carlisle patent that the neo-feudal dues were high – "there be a great custome imposed upon them [the settlers]" reported Captain John Smith[82] – but from the late 1640s until 1660 virtually no dues had been collected, and re-imposing them on the brass-necked planters would have required a serious military force.

The arrangement worked as follows:

1 Willoughby surrendered his lease of the Carlisle patent as of 1663 and the Crown wiped it out of existence. The patent had even less use to the Carlisle heirs than to Willoughby, for they had no chance whatsoever of enforcing their claims. Willoughby at least had the character to try, if that had been his only alternative.[83]

2 Francis Lord Willoughby was appointed Governor of Barbados and the Leeward Islands, not as proprietor (as he had been under the Carlisle patent) but during royal pleasure. When Francis Lord Willoughby died at sea in August 1665, the post remained vacant until January 1667, at which time his brother William Lord Willoughby replaced him.

3 As of September 1663, the Crown took with the approval of the local assembly a 4½ percent tariff on "all dead commodities" that were shipped from the islands. This was in lieu of the imposition of any other taxes for the maintenance of royal authority, and for such things as the repair of forts and public buildings on the islands. (In practice it was almost never used for such purposes.) In 1668–69 the 4½ percent duties raised 6,000 pounds of sugar (the local currency) for the Crown. This was an artificially low amount, because of the wars of the mid-1660s, but clearly, Montserrat was not the jewel of the Empire.

4 However, as a sweetener to Francis Lord Willoughby, he was granted one half of this tariff, which is to say that the Crown and the Governor of Barbados and the Leeward Islands each received 2¼ percent of the value of outward-bound produce. The Crown portion, however, stayed on the various islands and was used for public purposes. (In 1670, William Lord Willoughby farmed out the duty for

Barbados and the Leeward Islands for £7,000 a year. This should not be taken as being a direct indication of the total legal outward trade of the islands, for the framers of the duty intended to bring in more than they paid for the fee-farm.)

And, 5, there was a revolutionary part to the arrangement. In exchange for granting the 4½ percent duty (which was more than the dues that they were paying to the Carlisle estate, namely, none), the planters of Barbados and the Leeward Islands had their tenancies confirmed and received their lands in "free soccage." This was a confirmation of their land titles whereby major landholders and their minor tenants were granted permanent leaseholds on the lands they held. The lands could be bought, sold and passed on to future generations in testamentary documents. The soccage tenure was just one step short of freehold: the requirement that a symbolic annual payment of insubstantial value (sometimes called an annual quitrent, sometimes called a peppercorn rent) be proffered to the Crown.[84]

That was only a step away from freehold status. On Montserrat, they completed the revolution within five years. Perhaps it would not have been completed, but for a maritime accident. Francis Lord Willoughby was drowned on his way to fight the Dutch in August 1665 and he took with him to the bottom the Great Seal of the Leeward Islands, without which, it was believed, the documents granting the soccage tenure would be illegal.[85] Then, before this matter could be sorted out, a French invasion in 1667 destroyed almost all of the public records of Montserrat, and almost all of the leases, bills of sale, and kindred documents that had been in private hands. Very few people could prove legal title to the land that they occupied.

As a result, the assembly of Montserrat (with the approval of William Lord Willoughby) passed a series of laws designed to straighten everything out permanently. The procedure was based on the Tudor process of surrender-and-regrant, wherein the landholder surrendered title temporarily to the Crown and then was regranted the same land in clear title.[86] The pattern, as danced on Montserrat, also involved the 4½ percent duty. One act spelled out that duty, a second act repealed it, and a third re-instated it.[87]

That was one half of the equation: what was owed to the state. The other half was what was given to the planters. All claims on lands on the island of Montserrat were first pronounced null.[88] Immediately thereafter, the lands of all settlers were re-invested in them. The noteworthy point is that now there was no talk of soccage or of symbolic quitrents. The lands were granted "forever," and if the planters wanted this confirmed by a patent, they could have it so engrossed. There were exceptions: persons who had gone over to the

French in the recent war, and certain blocks of sizable property held by individuals who were letting them lie fallow.[89]

And so, fee-simple ownership had become a reality. The terms "forever" and "freeholder" crop up often enough in subsequent legislation to confirm that this was the real thing. But it was no panacea. An act of 1670 began: "Whereas there do arise many Differences betwixt the Inhabitants of this island touching the Bounds of their Lands"[90] and went on to prescribe the establishment of boundary viewers for each part of the island, pairs of senior property owners who would sort out the myriad land disputes between neighbours.

Two direct consequences followed upon the creation of the New World revolution in land ownership. The freehold system made planters much more willing to commit their resources to the sugar-slave economy, because the ownership of land in perpetuity greatly reduced their insecurity on the land questions. Secondly, as the system of fee simple ownership and the sugar economy evolved in the eighteenth century, it is clear that permanent land titles (backed, eventually, by a decent system of records) permitted the evolution of large-scale absenteeism on the part of land owners. Until land titles were permanently secured, personal occupancy of the land was important: leaving, even for a year, made one vulnerable to title-jumping at the island courthouse, or boundary-cheating by one's aggressive neighbour. By 1730, however, on Montserrat, owners felt confident in leaving plantations in the hands of agents, sometimes for years at a time. They may have been cheated on their annual accounts under such a system, but they did not have to worry about losing their land titles.

Just as a new theory and practice of land ownership developed after 1660, so a new theory and practice of local government emerged. As in the case of land, governmental change was messier in practice than it appeared in theory.

As mentioned earlier, Charles II in July 1660 peremptorily directed Francis Lord Willoughby either to resume his responsibilities under the Carlisle patent or nominate someone to take his place. Willoughby took charge himself of the governance of the Leeward Islands and Barbados. He needed to appoint local governors. He had in fact reappointed in February 1660, the then-governor of Montserrat, Roger Osborne.[91] This was sensible, because, despite Osborne's willingness to tug the forelock to Willoughby,[92] had this not been the case, removing him would have been difficult indeed. But, with Willoughby back in charge, with the Carlisle patent once again being honoured, and with Roger Osborne confirmed as governor of Montserrat, it appeared that nothing in government had changed since the 1650s.

Lots had. That became clear when Willoughby gave up the Carlisle patent in 1663 and took appointment as governor of Barbados and the Leeward Islands at royal pleasure (a post his brother assumed after 1667, following Willoughby's death at sea in 1665). So, from 1663 onwards, the administration was no longer neo-feudal but directly dispensed by the English state.

In 1671, the Leeward Islands, after nearly a decade of complaint by Leeward Islands planters against the domination of Barbados, were broken off as a separate administrative unit. When that occurred, the Irishman, William Stapleton, probably the most able administrator the islands ever had, was appointed governor of the Leeward Islands.

Locally, the most important development was the development of a form of representative government on each island. In the year 1668, William Stapleton had succeeded to the governorship of Montserrat – which confusingly was now styled the "deputy governorship," meaning that it was under the governorship of the Leeward Islands and Barbados (until 1671; thereafter it was simply under the governorship of the Leewards). William Stapleton arrived with a new remit, namely to create a simulacrum of the home government on the island of Montserrat.

Previously, there had been a council on the island. This was in the neo-feudal era, and its relationship to the governor of the island was analogous to the relationship of the medieval monarch and his privy council.[93] The council was expected to give advice and consent, but not criticism or dissent. It was not representative government by any stretch of the imagination, though its formal approval was necessary to pass laws on the island. Now, in 1668, a more modern model was adopted, and this too was a simulacrum of what was developing in the home countries. A structure of assembly-council-deputy governor followed the lines of commons-lords-monarchy.[94] The council consisted, in theory, of twelve substantial landowners, appointed by the lords of trade and plantations, upon nomination of the local governor. The assembly consisted of eight freeholders (four from each parish).[95] Thus, a broadly representative system of government (by late seventeenth-century standards) operated on Montserrat, subject to two caveats. One was that blacks of any sort (even the rare free blacks) were not allowed to participate in political life in any formal way. Second, Roman Catholics, while allowed to vote and hold some minor offices, and some appointed positions, could not sit on council, in assembly, or as deputy-governor, the surrogate monarch of the island. Catholics were allowed to serve in the militia: indeed, every white male between puberty and senescence had to serve. (The matter of Catholic disabilities – that is, things the Catholics were "disabled" from doing because of their religious adherence – is discussed in detail in the next chapter; here, the point is that one should be aware of those disabilities if one is to understand how the various sorts of Irish persons acted and re-acted in difficult times.)

Yet, if the post-1668 structure of government implied one set of behaviours, namely, local representative government, the fact that the laws after 1668 had to be sent to London for approval by the state authorities meant that the colonists were dependents. Therefore a state of forced governmental infantilism prevailed.[96] The contradiction frequently tipped over into confusion. Given that Montserrat statutes had to have London's approval, it was never clear the extent to which general statutes enacted in Westminster for England and (after 1707) for Great Britain, and (after 1800) for the United Kingdom of Great Britain and Ireland, were operative on the island. An act of the Leeward Islands Council and General Assembly attempted to simplify matters in 1705 by declaring that on the Leeward Islands the English common law took precedence. This, however, left murky matters of English statute law, especially those that contained penalty or criminal provisions.[97] This was especially confusing in the case of Roman Catholic disabilities. Therefore, it is appropriate that the most revealing discussion of the contradictions between the responsibilities implied in the island's governmental structure and the infantilism dictated by its colonial status is found in an argument put forward relating to Catholic disabilities. The argument is late – 1751 – and was put forward by an English lawyer who was arguing on behalf of Montserrat's Catholics against an act that would have deprived them of the right to vote. "The constitution of this island," he argued, "was limited in like manner as a corporation established by a charter, something betwixt that and a sovereign legislature – more extensive than the one and less than the other."[98] That Montserrat's laws had to be sent to the Lords of Trade and Plantation in London for their approval before they became law was of course based on a precedent that the Irish knew full well. The arrangements were the West Indies' version of Poynings' Laws of 1494.

William Stapleton was in charge of Montserrat from 1668 and of all the Leeward Islands from late 1671 to his death in 1686. His assignment was one of the toughest possible, especially concerning

Montserrat. During the 1660s and 1670s, that island had an unbroken string of bad luck, and that after the anarchy of the 1650s. The worst ill-fortune stemmed from a messy Anglo-French war in the West Indies, in 1666–67, which overlapped with the second Anglo-Dutch War of 1665–67. In 1667, Montserrat caught the full force of the French onslaught.

This occurred early in 1667 when a force of French soldiers (what would today be called marines) combined with ten periagoes full of Carib Indians, acting like a modern ranger unit, hit the island unexpectedly, and hard. By February 9, Montserrat was in the hands of the French and remained so until July[99] when the French withdrew and, immediately, a peasant rebellion followed. Tobacco warehouses and sugar mills were burned by the French; 649 slaves were taken.[100] Most of these never returned.[101] Given that there were 523 slaves on the island in 1672, probably well over half the slaves had been taken permanently by the French.[102] Over 600 of the inhabitants of Montserrat fled to Jamaica, "extremely plundered, even to their very shirts, so that many would have perished, had they not been relieved by the charity of the planters."[103] These were the lucky ones. Others were captured by the Carib and were taken to Dominica.[104] Eventually, after the peace of Breda between England, Holland, France and Denmark was concluded in the end of July 1667, the refugees and captives from Montserrat were free to come home. How many did so is unknown, but one suspects that a swirling of populations occurred throughout the Leeward Islands, all of which had been directly affected by the French war. Thus, one finds Thomas Lynch, the lieutenant governor of Jamaica, reporting in 1671 that Montserrat was better peopled than ever, for 300–400 settlers that "belong to St Christopher's" had gone there to settle.[105] Though Montserrat may have experienced a net population loss as a result of the French war, that loss was not so great as might be expected if one only pays attention to the distress figures.

When Lt-Col. William Stapleton took over as governor of the island in mid-1668, his qualifications were reported to the Lords of Council as follows: "A gentleman of known valour and integrity and born in Ireland, and therefore understands the better to govern his countryman."[106] That latter ability – to govern his countrymen – was of great advantage because during the French invasion of early 1667 a large body of the Irish had gone over to the enemy. This is well documented in both French and English sources. According to the French sources, the French commander of the invasion force, having seen how the Irish behaved, and that they were willing to promise faithfulness to his regime, let 500 Irish men and more than 1,500 of their women and children stay on the island, as French subjects.[107] This probably represented about two-thirds of the white population of the island in 1667 (we do not know exactly what the number was, but it probably exceeded somewhat the estimated 2,836 whites who were there in 1672).

About six months after the island was retaken from the French, a group of substantial citizens petitioned the English authorities for relief of their condition. They declared their loyalty to the Crown and noted that:

> We withall of his Majesty's loyal subjects of this island have so much above any other of our neighbours been devastated, wasted, and destroyed in the late unhappy war, not only by our enemies in the time of their short stay with us, but have likewise then as many times since in a most barbarous and unhumane manner been robbed, plundered, stripped and almost utterly consumed of all that we had in the world by a party of rebellious and wicked people of the Irish nation, our neighbours and inhabitants in such a sort as it is almost impossible either for men or pen to relate.[108]

What is here being reported is a jacquerie, a peasants' rebellion, that had lasted for roughly six months (the second half of the year 1667), after the French left the island. It was put down only by William Lord Willoughby's bringing a military force to the island in February 1668. He restored order by clamping down on Irish revolutionaries. "Some of them have been fairly hanged, and others he is hunting in the woods and will serve the same. The rest, about four hundred [men] swear to be loyal."[109] These men he resettled on their lands and, he hoped, in their minds![110] Three months later, he went back to Montserrat to check on its condition and found that the Irish now swore to be true, "and I believe them till an enemy appear."[111]

But who were "the Irish" and how does one judge their rebellion? From a far distance, say, the perspective of the London authorities, the categories of Irish and Catholic and treasonous overlapped. From nearly as far away, from the perspective of Irish resistors to the English conquest of Ireland, the categories of Irish and Catholic and heroic overlapped. But on the ground, there was more to it than that sort of cartooning. The seizure of control of Montserrat and the subsequent terrorizing of the ruling class meant that something more than religion and nationality was at work, though they certainly were there: social class rebellion also was involved.

That this is the case becomes clear when one realizes that not all of the persons of Irish Catholic background were involved. Many remained loyal to the Crown and suffered heavily from the jacquerie.

This is obvious when one examines the names on the remonstrance and petition that finally brought the colonial authorities to recapture the island. Of the twenty-seven names on the petition of loyalty to the Crown, eighteen are Irish, and an additional one was an English Roman Catholic. Of the Irish, some (David Gallway, Anthony Briskett, John Cormack, John Devereaux, and John Ryan) were Protestants, or at least willing to adopt Protestantism publicly, whatever their private religious practice. Most of the rest were Irish Catholic and not just of the "Old English" sort, but mostly of native Irish extraction (Dermott Sullivan, John Cahan, and John Lynch among them). That approximately half of the protestors against the Irish rebellion were Irish Catholic and substantial citizens makes clear the social class component in the rebellion.[112]

The complexity of the whole course of events as it concerned the Irish is underscored by one particular name on the remonstrance against the rebellious Irish: Anthony Briskett. This is Anthony Briskett II, Protestant, son of the first Irish governor of Montserrat, of the "New English" strand of Irish life, and very privileged. Despite the efforts of Governor Osborne to manipulate Briskett's patrimony while it was under his wardship, in 1667 Briskett still held three plantations: one called the "Forthouse Plantation" of about 525 acres; another, the "Waterwork Plantation" of about 573 acres; and a third, called the "Southside Plantation" of roughly 300 acres.[113] Of course Anthony Briskett II would be foursquare against the rebellious Irish. That is obvious.

Except that it is not. When the French conquered the island early in 1667, this same Anthony Briskett became the head of a tiny puppet regime. He accepted a French commission from Capt. de la Barre, the conqueror of the island, "to be governor over all, and more especially the Irish inhabitations of the leeward [that is southwestern] side of the said Island."[114] Thus, the ultimate old-settler figure on the island, the son of the Irish Protestant founder, had joined the Irish Catholic insurrection. When Willoughby convened the new assembly, in April 1668, one of the first laws passed was that depriving Anthony Briskett of his lands.[115]

Fair enough: Briskett had gone native and had to be punished. His defence, however, was intriguing. He argued that he had had a valuable estate destroyed by the French capture of the island (which of his plantations he did not say), and at the time "his Majesty's poor distressed subjects" pleaded with him to accept "a power from the French to protect them." That, Briskett says, he refused, until "their lamentable complaints, importunate tears, and most deplorable suffering" forced him to accept, for their sakes.[116] Given that he had assumed particular command of the southwest of the island (where, as our analysis of the 1678 census will show, most of the poorer Irish lived), this argument, that he was protecting the loyal subjects, must have rung hollow. In a subsequent petition, however, Briskett covered this flank by asserting that he was protecting "his Majesty's most distressed subjects from the fury of barbarous bloody Indians and others."[117] (This was always a good tactic in those days; when all else fails, wave the red card.) In petitioning against the attainder of his land, Briskett was forced to play off his back foot as most of his land was given away quickly. William Lord Willoughby, who was still in command of the Leeward Islands and Barbados at that time, gave the lower and more level parts of the Forthouse Plantation to the government of Montserrat for the situation of a town and fort near Kingsale. The rest of the plantation went to one Stanley, "an old planter" who had taken over temporarily as deputy governor of the island.[118] Briskett's second estate, the "Waterwork Plantation," was passed on by Willoughby's authority to the new deputy governor, William Stapleton: 573 acres to be held by him and his heirs forever. This was, as Willoughby explained, "for his better encouragement to plant and settle there."[119]

So, all that was left for Anthony Briskett, even if he were successful, was the "Southside Plantation" of 300 acres. As it turns out, he lost and the name Briskett disappears from Montserrat.

What Briskett's actions suggest is the same thing that those of the Gallway family indicated: namely, first, that one cannot stereotype the Irish: they went various ways and in the most unpredictable fashion. Second, they were frequently willing to change sides, whether in religion or in politics, depending upon their own self-interest, and on the interplay of their own self-interest and their consciences, items that frequently were negotiable.

In total, the French war with its sacking and theft, the consequent temporary depopulation of the island, the peasants' rebellion, was a massive piece of ill fortune. But there was more. In the autumn of 1670 both Montserrat and Nevis were "much ruined by hurricanes."[120] Then, on Christmas day, 1672, a severe earthquake hit the island. The stone buildings, so proudly raised in imitation of English civic, ecclesiastical, and estate architecture, were left as rubble.[121]

Next, the so-called "Third Anglo-Dutch War" of 1672–74 threatened the island once again with invasion. (It also threatened the islanders with cognitive dissonance, for during this conflict the French and the English were allies.) In May 1673, a Dutch fleet of nine men-of-war and six other vessels appeared at Montserrat, on the leeward side of the island, and fired from break of day until five in the afternoon at five ships that were riding at anchor in the harbour. They stormed one of the vessels, the "Michael," and took it. Apparently the Dutch were considering landing on the island and there is no question that they could have taken it, for they had 1,100 hardened marines on board their ships, and Montserrat had at most 1,000 men who could walk, ride, or shuffle to the island's defence. Surprisingly, the Dutch decided to leave without an invasion.[122]

Then, in 1678, the French and the English having fallen out as allies, almost began another serious war in the West Indies.[123] This series of misfortunes may be what led William Stapleton in 1679 to put forward a proposal to the Lords of Trade and Plantations that, in other circumstances, might have been taken as a skit. He suggested that in dealings with the French, it might be a good idea to acquire the French parts of St Christopher in exchange for Montserrat.[124] It is a sign of Montserrat's typhoid-Mary reputation that their Lordships considered the idea seriously for a brief time.[125]

What worried the islanders more than any of the skein of misfortunes already mentioned was the constant terror of Carib attack. The early settlers on Montserrat had been fortunate in that the island (in contrast to St Christopher) was not a permanent location of indigenous peoples. However, the island had experienced its first serious Carib attack in 1651, and from then on, they became the Amerindian nightmare. This was especially intense at times when the English and French governments were at war – or even at daggers drawn – because the French used the Carib, with whom they allied, as shock troops: as the captain who captured Montserrat in 1667 explained it, the Carib fell upon the English like demons, or savaged them from the woods, like wolves.[126] As discussed in chapter 2, the settlers' nightmares were in part self-induced, for they bought into the myth of the Caribs being cannibals (thus illustrating the universal truth that racism is frequently its own punishment). However, the Carib were frightening enough in reality, largely because of their mobility in the war canoes. This allowed them not only surprising speed, but permitted them to land at places to windward where vessels with sails could not approach. Thus, the whole perimeter of Montserrat became a sequence of potential invasion points. Towers, eight to ten feet high, of stone or timber were built around the island to serve as watch points and as signal beacons in case of attack.[127] William Lord Willoughby managed to conclude a truce with the Carib independent of the peace treaty of 1667 with the French. This agreement lasted until 1672, when the Caribs attacked Antigua, killed two settlers, and left two others badly injured. Some of these Indians (an estimated thirty) then took to the woods in Antigua and another segment took two periagoes to Montserrat to attack there. Montserrat's defensive measure worked, however, and Colonel Stapleton caught twenty-eight of them and put them in irons. Despite his own intense dislike of the Carib, Stapleton did not immediately give them "their due punishment" (by which he certainly meant death), because he feared Carib retribution upon English settlers on Dominica.[128]

The reason William Stapleton believed that it was worth staying his hand, in aid of the English settlers on Dominica, was that one secondary segment of the Carib was aligned with the English. This was the group headed by the extraordinary Thomas Warner, usually known as "Indian Warner." He was the son of Sir Thomas Warner, founding father of the Leeward Island settlements, by an Indian slave. Indian Warner, despite having been kept as a slave by his English stepmother, was predisposed to the English side in the French-English troubles and so useful had he been in that line that for a time in the mid-1660s he was deputy governor of Dominica.

Again, now, something of the Elizabethan gothic entered the story. Col. Philip Warner, a legitimate son of Sir Thomas Warner and thus the half-brother of Indian Warner, was in the 1670s the deputy governor of Antigua, one of the places where Carib frequently raided. Second, William Stapleton and Indian Warner were deep enemies. In part this must have stemmed from the murder on Montserrat of Thomas Russel some years previously. Indian Warner was generally reported to have been the chief leader of this raid. And (in 1671) William Stapleton had married into the Russel family, which centred on large plantations on Nevis. At one point (probably in 1674), Stapleton had taken Indian Warner prisoner and, blaming him for the attacks on Antigua, was about to hang him, when Philip Warner, half-brother of the accused, intervened. Indian Warner, being freed, made threats against Stapleton and against the island of Montserrat. After a further attack on Antigua in 1674, Stapleton authorized a major attack on Indian Warner's people on Dominica. This attack, according to Stapleton, killed eighty Carib. Of those killed, Indian Warner was one; and the man who was in charge of the actual expedition was Philip Warner, his half-brother. The latter, although deputy governor of Antigua, was charged with murder, and though he was finally cleared in 1676, the London authorities ordered that he forfeit his governorship.[129] In sum, it was about as nasty a business as possible, with William Stapleton hunting down the Carib with the same enthusiasm that the Dublin authorities in Ireland had hunted his own family earlier in the century.

In dealing with his London masters, Stapleton continually emphasized "the importance of destroying the barbarous heathens, the

Caribbee Indians, who in the war joined the French in the destruction of his Majesty's subjects, and have since murdered many in Antigua and had done the same in Montserrat."[130] Stapleton, who at the time of writing this was governor of all the Leeward Islands, noted that he often had to make expensive and dangerous trips by small boats to Antigua and to Montserrat to visit the planters and settle "their distracted thought of deserting them [sic] islands through apprehension of Indians inroads by murders, rapes, etc."[131] He added that the planters on those islands were more destroyed by having to watch and ward against the heathen than by any other cause. Many caught "malignant distempers" while serving their rotation on guard duty. Indian hunting remained one of Stapleton's obsessions throughout his career in the Leeward Islands, and most of his subjects would have enthusiastically approved.[132]

Montserrat's remarkable skein of bad luck, when combined with constant worries about Carib attack, made the island less than ideally attractive, despite the fact that it contained in the late 1670s at least 4,000 acres of farmable land still not allocated. In fact, it is estimated that only one-third of the island in 1676 was cleared.[133] (Whether or not it should have been cleared, given ecological considerations, is another matter; in the seventeenth-century planter mind, the only good land was cleared land, and land waiting to be cleared was profit waiting to be reaped.)

Thus one discovers a symptomatic, but curious, episode at the end of the 1670s. Captain John Carrol (var: Carrill, Carroll, Carryll) who briefly, in 1675, served as deputy governor of the island, complained to the governor of Jamaica that though he now was settled in Jamaica, with his family of twenty-five members (meaning that he was a moderate-sized planter), he had encountered great trouble getting his wife and some of his household off Montserrat. He reported that there was an act in force on that island which provided that no family should move from it, "owing to the desire of many families to be transported to Jamaica."[134] Carroll was in part right. From the late 1650s onwards, Jamaica had attracted planter families from the Leeward Islands, especially those who wanted to move from modest-sized farms to big sugar plantations. The really curious point is that the Montserrat law either did not exist, or if it did, was never engrossed on the statute books.[135]

William Stapleton, first as deputy governor of Montserrat, and then as governor of the Leeward Islands (with powers of nominating the deputy governor of Montserrat), was engaged in a major piece of social engineering. Of course that term would have been alien to him. He would have thought in terms of setting his dominion in proper order, but engineering it was. As discussed earlier, he introduced an entirely new system of land ownership: freeholds replaced neo-feudal tenancies as the primary form of land usage. He introduced a form of representative government based upon the Westminster model, with a bicameral structure and the Crown representative. He did this, and a great deal more, while on the one hand trying to wipe out the indigenous peoples of his satrapy and, on the other, keeping the potentially contumacious Irish proletariat quiet.

Further, the importance of Stapleton's creation of a formal legal structure on the island should not be underestimated. The regular publication of public acts was an innovation. One of the first acts of Stapleton's regime was to determine a fee structure for the office of the secretary of the island and for the marshall, the two legal functionaries on the island. The annexes to the act look like the wine list at a strange restaurant. Three pages of secretary's fees were defined, ranging from the licensing of a victual and tap house to writing up a special warrant of arrest. The marshal's fees included those for serving warrants, taking prisoners into custody, and specified the amount the marshal was due from the government for every twenty-four hours he kept someone imprisoned. (Significantly – the year is 1668 – these tariffs are given in pounds of tobacco and not in sugar, an indication that the economy still was predominantly a small-holder, tobacco economy.)[136]

A considerable number of local laws of the Stapleton era attempted to establish economic order. Some of them, such as the licensing of taphouses, had a double intention: to control one form of economic activity, but also to limit social disorder; then as now, shebeens were a source of fights and crime. Interestingly, the act set out a price scale for drink, since many of the taphouses were overcharging their customers.[137] Another set of laws tried to keep trade reasonably honest: an old act (pre-1668) governing the accuracy of weights and measures was re-enacted,[138] as were measures governing the quality of tobacco,[139] indigo, and sugar.[140]

In-coming trade was to be limited to three towns: that of Briskett Bay (coming at that time to be known as "Stapleton," the New Fort (from the Fort plantation recently seized from Anthony Briskett II and "usually known by the name of Kingsale'") and Plymouth, identified by the "Church gut" of St Anthony's parish church. Of course one of the purposes of this statute was to reduce smuggling. However, recalling the recent war with the French, it had another purpose: to concentrate the forces that might be put into readiness if an invasion should be threatened.[141] That was not mere posturing, for the late French invasion was deeply seared into the minds of the substantial landholders who dominated the council and assembly.

An act of 1673 noted that there had been "several complaints of labourers on this Island of their being much damnified for want of their due payment, and the Courts being usually suspended in the latter part of the year, by which means many persons take advantage to defraud the labourer of his payment for the said time," it was therefore enacted that any justice of the peace could intercede. The JP could determine the labourer's wage complaint and order legal processes for payment of those wages.[142] This enactment, one may reasonably suggest, stemmed not from humanitarian concern for the labourers, but from a memory of what had happened six years earlier, when the Irish Catholic segment of the agricultural proletariat had expressed its displeasure by seizing control of the island for a period of six months.

Most of the economic legislation of Stapleton and his successors on Montserrat was market-freeing work: the removal of impediments to trade, especially unfair business practices which precluded the trust required for a functioning local market economy. A few acts, however, were pro-active, and interventionary. For example, the shortage of "real" money on the island (as, indeed, throughout the West Indies) being notorious, a measure of 1670 provided that Spanish, Mexican, Peruvian and New England money would be acceptable currency for payment of all debts and anyone refusing to accept them would be fined 1,000 pounds of sugar for each refusal.[143] Another important intervention began "Whereas there hath been of late a general complaint over the whole island of the great want of provisions." Some of this scarcity, the act acknowledged, was caused by recent hurricanes, but mostly "the cause thereof being by the general neglect of the inhabitants."[144] Therefore all families living on the island were required to grow provisions in the proportion of one acre for every two working persons, white or black. Potatoes and cassava were prescribed and the provision gardens had to be kept clean and in good order. There were other requirements and provision-viewers were appointed to enforce the rules. Now, on most of the West Indies, as sugar became king, provisions became short, and this sort of legislation became commonplace. This 1669 act, however, is specific to Montserrat and should not be taken to mean that the place had turned to King Sugar: a French war, a local rebellion, and a hurricane had preceded this enactment. In that context, and in the context of Montserrat still having a good deal of unused arable land, the real local meaning of the act was that there was a considerable potential for (a) the importation of provisions, especially things like Irish beef, by sharp-edged merchants such as the Blake family, whom we discussed earlier; and (b) chances for both small and large farmers on the island to get into a profitable provisions trade. The small ones' opportunity is obvious: they could grow root crops and maize for the provisioning of slaves on the emerging sugar plantations. The large ones, however, like the Gallways, could use their land for cattle ranching, and – as discussed earlier – that is what the Gallways did with most of their land.

Even though Montserrat was a tiny island, its economy in the seventeenth century was much more complicated than the term "sugar island" implies. Sugar was probably evenly balanced in 1680 by other commodities, such as home-grown provisions and livestock, as well as tobacco. One reason that the economy stayed this complex – this balanced – was explained by William Stapleton to the Council for Trade and Plantations in 1672, when he told their lordships that "the ordinary obstructions to the improvement of trade are want of slaves, servants, horses, and frigates to countenance them."[145]

To keep trade in order was an easy task compared to keeping some of the Irish in line. One of the first statutes for which William Stapleton was responsible, was "An Act against opprobrious language," which came into effect 1 December 1668. Opprobrious language had nothing to do with blasphemy, as one might expect, given that it was a seventeenth-century statute. Rather, it dealt with a social control problem: namely, that some segments of the population were undercutting the civil government by "their scandalous, ruinous, and opprobrious speeches." These "over-shadow the good government and administeres [sic] in this island with the staple clouds of reproach and infamy" to the danger of public peace and the discouragement of these public officers.[146]

We are viewing here the aftershock of the French invasion and the subsequent peasants' rebellion. Although the rebel servants on the island still had been disciplined by Lord Willoughby, that does not mean that they would lie down. Clearly, this group – mostly Irish – contrived to make life pure hell for the public officials. Thus, any who "shall presume either by writing, verbally, or other ways or means, to scandalize or abuse"[147] any of the members of the council of the island was to be liable upon conviction for each instance, to a fine of 5,000 pounds of sugar (or its equivalent in tobacco, cotton, wool, or indigo), and if the person could not pay, he was to be corporally punished which, presumably, meant a public beating. Interestingly, the act implicitly affirmed the principle of hierarchy in that anyone who scandalized or abused members of the Montserrat assembly was liable to a fine of 500 pounds of sugar, one-tenth of the rate for slagging legislative councillors.

There was more to opprobrious language, however. The Irish and everyone else were continually badmouthing each other and this frequently led to violence:

> And whereas also there are several persons of his Majesty's subjects of his three nations, that is to say, England, Scotland, and Ireland, residing in the Island, and oftentimes as well in Drink as sober [a nicely balanced phrase that, the more effective for its placing the rule before the exception] ... certain words of distinction do arise between his Majesty's subjects of the said three nations [what words?] ... as English Dog, Scott's Dog, Tory, Irish Dog, Cavalier, and Roundhead, and many other opprobrious, scandalous, and disgraceful terms, [leading to] the Breech of his Majesty's Peace etc. and by certain Quaralls that may arise by reason of such ill language...to the endangering the loss of the lives of many of his Majesty's good subjects of the Three Nations.[148]

This had to be stopped. So, in what was probably the English Empire's first (but, one suspects, not the last) Multicultural Language Enforcement Act, anyone using these terms was to be, in the first instance, subject to the fines or corporal punishment for breaking the peace. However, if "any affrays, murders, bloodsheds, riots, routs, or unlawful assemblies shall be had, made, or stirred up in this Island, by reason of any such word or words of distinction before mentioned, or any other"[149] the penalties were to be the same as for mutiny, which is to say serious imprisonment or capital punishment.

In managing Montserrat, William Stapleton never forgot for a moment that he was managing Irish people and that they never were standard-issue items. Outsiders, such as the London authorities, might refer to "the Irish" in the West Indies as if they were an entity, but Stapleton understood that they were neither homogeneous nor predictable. Thus he took nothing for granted, save that the English administrators did not have a clue as how to deal with them. (An observation that is well documented by the odd few hundred years of Irish history both before and after Stapleton's era.)

Therefore, after Stapleton's promotion from deputy governor of Montserrat (which he held from 1668 to late 1671) to the governorship of the Leeward Islands (which he held from late 1671 until his death in 1686), he took few risks with Montserrat. It might not be the most expensive bauble in the West Indies, but it was the most likely to shatter. So he did exactly what Irish petty kings had done in ancient times when faced with the necessity of being in two places at once: he placed a member of his family in charge of part of his domain. In this case, from 1672–79, Stapleton's elder brother, Edmund, was in charge as deputy governor of Montserrat and later, his younger brother, Redmond, was deputy governor from 1685 until his own death in 1687.[150] (When Edmund was away for a time in 1675, John Carroll, another Irishman of Old-English background, served as deputy governor of Montserrat.)[151]

After Edmund Stapleton left the deputy governorship in 1679, he was briefly replaced in 1679–80 by a large Montserrat planter of English background, Peter Cove,[152] and then, very quickly, another Irishman was in charge, a fellow soldier from William Stapleton's adventuring days, one James Cotter (1680–85).[153]

Thus, except for one very brief period when the Englishman Peter Cove stepped in, from 1632 to 1687, Montserrat was controlled by Irishmen. Even if one excepts John Carroll as being a local planter, his period in charge was so brief as not to threaten the generalization: namely, that from 1668–87, Montserrat was controlled by a particular sort of Irish adventurer: very adaptable men of Old English or native Irish background. The cases of Edmund and Redmond Stapleton will be made in just a moment, when we turn to the great mystery, the man we have been saving until last to interrogate, the great William Stapleton.

But consider first, his friend and ally James Cotter (var: Cottar) who served as deputy governor from 1680–85 (sometimes more in absence than in presence). Coming from a native Irish, County Cork family of good connections (related to the FitzGeralds, Plunketts, and Butlers), Cotter was both royalist and Catholic, which meant that his family was dispossessed during the Irish Civil Wars. He stayed fiercely loyal to the Stuarts and clearly had done them trustworthy service, for soon after Charles II's restoration, James Cotter was entrusted with tracking down one or more of the regicides who had ended the life of Charles I in 1649. Thus, Cotter became a royal hitman. The operation he ran tracked down one of the regicide leaders, Col. John Lisle, in Switzerland. Lisle was successfully dispatched by a gunshot, when on his way to church. (Whether Cotter or his subordinate fired the shot is unclear, but Cotter planned the operation.) That was in August 1664. Cotter's next major action was in 1667 when he joined William Stapleton (whom he probably already knew from civil war days) in an unsuccessful attack on the French on St Christopher, which at that time was held entirely by the enemy. Now Cotter, like his friend Stapleton, had no inclination to spend his life as the typical Irish hero, handsome, charismatic and unsuccessful. He intended to do well for himself, and devil take the rest. When, in 1672, William Stapleton became governor of the Leeward Islands, he endorsed Cotter's petition to King Charles II for appointment to the new offices of secretary and marshal of the Leeward Islands, separate offices which, when combined, handled almost all of the legal documentation relevant to the Leeward Islands as a whole. This was granted, in 1676, as an appointment for twenty-one years. This quasi-judicial post may explain why Cotter was enumerated in the 1678 Montserrat census along with ten prisoners in the local lock-up. When, in 1687, Cotter was appointed deputy governor of Montserrat by his old friend William Stapleton, he simply farmed out his two legal offices and kept taking the income. He continued to do this even after he returned to Ireland in 1682.[154]

A sense of the religious ambiguity of the whole situation in the Leeward Islands after the Restoration is found in the fact that Cotter, despite his Catholic background, was willing to assume the guise of an Anglican in order to hold his judicial posts and to be the deputy governor – the viceroy – of Montserrat. So, it is a suitable twist to a careerist's career, that in 1689, after an investigation by the attorney general of England of Cotter's farming out of his legal posts in the Leeward Islands, he was deprived of these offices and was declared "a papist and a rebel."[155]

His friend and mentor William Stapleton was of the same cut of cloth, only tougher. Of an Old-English Catholic family from County Tipperary, with branches in County Limerick, he too saw his family estates forfeited for the family's combination of royalism and Catholicism. Leaving Ireland, he fought in France and Spain, a soldier for hire. After the Restoration of 1660 he returned to England and took a lieutenant-colonelcy in a regiment commanded by Sir Tobias Bridge. This regiment was raised specifically for the French War, and was ordered to Barbados in 1667, conveniently for William Stapleton. He was in Newgate Gaol at the time on a murder charge. He was granted a King's pardon on the charge and allowed to sail. From Barbados, he was sent in command of a unit to attack the French on St Christopher and though he was unsuccessful, he was conspicuous by his bravery. When the peace with the French was signed (the Treaty of Breda which also involved the Netherlands and Denmark), there were myriad local details to work out and Stapleton, being fluent in French, was appointed as one of the commissioners to treat with the French.[156]

Scant wonder that the governor of Barbados and the Leeward Islands found William Stapleton the perfect man to place in charge of the West Indies' messiest little colony, Montserrat. Stapleton did not mellow, despite his new dignities as deputy governor of Montserrat and then governor of the Leewards. He wrote to a man who had accused him of an injustice that "Were I near you I would dash your teeth and your words down your throat," and, while governor of the Leeward Islands, he once drew his sword on one of his deputy governors and made several thrusts at him.[157] His version of direct management techniques included hunting Carib Indians as if he were harrying rabbits with hounds. One reason, I would suggest, that he was able to control the Irish in Montserrat so well is that the Irish, all sorts, had the good sense to be afraid of him. He was a man of a good deal of worldly wisdom, as his governmental and economic reforms show, but in the world in which he lived, wisdom was of no value without a strong sword hand.

From his official posts, Stapleton did not make money. Indeed, I suspect he lost, given that he frequently had to pay militia expenses out of his own pocket, and then fight for years for reimbursement.[158] But he became immensely wealthy by acquiring land and slaves. His first piece of land was that given him by William Lord Willoughby, land that had been confiscated from Anthony Briskett II, the "Waterwork Plantation," near Plymouth on Montserrat, of 573 acres. This he acquired in 1668, as newly appointed deputy governor of Montserrat.[159] Then, shrewdly, he paid court to Anne, daughter of Lt-Col. Randolph Russell of Nevis, and a niece of Sir James Russel, also of Nevis, who came as close to being planter aristocracy as the Leeward Islands offered. He married her in June 1671, and although this probably did not bring him any direct financial benefit (as her dowry did not include fee simple lands), it did him immense good socially.[160] In turn, this social advantage became a material lever for, in July 1680, he was able to purchase an estate, the "Windward Plantation," that the Crown – he was the Crown! – had granted to his brother-in-law on Montserrat in May 1678. This was recorded as being for 100,000 pounds of muscovado sugar.[161] The whole thing has a plangency that anyone who has studied the interaction of Irish land speculation and state intervention from, say, Henry Tudor to Charles Haughey, will immediately recognize. However, because Stapleton was careful to keep his own estates out of the lands described in the 1678 census of Montserrat (and who can blame him?), we cannot know their full extent.[162]

In a similar transaction in Antigua, William Stapleton granted a total of 1,025 acres to his younger brother Redmond in January 1681. He then purchased the same plantation for himself, from Redmond, for 100,000 pounds of sugar in mid-July 1682.[163] I suspect this was a purely nominal transaction. Effectively, Stapleton gave himself Crown lands. (He later repaid his brother Redmond by making him deputy governor of Montserrat.)

On Nevis, which became his favourite island, Stapleton again flipped land, only blindingly quickly this time. By a patent of May 1678, he (as Crown) granted to one Major Charles Pim a plantation of 502 acres. On the very same day he purchased the plantation from Pim for 400,000 lb of sugar.[164] Heaven only knows if any part of this transaction was real, save the parcel of lands ending up in William Stapleton's collection of plantations: maybe Pim received something for his trouble.[165] In any case, Stapleton came to love this particular place. Although as governor of the Leeward Islands, he was supposed to live on St Christopher, he argued strongly that the London authorities should permit him to live on Nevis.[166] When they failed to grant permission, he ignored them and his Nevis estate became the social centre of Leeward island life.[167]

Strangely, only very late in his career did Stapleton acquire lands on St Christopher, and then in a very unusual way. He was given the gift (subject to the lifetime usage of the donor) of a plantation by Philip de Nogle (var: Philip Nagle or Nangle), who was known as "the Father Hermit."[168] In just a moment, that gift may not seem so strange.

During the early 1680s, Sir William (he had been knighted in 1679) began to feel the wear and tear of his hard life. In June 1683, he requested a furlough or, alternately, permission to retire. He finally arrived in England on furlough in 1685. Even though he now was in poor health, it was evidently expected that he would return to the islands, so a new commission was prepared for him by the London authorities. His health did not improve, however, and he died in Paris in August 1686 where, with his wife and sons, he had gone for a cure.[169] He left behind several square miles of choice plantations on four islands, lands in England, and some hundreds of slaves.[170]

Testamentary matters involved Stapleton's London agent, an Irishman by the name of Sir Patrick Trant, who was also a commissioner of excise and hearth money, and an all-around scoundrel. Stapleton had engaged Trant in 1681 to look after his London affairs, when his previous agent proved unsatisfactory. Now Trant was Irish. Trant was Catholic. Trant had several relations by that surname on Montserrat. Trant was part of a County Limerick–based family of Catholic landowners, the locale of one branch of the Stapleton family. And Trant was the cousin of Stapleton's old war chum James Cotter! (That a small Catholic mafia, or rather, Murphyia, ran Montserrat becomes increasingly clear.) Sir Patrick Trant was also an embezzler and after Stapleton's death on 3 August 1686, it was found that Trant had made off with £8,000 in the governor's funds. Stapleton's widow sued, and won, but the judgment did her scant good, for in the meantime, Trant had been declared an Irish traitor and deprived of his estates.[171] Of course Trant had not been appointed to his trust because he was a crook. He had been appointed because (like Cotter) he was a man whose personal views were palatable to Stapleton; and also, one supposes, because Stapleton did not have to explain to him the fine religio-political line the governor's career was taking. It is probably just as well that Stapleton died before the English and Irish revolution of 1688–89, as he would have had to make a hard choice: I suspect that he would have been not a Williamite, but a Jacobite.

More directly revealing of Stapleton's politics and religion was that in 1685 he and his wife had taken their three sons to France and enrolled them in a Catholic convent school. The baroque twist was that when Stapleton died, Sir Patrick Trant gave instructions to the convent to lock up the three boys and to prevent their mother from taking them away, since she would raise them as Protestants. The eldest lad, James (now the second baronet) was sent to the Douai, one of France's leading educational institutions and a favourite of the wealthy Catholic Wild Geese of Ireland. He managed to escape to England, but died in 1690 on board the vessel the HMS *Jersey*. His brother William became the third baronet and was a firm Roman Catholic.[172]

That plays us back in time to a minor dynastic event of the year 1679. In that year, James Cotter – soldier, papist (and again to be rebel) – married Mary Stapleton, who was either William Stapleton's eldest daughter or his sister.[173] In the former case, Stapleton would have been agreeing to a marriage in which his own grandchildren certainly would have been raised as Irish Catholics; in the latter case, this would have occurred with his nephews and nieces. (Incidentally, James Cotter's willingness to take charge of this female from the Stapleton household – whatever her actual position – is yet another reason that Cotter was appointed to the deputy governorship of Montserrat. One takes care of one's own.)

And now, one further step backwards. In 1674, when he had been governor of the Leeward Islands for about two years, Stapleton came very close to losing the whole golden chain. The previous incumbent of that office, Sir Charles Wheeler, had held it for just over a year and had departed in disgrace. Appointed in January 1671 to be governor of the Leeward Islands (which were not then separated from Barbados), Wheeler was commissioned in mid-March to negotiate with the French about those English estates and goods on St Christopher which had been seized by the French in the 1666–67 war. Their owners wanted compensation. Unfortunately, Wheeler was so generous to the French that he was recalled in early February 1672. Just before the official notice of his recall reached him, Wheeler, having received unofficial word of his disgrace, bolted, taking the Great Seal of the Island with him and leaving the two companies of soldiers he had stationed on St Christopher, in arrears of their pay and ready to turn nasty. To top off his incompetence, he lost the Great Seal, literally.[174] So, when William Stapleton stepped in, he had a nasty mess to clean up. This he did quickly and efficiently, but not without documenting the bad conduct of his predecessor. Wheeler, therefore, became a lifelong enemy of Stapleton, because Stapleton permitted (indeed, one supposes, encouraged, although he denied it) the assembly, council, and deputy governor of St Christopher to seize Sir Charles' plantation and sell it to raise payment for the soldiers who were a year behind in their pay.[175]

Sir Charles Wheeler was an implacable enemy, and his most effective move came in 1674 when he accused William Stapleton of being of the Romish religion. Now being a Roman Catholic was not in England of the time an actual crime. What was a crime, was being a too-visible and too-powerful Papist. Charles II was implicitly tolerant of Catholics, but he had to be wary of the more Protestant wing of parliament. In 1672, the English parliament overcame the resistance of Charles II and passed the Test Act. By its provisions, every holder of a civil or military office had to take communion (the "test") according to the rites of the Established Church, and also to take the oaths of supremacy and allegiance. These oaths had been on the books in England and Ireland for some time previously. They ascribed the headship on earth of the church to the king, and renounced the temporal deposing power of the pope. Some Roman Catholics could take them without bruising their consciences, others could not. What was new was the requirement for the "test," and also a declaration against the doctrine of transubstantiation, items that no Roman Catholic could affirm in good conscience.

So long as William Stapleton was far away in the West Indies, and quiet, the Council of Trade and Plantations was not concerned about his religion. The council cared about how effective he was as a colonial governor and at that he was very good indeed. The Council for Trade and Plantations, however, had to inquire into Sir Charles Wheeler's allegation and, were it proved, Stapleton's career as a governor might have ended in 1675.

Stapleton's response was a rhetorical gem. He worked himself into a mixture of righteous indignation and hand-over-heart patriotism:

> Whenever the King my superior calls me to a religious account, I shall fully declare my trust in religion. I hope I have enough of it through God's mercy

to save my soul. [T]hat little I have, I learnt it among the noises of drums and trumpets and that in his Majesty's service at home and abroad; I pray God it may do me no good if I do not venture my life and 1,000 if I had them, to defend my sovereign's rights and titles or to kill and destroy all manner of persons, emperors, kings, popes and prelates on their invading any part of his Majesty's territories.[176]

A tiny masterpiece: Stapleton had not perjured himself. He had not even denied that he was a Catholic. Instead he had resoundingly asserted his loyalty to the Crown, reminded his readers of his own past service during the civil war ("service at home and abroad"), and had implicitly stated his rejection of the pope's temporal deposing power (he would fight "all manner of persons, emperors, kings, popes and prelates" who invaded any part of the home islands or empire). This latter affirmation he achieved without having to use the words of any of the distasteful oaths whereby Catholics abjured the power of the papacy.

It worked. The Lords of Trade and Plantations were not fools. They knew what Stapleton was doing, and from their viewpoint it was enough. Stapleton, though a Catholic, was left in place because he was unswervingly loyal to the Crown, a very able governor, smart enough not to make an issue of his Roman Catholicism and, when necessary (as it sometimes was in the islands), to adopt and support the forms of the Established Church.

In early sections of this chapter, I have suggested that plasticity characterized the religious practices (and, probably, beliefs) of many of the Irish. One reason put forward for this was that people on a frontier often want religion, and they will go towards any opportunity that promises to slake their religious thirst. Secondly, as Brian McGinn has well argued, many of the Irish Catholics were able to be both Protestant and Catholic, in some cases simultaneously. Thirdly, it is undeniable that some of the Irish must have changed their religion (some permanently; others, like Cotter and Stapleton, only on the surface), for their own economic and social advantage.

This later set of actions, easy to condemn as mere careerism, must be viewed in a larger context. In fact, it is the behaviour of much of traditional Gaelic society in Ireland in the late sixteenth and seventeenth centuries. Religion is only one part of a larger cultural constellation. Dr Art Hughes has shown that among the most privileged and most highly cultured of the old Irish social order – those Gaelic poets who had family lands which they held permanently – many shrewdly changed their patrons as the seventeenth century wore on. They moved from the courts (soon to be destroyed) of Gaelic nobles to being civil poets for the new regime. Thus, as early as 1586, Eochaidh O'hEodhasa was writing, "King James is the dispersal of all mist," and the same king paid 100 guineas for a praise poem from Fearghal Mac an Bhaird. One of the O'Gnimh (Agnew) poets was willing to declare:

> Though we both be of one descent
> I and the stock of Eochaidh Duibhlen
> 'Tis the English who are my cousins
> And not the blood of Eochaidh.[177]

Or, to put it otherwise, in the real world power and patronage are worth more than blood and belief.[178]

So, what people such as William Stapleton, James Cotter, the Gallway family and scores of others were doing was not apostasy in any significant sense (whatever canon law may have said about it), but rather a working out on a narrow edge of England's empire, what was being worked out at home, in Ireland, the biggest and most central of England's colonies of the time. Like the Gaelic poets, these men were finding alternate patrons. And like those poets, whenever possible they stayed true to the old patrons, the old compacts and covenants, but they were not about to save their souls at the expense of their stomachs.

One further detail of the adjustment of the Gaelic poets to the seventeenth century is important. Some of them acquired Protestant patrons in Ireland.[179] Consider what that means from the Protestant side of the equation. The Protestants, in going a bit Gaelic, were hedging their own bets. They hoped that their own kind would continue to roll over the Catholic Irish, but they knew that history reversed itself frequently in Ireland. Thus, though supporting Gaelic culture was expressly forbidden in a number of statutes, they did so anyway. This had resonance on Montserrat in the strange career of Anthony Briskett II who, though son of the Protestant founder of the colony, ended his career there dispossessed of his estates, having served as the collaborationist governor of the island while it was first in the hands of the French, and then under the rule of Irish Catholic rebels from the least-wealthy sectors of the island's white community. That the Irish revolutionaries later turned on Briskett and necessitated his keeping a guard in his house nightly until the arrival of the English fleet[180] does not call into question the reality of what he had done, but only the quality of his political judgment.

The adaptation on Montserrat of those three great, diverse, and confusing strands of Irish culture – Old English, native Irish, and

New English – to their new environment was not a simple thing, but it was hardly unique. Similar adaptation was taking place at home and, increasingly, all over the New World. The tiny size of the Montserrat community has the advantage of making more readily observable what is less easily seen in other venues.

Fortunately, while spending their time doing what counted, the governors of Montserrat spent some of their time counting. The Montserrat enumerations of 1678 and 1729 are far from perfect (as the discussion of them in Appendices A and B indicates) but, nevertheless, taken together they represent the most useful systematic social profile sketched any place in the English empire in the seventeenth and eighteenth centuries.

The great virtue of the 1678 enumeration is that it can be tied to a first-rate, if unusual, piece of cartography, the so-called "Blathwayt Map" of 1673. This is an extraordinary production, thought by the best authorities to be done by William Stapleton himself. It is a mixture of three cartographic styles, planimetric (straight above), scenographic (bird's eye view) and coastal profile (as if from a passing ship). Despite the mixture of styles, it is a gold mine of information because it provides an indication of settlement patterns and of the major features of domestic and civic architecture that otherwise would no longer be discernible. That is good fortune. The good fortune doubles, because the map has been reproduced at the highest technical level as part of a major historical cartographic project of Brown University, which owns the document.[181] Then, Lydia Mihelic Pulsipher decoded the map's eccentric qualities, integrated the information it holds, and tested by archaeological methods the accuracy of the map, which was confirmed.[182] And, finally, Pulsipher went through an extremely difficult exercise of taking the cartographic information of 1673 and using it to hypothesize what the actual census districts were for the enumeration that William Stapleton completed in 1678.[183] This last sounds as if it were an easy task; it was not, and all subsequent historians of Montserrat are in Pulsipher's debt.

In 1672, soon after taking over as governor of the Leeward Islands, William Stapleton conducted the first fairly trustworthy census of the four main islands. It was only an enumeration of males, however, and though this made sense, given that Stapleton's immediate concern was getting the militia up to scratch, this limits its utility, and opens the way to misinterpretation. Nevertheless, it provides a useful context to the later, more accurate enumerations.

Table 1
Adult Male Population of the Main Leeward Islands, 1672

	Column 1		*Column 2*		*Column 3*			
	White Males of Military Age (c. age 16–65)	*% of Total Adult Male Population*	*White Armed Males*	*% of Total Adult Male Population*	*African Slaves (Male)*	*% of Total Adult Male Population*	*Total Adult Male (Cols. 1 and 3)*	*%*
Montserrat	1,171	69.1	700	41.3	523	30.9	1,694	100.0
Nevis	1,411	44.8	1,330	42.2	1,739	55.2	3,150	100.0
Antigua	??	??	1,052	??	570	??	??	100.0
St Christopher	886	48.2	811	44.1	952	51.8	1,838	100.0

Source: Accounts of William Stapleton, enclosed in Stapleton to Council for Trade and Plantation, 17 July 1672, *CSPCS 1669–1674*, 393–4.

Because this is the first fairly reliable social enumeration we have of the Leeward Islands, let us derive one simple index number. This is the ratio of armed white men to black male slaves:

Montserrat	1 armed white male to each	0.75 black male
Nevis	1	1.31
Antigua	1	0.54
St Christopher	1	1.17

Without being in any way facetious, I would suggest that this is a double-surrogate. It could be named the "Big Plantation index." The higher the ratio of black males to armed whites, the farther along the path to industrial-commercial plantation agriculture; the smaller the number, the closer the island was to individual proprietorships as the dominant form. Secondly, the index could be called the "Fear of slave index." The larger the number of adult blacks to armed whites, the greater the society was in fear of slave revolts. The reason that Montserrat in this era did not show in its legislation the great concern with controlling and punishing blacks that it later was to evince is that in this era, the black population was controllable by individual slaveowners. The baroque and bizarre punishment schedules that later emerge were not yet necessary. A reasonable suggestion is that when these societies moved beyond the ratio of one armed white to one adult black male, they were moving into a new and different world, in terms of both economic organization and social comfort. For whites, the world of big plantations necessarily was a world of scared planters.

Table 2

Population of the Main Leeward Islands, 1678

Adult White Males	% of Total Pop.	Adult White Females	% of Total Pop.	White Children	% of Total Pop.	Sub-total White Pop.	% of Total Pop.	Adult Black Males	% of Total Pop.	Adult Black Females	% of Total Pop.	Black Children	% of Total Pop.	Sub-total Black Pop.	% of Total Pop.	Total Pop.	%
MONTSERRAT																	
1,146	25.1	589	12.9	941	20.6	2,676	58.6	?	?	?	?	?	?	1,894[1]	41.4	4,570	100.0
NEVIS																	
1,534	20.8	828	11.3	1,159	15.7	3,521	47.8	1,422	19.3	1,321	17.9	1,106	15.0	3,849	52.2	7,370	100.0
ANTIGUA																	
1,236	27.6	544	12.1	528	11.8	2,308	51.5	805	18.0	868	19.4	499	11.1	2,172	48.5	4,480	100.0
ST CHRISTOPHER																	
695	20.8	539	16.2	663	19.9	1,897	56.9	550	16.5	500	15.0	386	11.6	1,436	43.1	3,333	100.0

Source: PROL, C.O. 1/42, as presented in Dunn, *Sugar and Slaves*, Table 12, 127, and, for Montserrat, sources specified in Appendix A.

[1] See Appendix A.

Table 3
Ethnic Composition of the White Population of the Main Leeward Islands, 1678

	No. of Irish	*% of White Pop.*	*% of Total Pop.*	*No. of English*	*% of White Pop.*	*% of Total Pop.*	*No. of "Other"*	*% of White Pop.*	*% of Total Pop.*
Montserrat[1]	1,845	68.9	40.4	783	29.3	17.1	48	1.8	1.1
Nevis	800	22.7	10.9	2,670	75.8	36.2	51	1.5	0.7
Antigua	610	26.4	13.6	1,600	69.3	35.7	98	4.3	2.2
St Christopher[2]	496	26.1	14.9	1,003	52.9	30.1	398	21.0	11.9

Sources: PROL, C.O. 21/42, as presented in Dunn, *Sugar and Slaves*, Table 12, 127, and, for Montserrat, sources specified in Appendix A.

1 For Montserrat, see Appendix A.

2 For St Christopher, although the ethnicity of the adult males was distinguished, for adult females and for children, English and Irish persons were lumped together. These amalgamations have been decombined, by allocating women and children to the Irish and English categories in the same proportions as the adult males were reported to be in those two categories. This is a notional enumeration, therefore.

In 1678 another enumeration was ordered by Stapleton and this one was more complete than the previous one (although, again, far from perfect). The results for the Leeward Islands are found in Tables 2, 3, and 4. (I would suggest that the reader refer to Appendix A for an indication of the character of the Montserrat enumeration and of the flaws in it and of the way some of those can be corrected.)

The most obvious conclusions these data indicate are, first, that Montserrat was proportionately the most "white" of the Leeward Islands. This is an indication that the evolution of the island into a sugar-and-slave economy was less advanced than on the other islands. It also means, probably, that the fear of slave risings was less than elsewhere. On Montserrat in 1678, "the Irish" were still perceived as more of a danger than were the blacks. Secondly, unlike the three other main Leeward Islands, the white group on Montserrat was largely Irish. This is what had always been held to be the case in anecdotes, letters, and so on, but this census established the fact firmly. That Montserrat was (by my estimates) 68.9 percent Irish in its white population, and 40.4 percent of its total population, inclusive of slaves, means that Montserrat in 1678 registered the highest concentration of persons of Irish ethnicity of any colony in the history of both the first and the second English empires (excluding groups of two or three dozen persons in the Amazon earlier in the seventeenth century). Among real colonies, it was the most Irish: ever.

Table 5 provides the census of 1678 district-by-district, and indicates ethnicity. Because of the ways the data were collected, one

Table 4
The Gender and Dependency Composition of the White Population of the Main Leeward Islands, 1678

Irish Adult Males	*Irish Adult Females*	*Irish Dependent Children*	*Ratio of Irish Adult Males to Adult Females*	*English Adult Males*	*English Adult Females*	*English Dependent Children*	*Ratio of English Adult Males to Adult Females*	*"Other" Adult Males*	*"Other Adult Females*	*"Other" Dependent Children*	*Ratio of "Other" Adult Males to Adult Females*	*Total Adult Males*	*Total Adult Females*	*Total Dependent Children*	*Ratio of Total Adult Males to Total Adult Females*
MONTSERRAT															
(a) observed															
747	?	?	?	?	?	?	?	?	?	?	?	1,146	589	941	1.95
(b) inferred[1]															
747	409	689	1.83	370	174	239	2.13	29	6	13	4.83	1,146	589	941	1.95
NEVIS															
450	120	230	3.75	1,050	700	920	1.5	34	8	9	4.25	1,534	828	1,159	1.85
ANTIGUA															
360	130	120	2.77	800	400	400	2.0	76	14	8	5.43	1,236	544	528	2.27
ST CHRISTOPHER[2]															
187	127	182	1.48	370	272	361	1.36	138	130	130	1.06	695	539	663	1.29

Source: PROL, C.O. 1/42, as presented in Dunn, *Sugar and Slaves*, Table 12, 127, and, for Montserrat, sources specified in Appendix A.
[1] See Appendix A.
[2] See note 1, Table 3.

Table 5
Ethnicity of Adult White Male Population of Montserrat, 1678

			Irish									
	British (= Non-Irish)		*"Native Irish"*		*"Old English"*		*"New English"*		*Subtotal of Irish*		*Total Population*	
Census Area	*No.*	*%*	*No.*	*%*	*No.*	*%*	*No.*	*%*	*No.*	*%*	*No.*	*%*
Admin. Div. of St Peter's:												
Northward section	55	51.9	36	34.0	13	12.2	2	1.9	51	48.1	106	100.0
St Peter's Parish	43	58.9	24	32.9	6	8.2	0	0.0	30	41.1	73	100.0
Admin. Div. of St George's:												
Capt. Peter Cove	50	49.0	39	38.2	13	12.0	0	0.0	52	51.0	102	100.0
Admin. Div. of St Anthony's:												
Capt. Nicholas Mead	46	39.3	52	44.4	16	13.7	3	2.6	71	60.7	117	100.0
Capt. John Devereaux[1]	39	39.8	47	48.0	12	12.2	0	0.0	59	60.2	98	100.0
Capt. Richard Basse	23	19.3	80	67.2	15	12.6	1	0.9	96	80.7	119	100.0
Admin. Div. of St Patrick's:												
Major David Gallway	30	23.4	84	65.6	13	10.2	1	0.8	98	76.6	128	100.0
Lt. Col. Cormack	47	33.1	75	52.8	18	12.7	2	1.4	95	66.9	142	100.0
Capt. A. Booth	56	37.3	81	54.0	12	8.0	1	0.7	94	62.7	150	100.0
Cove and Palmetto Point[1]	10	9.0	81	73.0	20	18.0	0	0.0	101	91.0	111	100.0
Total	399	34.8	599	52.3	138	12.1	10	0.9	747	65.2	1,146	100.0

Source: Census of 1678.

[1] See Appendix A concerning the distribution of an "unknown" category in the Devereaux district (32 men) and in the Cove and Palmetto Point district (45 men).

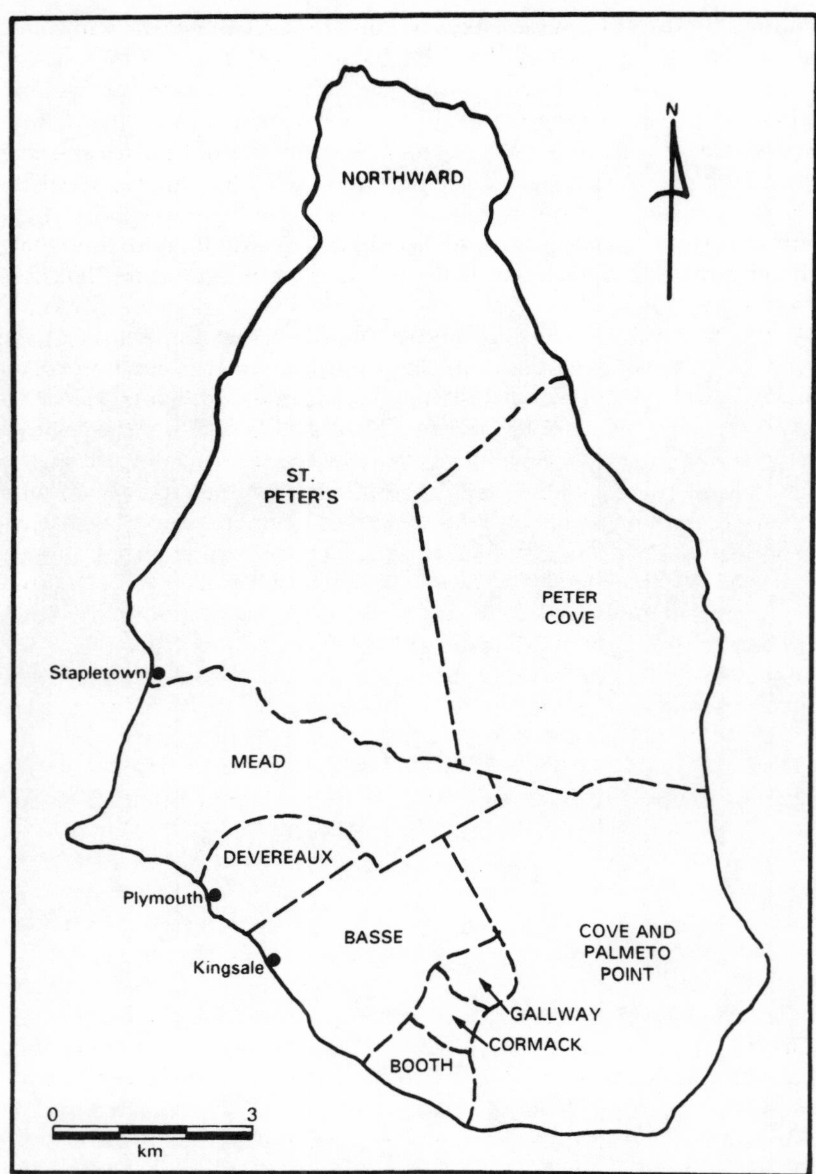

Map 3 Census divisions, 1678

cannot do a direct ethnic breakdown of women and children in each district. However, the male situation is revealing.[184]

The census districts (see Map 3) were nicely comparable, as Table 5 indicates, because they were all of roughly the same size. (This occurred because the districts were based on the militia rolls, each district representing a unit.) Even so, the census's ethnic pattern is better appraised visually than simply numerically. Map 4 indicates, with a certain appropriate, but accidental, irony, that in terms of ethnicity, the population gradient was like that of Ireland itself at the same date. That is, there was a strong gradient from north to south. The north of the island was slightly more British than Irish; the far south was overwhelmingly Irish; and portions in the middle of the eastern coast were evenly divided between Irish and British populations. This map is misleading in one aspect, however, for it leaves the visual impression that Montserrat was flat as a piece of clear cardboard, and just as empty. This was anything but the case. Map 5 includes Lydia Pulsipher's inferences as to how much land had been cleared in 1673 (using the Blathwayt map as a guide); when combined with topographic lines, it shows that, in fact, the populated areas were much smaller than at first appears. Essentially, one can "move" the population to the three main towns, to the areas that are obviously cleared, and to the margins of the cleared lands, those limbic regions where the bush was still being beaten back by provision-growing and small crop production.

Were the Irish "ghettoized"? No. In any population, the degree of segregation is expressed as a deviation from a norm. Since the Irish were 65.2 percent of the adult white population, it was hardly a case of segregation or ghettoization to find them comprising 60–67 percent of the adult white population in four census districts. Nor was their being on a fifty-fifty basis in one district and their comprising 41–48 percent of the white population in two others, any indication of ghettoization. What was noteworthy was that in a small part of the south – in three census districts, that formed a settlement area shaped like a horseshoe – they were between 76 to 91 percent of the population. Although that horseshoe of population held a minority of the adult males of Irish ethnicity (almost exactly 25 percent of the Irish cohort), it was those districts which gave the Irish of the whole island a reputation for being difficult in the best of times, and rebellious and potentially traitorous in the worst. It was in those areas that in 1667 the French had found their allies. And from thence came the temporary rulers of the island, during the 1667 jacquerie.[185]

Only three of the island's ten enumeration districts provided direct information on family structure and on wealth, and thus one cannot

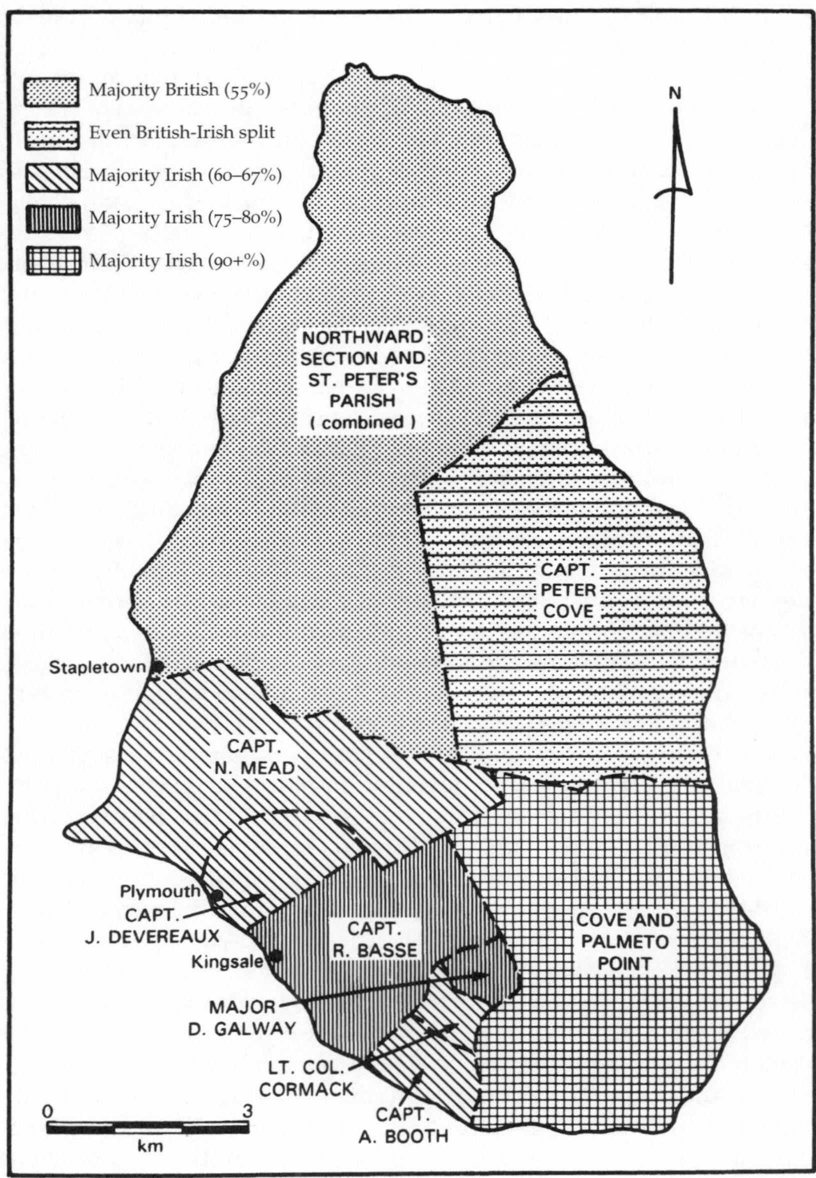

Map 4 Census tracts, by ethnicity, 1678

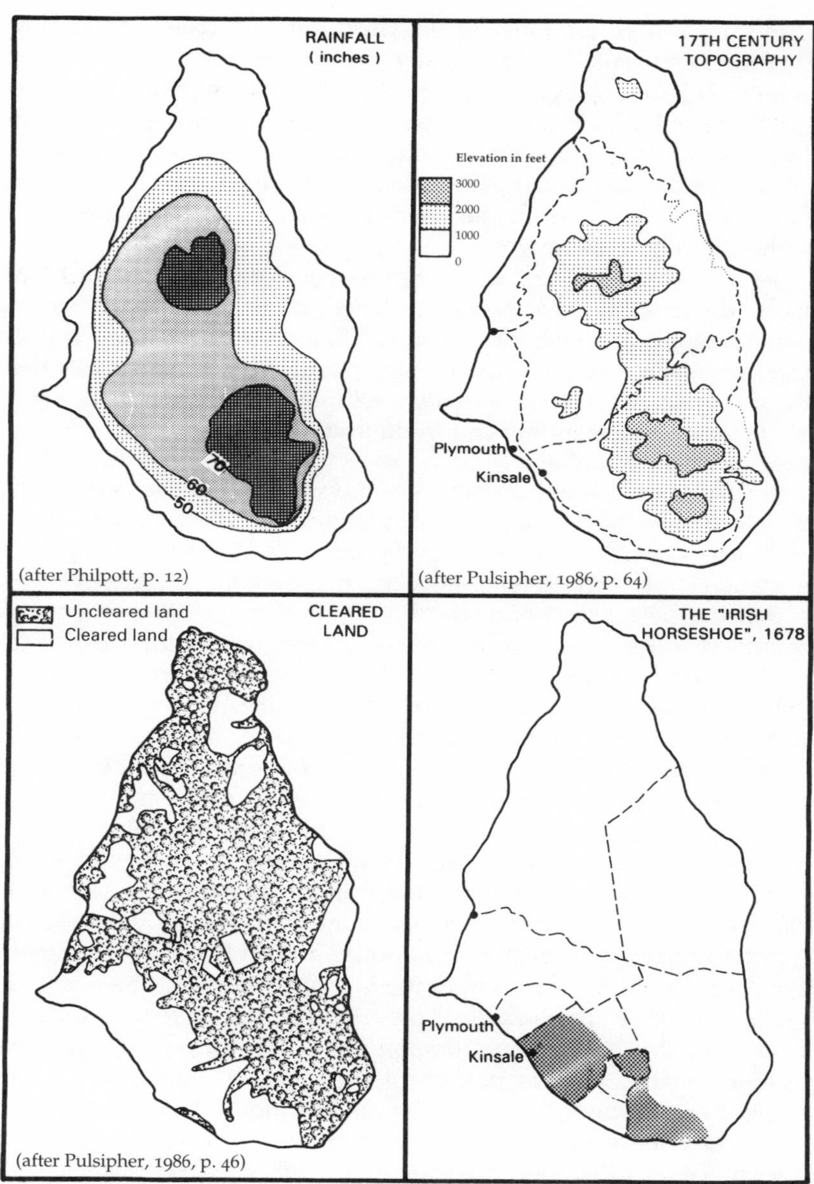

Map 5 Rainfall, topography, and settlement patterns

draw up a table for the whole island; but fortunately, these three districts represent the three major types of community structures: Cove and Palmetto Point which was the most Irish part of the island (91.0 percent of adult males) were of Irish ethnicity; Northward Division which had a British majority (51.9 percent); and Devereaux's Division where the distribution was near the island's norm (60.2 percent Irish). Thus, the spectrum at least can be defined, even if the shading is missing.

The social physics that emerge make considerable sense, but have to be dealt with almost syllogistically, or the force of the several vectors will be missed: for, like a building constructed on a hillside, the social structure not only has shape, but it has force vectors built in, and these, though not visible, are fundamental.

Six basic social realities ran throughout the island:

1 A surprisingly low proportion of the white male heads of household owned slaves (or, more accurately, owned adult male slaves, which is what the enumeration recorded): an island-wide figure of 15 percent is a reasonable speculation, based on the three available districts. The largest plantations (or, if one prefers the term, farms) tended to be in the north, the smallest in the south. Most of the slaves were owned by persons who also owned plantations of significant size. However, against this ran another social gradient. Namely that although the large plantation owners were the owners of most of the slaves, small self-operators (small tobacco, indigo, provisions or sugar farmers) were more apt to be the owners of slaves than anyone save the very biggest plantation owners. Persons of Irish ethnicity were more apt to be small individual proprietors than were the British. Therefore, paradoxically, persons of Irish background were more apt to own slaves than were persons of British background. Thus, in the Northward division, fewer than 10 percent of the heads of household owned adult male slaves. In the middle of the island (the middle both in terms of location and of ethnic demography), the Devereaux division, slightly more than 13 percent of the heads of household owned adult male slaves. But in the far south – the heaviest Irish district – the proportion was almost two-and-a-half times that: nearly 32 percent of the households owned adult male slaves.
2 Within the Irish ethnic group, there was a sharp economic and social distinction between those Irish slaveholders who ran large plantations in the north of the island, and those Irish slaveholders (most in the far south of the island) who kept one or two adult male slaves. Therefore, Irish slave owners were not a single group,

and one infers that the method of using and abusing African slaves was quite different as between the two sorts of Irish slave-owners.

3 Large plantations or large merchants employed most of the island's waged labour (mostly to oversee the slaves) and most of the indentured servants. However, the households of small proprietors (the bulk of whom were Irish) were more apt to have within them servants or free labourers than were larger operations. They did not, of course, employ them in large numbers, just one or two in some households.
4 The people of the Irish "horseshoe" in the far south had the worst land on the island, at least as far as cleared land was concerned. The ground was steep and communications difficult.
5 Within the Irish ethnic group, there was a further gradient. The farther south one went, the greater the proportion of the native Irish in the cohort, and the lower the proportion of the "Old English."
6 The Irish were more apt to be married than were the British. Or, to put it more precisely: Irish male heads of household were more apt to have an adult female in their household than were British heads of households – whether or not they were married, no one knows. A geographic gradient also existed. Families (as compared to single males) were proportionally more frequent in the south of the island.

What this converging matrix of social gradients dictates is a two-fold conclusion. First, that Montserrat in the later seventeenth century operated as a single economic and social system (every sort of economic activity, every major sort of household unit, and every ethnic background was found in each of the island's administrative districts). Yet, second, within this single system were distinguishable sub-systems: (a) that of most of the island, wherein the British and the Irish were roughly social equals. Each group was distributed through all the rungs of society. The governor was Irish and took care of his own. A bit more than half the population was Irish in background. And (b) the southern "horseshoe" which was in many ways separate. The population in this area was overwhelmingly Irish, and strongly loaded towards persons of "native Irish" background. The household there (taking the Cove and Palmetto section as representative) was more broadly based than on the rest of the island in that individual households were more apt to include agricultural labourers or indentured servants or slaves than were the households of the rest of the island. That is, extended family units were more common. Most importantly, it seems highly probable that the overwhelming bulk of the Irish population in the south lived in a traditional male-female unit. Only four adult Irish males, from a total Irish male population in Cove and Palmetto district of 101, lived in households in which no adult white female was present.

This defines the major paradox of Montserrat. If European standards are invoked, the portion of the island that was most troublesome, most apt to be contumacious, rebellious and generally cantankerous was actually the most normal place. Individuals in the far south were the most apt to live in European-style extended households in which an adult white woman was present. Isolated adult males, the mark of a new and raw settler society, were rare in the Irish-dominated south.[186] No part of Montserrat would ever make it all the way to European normalcy (sugar and slavery precluded that), but the closest, in terms of family structure, was the south.[187]

And it was the most normal in terms of community. Culturally, the southern horseshoe was dominated by the "native Irish" and, if family names and the known migration history do not betray us, overwhelmingly from Munster. The inhabitants of the southern horseshoe had a shared culture. They were a community, social order based upon family units. This was a great contrast to most of the New World frontier, where migrant males were the dominant life form and flux the format.

This is not to say that their community was a moral Eden. These Irish small proprietors of the south of the island were the people most apt to buy and to use African slaves as part of their household economy. It is hard to imagine that being a slave, or even a wage labourer, for these small proprietors was anything but beastly. Still, the Irish of the southern horseshoe comprised the one part of the island that worked as a European-style community.

That is why they were always potentially troublesome. People who have something they treasure, and who distrust the people outside their own little world, especially if the outsiders are the sort they understand only too well – the old landlords from Ireland, the "Old English," or the new landlords, the "New English" – such people are potentially rebels. And, when it occurs, their rebellion may have something to do with religion, and something to do with political loyalty (to the pope or, later, to the Jacobite cause); and it may have a good deal to do with socio-economic issues. But always, and at its centre, their rebellion has to do with hearth and with community. People like that are hard for outsiders to control. Any wise colonial governor would have said his prayers regularly, and petitioned that these terrifyingly normal people would cease to terrorize him.

4 Capitalism at a Gallop, 1680–1730

Having passed from neo-feudalism to the Restoration imperialism of Charles II and his parliament, Montserrat now entered the era of capitalism-without-restraint and became a slave economy. That being the case, the transition appears simple enough, particularly as it affected the Irish. The change could be defined, one might argue, by four simple figures. The first two are the number of blacks on Montserrat:

1678 1,894[1]
1729 6,063

The second two are the number of persons of Irish ethnicity on the island:

1678 1,845
1729 641

Obviously, the growth of the sugar economy had as one of its effects the displacement of Irish by blacks. The Irish, being disadvantaged within white society, were the natural victims of this displacement within England's empire, and they suffered first and worst.

Obviously, perhaps, but not actually. The optics here are very misleading. The apparent situation is very much like that presented by economic analysts of the 1930s, who related economic events to sun spot cycles. They had two observable phenomena – the world's economy, and information on solar emission – and each was a spectacular occurrence, and therefore, must be directly related to each other. So they argued. Now, in fact, the two sets of events may have been related, but very indirectly (through, perhaps, sunspots affecting crops production on marginal lands), but the mechanism was so complex, so indirect, and so causally tertiary, as to be of minor importance. That, I think, is the situation here.

Nevertheless, things *look* clear. For example, it is obvious that both the British and the Irish lost total population, but that the Irish lost proportionately more.

	Population in 1678	*Population in 1729*	*% loss*
Irish	1,845	641	65.3
British	831	514	38.1

This appears to indicate classical imperialism: the master class, the British, not only stripped the surplus value from the African slave population, but ground down the intermediate class, the Irish, the wheels of capitalist economic change moving irrevocably towards the exploitation of the blacks and the extrusion of the Irish.

In the chapter that follows, I will suggest other hypotheses. Given the nature of the documentation, probative material can be presented, but actual law-court-solid proof cannot: too many hurricanes have taken away too many records. Basically, I will argue that everybody on the island took several hard hits during the years 1680–1730, through events over which they had no control. This is almost a sub-bass in the history of the island, for Montserrat seems to have had more than its fair share of natural and man-made disasters. Secondly, and more important, as it affected the Irish, were matters related to the communal identity. Roman Catholics were placed in the position of being slightly disadvantaged, but not of being actively persecuted. Nothing like the full penal code of eighteenth-century Ireland developed, but the adoption of Protestant forms was necessary if one were to have full weight in the island's official affairs. That (as we have seen) was not much of a problem for many Catholics; they simply took the necessary Protestant oaths in public and went about their own religion in private. But such anti-Catholic legislation was also a reminder of a second-class national (or ethnic) status. Further, the displacement of the Stuarts by the Williamite succession in 1688–89 hit some very deep, instinctive loyalties, and it is such events, more than economics in the narrow sense, that taught the Irish to think of migrating to other, freer New Worlds. (Mind you, several of the American colonies were viciously anti-Catholic at this period, but there were always the Carolinas and Maryland.)

Thirdly, I think that we should abandon the idea that all those who left this island – Irish or British – necessarily did so under financial duress. The evidence of the period is of a great demand for white labour and of a market for the ready sale and purchase of land. As established in chapter 3, the great bulk of the white labour force in the 1670s was free labour. Indentured servitude was hard time, undeniably, but when indentured servants became free and received £10–12 sterling in freedom-dues or the equivalent in some other currency or in local produce, they had a fair chance at purchasing freehold land and an even easier time if they wanted a tenancy. The going price for freehold land in 1678 was roughly thirteen shillings sterling an acre.[2] Just as it was easy to move into land holding, it was easy to move out. When, eventually, the small proprietors-cum-free labourers sold their holdings, they left Montserrat after having worked in a labour-short market and after having sold a piece of freehold ground or a tenancy that had real value. Remember that many of the Irish households owned slaves in 1678; by 1729, almost all did. These were valuable property indeed, and they could either be sold or transported as storehouses of value by their Irish owners as they moved onward. The Irish, when they left Montserrat, had done well, but now they thought to do better elsewhere.

Finally, I shall argue that those Irish who stayed behind not only did well, but became more economically powerful than did the British. This conclusion follows whether one measures aggregate wealth by ethnic group or on their average success, enterprise by enterprise. And this success occurred despite the tilt of the official world against the Irish because of the preference most of the Irish had for Roman Catholicism. This economic victory was no moral triumph, however: the Irish who stayed on Montserrat did so well because they well knew how to be hard and efficient slave masters.

First, the disasters. Like all such phenomena, they were ecumenical experiences. As St Matthew reminds us (5:45), the rain falls on the just and the unjust alike.

The Carib Indians continued to be a source of some damage and the cause of great fear. They had not struck Montserrat successfully for some years since their démarche in 1667, but in November 1682, they landed seven periagoes on the island at a remote and undefended site. They killed two young blacks, burned a sugar factory, and carried off a few adult slaves.[3] Further raids on Montserrat and Antigua in April 1683 set William Stapleton on one of his vigorous Carib-hunting trips.[4] The Carib remained a constant threat, more in mind than reality, but frightening nonetheless, until 1796. At that time they were moved, through *force majeure*, from their then-home base on St Vincent to the island of Ruatan and they ceased to be of trouble to the Leeward Islanders.[5]

During the spring of 1684, Montserrat became a sink for smallpox. The other islands, especially Nevis, worried about how to keep the epidemic confined there.[6]

Weather was always a problem. Brutal storms were an annual danger. In 1707, most of the houses on the island were destroyed by hurricane.[7]

And always, almost like background noise, was the knowledge that one lived in a tough neighbourhood, and could easily be mugged. Although from 1670 onwards the commissions of various buccaneers who had fought on the British side against Spain were revoked, many of the buccaneers transformed themselves into privateers or, more accurately, pirates.[8] Matters in the Leeward Islands were so bad that in 1683 a frigate with 300 soldiers on board and three full years' provisions was ordered by London to the Leeward Islands to fight piracy.[9] The problem with the pirates was that they did not confine their piracy to the high seas. One or two ships of these hellions could sweep down and capture many, perhaps most, small towns. The pirates' capacity for pillage on land was, if anything, greater than on sea. Further, they could ally with England's enemies (meaning, usually, the French), and serve as shock troops in the geopolitical game that was forever being played. In 1678, for example, 800 pirates landed at St Christopher and fought for the French.[10]

In early October 1693, a French pirate party landed on Montserrat and carried off a militia captain and forty African slaves.[11] Given that yet another war with France was in progress, this attack was the stimulus for a general militia act for Montserrat which began by declaring "the continual danger this island is in of being attacked, or surprized by enemies, privateers or pirates."[12] Every white male between fifteen and sixty years of age was put on alert. If privateers or the French (who were feared as much as the pirates) were to arrive, at first alarm all the island's cattle were to be driven to the windward part of the island. Arrangements were made for billeting three companies of an English regiment upon the people of the island, and two large guns were sent to Carr's Bay. All the slaves in the middle division (meaning St Anthony's parish) and the windward division were required to work at building fortifications.[13] What's important in all this is the pervasive terror, the knowledge by everyone on the island of how vulnerable they all were to thugs, whether pirates or the servants of some European monarch. The situation in the Leeward Islands was summed up in July 1695 by an Antiguan planter. "This part of the world is full of privateers. The

French have fourteen small craft with six hundred men in them, which are daily watching these islands, and know all that passes as well as ourselves."[14] That same planter detailed several recent privateers' attacks, and then concluded his report with a late postscript. "Since I wrote the above, Antigua, Montserrat and Nevis have resolved to fit out three sloops, man them well with landsmen, and give officers and soldiers their diet and the King's pay, for which purpose, they have made a levy of eighteen pence a head on all negroes, great and small. Thus they hope to disperse the swarm of privateers."[15]

This worked for a time, but in 1707 French buccaneers raided the island.[16] The next year, in December 1708, they hit again, and this time they robbed the same man (Captain Edward Buncombe) who had been captured and had lost forty black slaves in 1693. This time they took twenty-nine slaves, his family plate, and household goods. According to three valuers sent to confirm Buncombe's loss, the total value was a bit over £1,330.[17] Then in 1712, a large squadron of French privateers first prepared to storm Antigua, but withdrew when the militia gathered in force; and then sailed on to Montserrat. There the force of 3,500 was put ashore near Carr's Bay, near the northern tip of the island. The Montserrat militia fought well, but were heavily outnumbered. The result was that the island was efficiently pillaged. An estimated 1,200 slaves were taken, sugar-making machinery was lifted, and all the valuables the pirates could lay their hands on were taken.[18] This last raid ruined a number of the planters. Under the Treaty of Utrecht of 1713 the French were supposed to compensate the Montserrat planters for their losses in this raid, but by 1724 nothing had been paid and many planters could hold out no longer.[19] Like the residents of any tough neighbourhood, many islanders must have reached the point where they said no, living under this degree of aggravation just is not worth it, and they moved elsewhere.

The demoralizing effect of these various calamities is documented in a bill passed by the Montserrat legislature soon after the October 1693 raid by French privateers. It began: "Forasmuch as this Island hath by the last Expedition, sickness, and other great casualties, sustained great loss in the death of white men, to the great weakening of the same."[20] There it is: disease, piracy, death, population decline. The remedy proposed was one widespread in the British Caribbean: to build up the white population by providing bonuses for those who imported white servants. Any vessel that brought in twenty or more white male servants at one time would be freed from all port charges and customs duties. Individual merchants, masters, and employers of white servants on Montserrat were to be paid out of the public treasury, for each eligible servant, 2,500 pounds of good merchandisable sugar, this to be delivered to some convenient shipping pound on the island. There were three provisos. The servants had either to be indentured or, by free contract, to agree to serve on the island for four years.[21] The bounty was paid only for men in the age group from sixteen to thirty-nine. And – this is significant – it was for each "English, Scotch or Welsh man."

After the Treaty of Utrecht ended the immediate pressures to leave the island for reasons of safety of property and persons, a variety of opportunities elsewhere in the West Indies drew down further the pool of able-bodied white men. For example, in 1717, a group from the Leeward Islands, "particularly from Montserrat," formed a settlement upon the island of Tortola.[22] At first the then-governor, Walter Hamilton, thought this was a good way to extend the royal domain, but a year later, when another group from the islands (including Montserrat) took off for Crabb Island, near Puerto Rico, he began to worry. Only forty-odd white men and twenty to thirty slaves went on this voyage, but the governor began to think that the white population of Nevis, St Christopher, and Montserrat was running thin.[23] During the early 1720s, significant numbers from Montserrat settled in the "French lands" on St Christopher, thus causing a noticeable drop in the numbers in Montserrat's militia.[24]

These documentable instances of white settlers from Montserrat moving to other places in the West Indies where opportunities appeared to them to be greater are, I think, representative of a larger process. Disease, military raids, privateering, cost lives, but the population was more strongly diminished by voluntary out-migration. Some of the planters were "ruined" in the sense that, say, before the French raids they had been wealthy, possessing a score or more of slaves, and now they had fewer. Their being "ruined" did not mean that they were penniless, just brought down in the world. The men who went to places like Tortola, Crabb Island, or to the former French part of St Christopher were attempting to do better, or on a larger scale, what they had already tried to do on Montserrat: earn a living by running a small plantation. Lost in the discussion of migration to other places in the West Indies is the strong probability that most of the migrants passed onwards, perhaps through Jamaica or Barbados, to the American mainland colonies. A heterogenous band, forever hopeful, lost to history.

No one could reasonably suggest that the island of Montserrat in the late seventeenth and early eighteenth centuries was a religious place in the sense of the population possessing a culture that was deeply embedded in institutional religion. It was not, nor could it have been, given that neither of the two main denominations, the Roman Catholic church and the Established Church, served the islanders in any but the most sporadic fashion. However, religion at that time often was tied in with other matters. These ranged from imperial policy and the problem of England's relationship to the continental European powers, to matters of dynastic loyalties (which becomes especially important with the end of the Stuart monarchy in 1688), and also to assertions of cultural identity (in the case, for example, of some of the Irish Catholics). So religion was important, even if institutionalized religion was not.

The institutional situation in the period was very simple indeed. It had four characteristics. The first of these is that there was no resident Roman Catholic priest on the island, and there would not be until 1756. However, priests from various sources – the French islands, and perhaps from Ireland – passed through Montserrat. One finds in 1708, for example, the governor of the Leeward Islands complaining to the London authorities that the papists on Montserrat had an Irish priest with them. The governor complained that "notwithstanding I have several times gave orders for taking him up, yet, I cannot get it done."[25] There is no way of knowing how often such priestly missionaries came to Montserrat, but I suspect that it was infrequently, because otherwise Catholic historians (particularly Aubrey Gwynn) would have documented the fact.

Secondly, in this period there was no Catholic chapel. This does not mean that we should invoke a dramatic picture of clerics being limited to fleeting visits to a clandestine mass rock, as in the worst days of the Irish penal codes of the eighteenth century. One suspects (and here again, it can be only speculation) that the house of a Catholic proprietor was used for religious purposes. This speculation stems from the fact that in the mid-eighteenth century, the very substantial Plymouth house of one of the island's Catholic landowners became the site of Catholic worship, long before a permanent church was erected. Similar arrangements could have been made earlier.

Third, the Anglicans were scarcely better off in terms of religious matters. As mentioned in chapter 2, a stone church, famous for its beauty, had been built by Anthony Briskett, the first governor, and it of course was an ornament of the Established Church, as Briskett had so proudly pointed out to his royal master. This was St Anthony's church, Plymouth. However, by the 1660s, a second Anglican church had been built, the location for which is not known with any certainty. These two buildings were wrecked by the French in 1667 and then rebuilt on the orders of William Stapleton on his arrival as deputy governor of Montserrat in 1668. These same buildings were levelled to the ground by the Christmas Day earthquake of 1672. Stapleton, in reporting this to London, noted that "had the people been in the afternoon at church they had been knocked in the head,"[26] by which he either meant to indicate great good fortune, or a pretty good reason to become a non-attender. Both churches were again rebuilt.[27] These two structures made it to 1733, but were totally destroyed in the great hurricane of that year.[28] Thereafter St Anthony's church was rebuilt.[29] This was done at public expense and, to protect their spiritual investment, the assembly and council provided that a sexton would look after the building. And "whereas Negroes and Cattle are very often apt to destroy the fences made" – the former would be given thirty-nine lashes on conviction of stealing church stones (presumably, one lash for each of the Church of England's Thirty-Nine Articles), and the owners of trespassing animals would be fined three shillings per beast found within the church enclosure; and, "whereas it has been found by Experience, that the burying of Bodies in a church or very near it, in this hot Climate, has been very nauseous to the people assembled together at Divine Service," a £100 fine (in local money) was to be paid by the executor of any estate who interred a body within a church.[30] That such regulations were necessary speaks volumes about the respect with which the Established Church was held on the island.

Fourth, having a church and having a pastor were two different things and, until 1668, the governors of Montserrat had been content to fulfil their duty to the state church by erecting buildings, and letting them be used by the occasional visiting cleric from the other islands, who performed marriages, christenings and, sometimes, funerals. This was shrewd, given that the bulk of the population was Roman Catholic and that many of the leading citizens were Irishmen who were Catholic by background. These substantial citizens, though willing to conform occasionally to the Established Church, did not appreciate anything that raised the specificity of religious differentiation on the island: as long as things were kept fuzzy, they could be all things to all men, in the true Christian manner. Significantly, it was William Stapleton, a Catholic, willing to conform to the Established Church, who in 1668 oversaw the passage of an act to appoint a Protestant clergyman. This was to be an "Orthodox Minister" who would preach and conduct divine service according to the rubrics and canons of the Church of England. He was to be paid 14,000 pounds of sugar a year, or an equal amount in value in indigo and tobacco, cotton and wool. In addition, the clergyman could demand up to 100 pounds of sugar for each marriage. Christenings, the churching of post-partum women, and funerals were to be done gratis, unless, in the case of a funeral, the executors wanted a sermon in addition to the reading of the burial service.[31]

Does not Stapleton's seeing through the appointment of a Protestant cleric contradict the earlier observation that leaving the pulpit empty was in many ways preferable? Yes, and this is because Stapleton's own position was contradictory to that of his fellow Irish Catholics. Unlike them, he had to be seen to be totally trustworthy, as an operative of the London authorities. His crypto-popery could be overlooked by London so long as he was a strong representative of English interests. But, especially in the early years of his appointment, he had to be extremely careful. Making the Established Church for the first time an actual church on the island, protected him. Moreover, although the appointment of a rector for the island was officially done by the Bishop of London, the appointment really was Stapleton's. Considering that a living on Montserrat must have been one of the least desirable preferments in the entire Anglican world,[32] Stapleton did well.

Indeed, he found the perfect man – one well able to blend his own and local needs. The Rev. Richard Molineux settled into his charge in 1678. Because Molineux is a major name in Irish politics in both the seventeenth and the twentieth centuries, one must emphasize that this man was not Irish, but English. He was the son of an Established Church parson of Garsington, in the County of Oxford. He was very young (indeed, only twenty-one when he arrived, which was below the canonical age for ordination), and therefore was very malleable, and, as his later career showed, very quick to recognize his own self-interest. He went along and he got along. He married locally, the daughter of William Irish, a medium-sized plantation owner. In 1697 he became a member of the legislative council of the island and in 1699 received a legacy from William Irish of some size: he was able to give up half his clerical income, splitting it with the Rev. James Cruickshank, a junior cleric (who probably did all the work, in established tradition).[33] Richard Molineux died in 1721 and was buried at St Peter's Church, Montserrat.[34]

So, we have four clear observations: the Catholics had no church and had few clergy visits; the Anglicans had two churches and a malleable, amiable clergy. After that, things become very unclear, because one enters an area deliberately made murky by contemporaries. The key question is: to what extent an Establishment regime actually operated in the widest civic sense on Montserrat. That question would be difficult to answer even if Montserrat possessed ordinary documentary resources, which it does not.

Contemporaries had two conflicting views. The one view taken, for example, by a governor of the Leeward Islands who surveyed the matter in the 1730s, was that Montserrat was far from being run according to the template of the Established Church. In particular, he noted that although Anglican parishes determined the civic boundaries (for census and militia purposes), never had the parishes been governed ecclesiastically by vestries or church wardens, nor had the rector been paid by a parochial levy. Instead, the island had a single central local government and the clergy had been paid by public levies (that is, by local government taxes) and in some years the levy was not raised and the poor parson nearly starved.[35]

That was an outsider's view. The islanders' view was expressed with lapidary reserve by the Council of Montserrat in 1680, when it reported to the Lords of Trade and Plantations that "Our ecclesiastical affairs are to the best of our endeavour agreeable to the canons and constitutions of the Church of England."[36] Considering that six of the nine men who signed the letter had been Roman Catholic and that at least three of them still were, the reserve is admirable, for the best of their endeavour was not very much. In 1676, William Stapleton had reassured the London authorities that "In Montserrat most part are Roman Catholics, it being first settled by those of that persuasion, yet they give no scandal to the Protestant Church, which is the prevalent persuasion. Every licence of marriage, probate of will, and all other ecclesiastical acts according to the Church of England."[37] Stapleton and his legislative councillors wanted it to appear that the classic English ecclesiastical-cum-civic situation operated. A strange situation indeed, wherein the more Protestant one was, the more one was apt to decry the island's deviation from Anglican orthodoxy – and the more equivocal, or more Roman Catholic one was, the more apt one was to claim that the place was cut from the standard Anglican template.

In fact, the place was not standard at all, and that was because of its religious population profile. Therefore, before engaging the nature of the religio-temporal mix, we must briefly survey contemporary estimates of how large a proportion of the population was Roman Catholic. There was never a direct census of the Catholic-Protestant divide, and there is no surrogate for that division (obviously, one cannot use Irish names as an indicator of Roman Catholicism; dozens of examples of persons with Irish surnames embracing Protestantism, at least nominally, are easily to hand). We can, however, set an upper boundary of the percentage of Catholics as being the percentage of Irish-less-something. What "something" is, is hard to say, but the formula gives one licence to discard the more hysterical estimates of popish numbers. Those tended to arise at times of external crisis, such as the wars with the French. So, in practical terms, contemporaries who suggested that more than two out of three white inhabitants were Roman Catholic, were vapouring, or had an axe to grind. That said, here are the contemporary estimates. In 1676, before he engaged in his great Leeward Island census of 1678, William Stapleton thought that the people of Montserrat were divided in a Catholic-Protestant ratio of six to one, that is, 86 percent Roman Catholic.[38] A panicked military appraisal of 1701 claimed that the island was twenty Catholics to one Protestant (95 percent Catholic).[39] More realistic, but still high, was the estimate of Christopher Codrington in 1689, that the ratio was 8 to 3 (that is, 72 percent Catholic).[40] Now, the interesting thing about those estimates is that they all were made in times of possible Catholic rising, or Catholic alliance with the French. At such times, the Irish Catholic numbers looked bigger than they really were.

Conversely, in times of stability (roughly from 1715 onwards, as will be discussed in a moment), the Irish Catholic numbers looked smaller. In 1724, Col. John Hart, governor of the Leeward Islands, estimated that two-thirds of the white population were papists.[41] Significantly, not only was it peacetime, but Hart had previously been governor of Maryland,[42] so he did not panic at encountering a Catholic. A 1734 estimate, though critical of the lack of Protestant civic institutions, thought that only slightly more than half of the island was Catholic.[43] In light of the ethnicity of the island (see Table 6), this seems to me to be the most sensible estimate for the first half of the eighteenth century.

Thus, in the matter most affecting the historical depiction of the Irish on Montserrat, we encounter sets of lenses whose effects are to provide opposing sets of distortions. One of these sets exaggerated Catholic numbers in tense times; in calm times a more realistic lens was in place. Simultaneously, as described earlier, one set of individuals with state power, the Protestant party (if one can use such a phrase), viewed and exaggerated the divergence of the religio-civic arrangements from the Church of England ideal. On the other side, the party most associated with the religiously ambiguous Irish elite on the island, used a lens that overemphasized the closeness to the Establishment ideal. These incompatible lenses make it very difficult to see clearly what little evidence there is about the really key question: to what extent was there an anti-Catholic penal code on Montserrat?

Let us break this question into two parts, before the Williamite Revolution of 1688–91, and after.

If one reads all the statutes of Montserrat for the Stapleton era (that is, up through 1685), one finds no act that could be considered a penal measure. For someone trained in Irish history, where the anti-Catholic penal legislation is so overt and, indeed, overlapping and rebarbatively luxuriant, it is tempting to see the island as a sanctuary. But it was not. I think what we are viewing is (1) a largely invisible, but real, penal code and (2) a countervailing set of resistances against the code, the most important of which came at the top of the social system, with William Stapleton and the other leaders of the Irish Catholics disabling the penal system as much as possible.

Consider: although there was no overt anti-Catholic legislation, recall that in 1676 William Stapleton had reported to London that a situation prevailed of which, he strongly implied, the authorities would approve. "Every licence of marriage, probate of will, and all other ecclesiastical acts," were according to the Church of England canons.[44] That was how one phrased the situation if one were trying to make the Lords of Trade and Plantations and their parliamentary and royal masters happy. Placed in the local context, a more apt phrasing would have been: "Catholic marriages and testamentary documents are not legal; Catholic children are bastards in law, and the inter-generational transfer of property by Catholics is vulnerable to later legal challenge, unless the Catholics have filed and probated the last will and testament according to Anglican forms." Such a penal practice might not hurt the very small proprietor or the wage labourer, but any Catholic of modest substance was likely to be affected by these matters.

With that as background, the meaning of a seemingly inconsequential act is clear: in 1678, Deputy Governor Edmund Stapleton (brother of William who was now governor of the Leeward Islands), and the Montserrat Council and Assembly passed an act that claimed they had given "their serious consideration" to "the great scarcity of ministers." Wishing "to prevent the manifold sins of incontinency," they decided, therefore, to permit justices of the peace to perform marriages. Children of such marriages were legitimate, "and capable to receive all such privileges as are usually appertaining to Children lawfully begotten. Any Law, usage or Custom in this island to the contrary in any wise notwithstanding."[45] Although outsiders would have missed the fact, this was what later would be termed a "Catholic relief act." Although passed under the guise of protecting public morals ("the manifold sins of incontinency") it was in fact a protection of Catholic property rights. If Catholics were willing to take the step of having a justice of the peace solemnize their union, then their children were legitimate and their lands transferrable. This was the kind of situation which (assuming that a Catholic ceremony was also conducted) the church authorities were reluctantly accepting in countries where the Catholics were a persecuted minority. The arrangements were far from ideal but, from the viewpoint of Catholic authorities, were preferable to having large numbers of Catholic landowners go through Protestant services, which many would do rather than lose their lands. A telling point is that this act – which claimed a "great scarcity of ministers" – was passed just at the moment when the first permanent Anglican rector was scheduled to arrive on Montserrat. So, it was not only a relief act, it was a preemptive move: it precluded the new rector from bringing pressure to bear (were he so inclined) on the Catholics to conform to Protestantism on central matters of family formation and legitimacy of children.

Thus, we are detecting, rather in the manner of enthusiasts who do rubbings of old, illegible gravestones, a pattern that is not normally visible. It conceals the existence of a penal code, one that was dictated by external authorities and which left few overt local imprints; and, simultaneously, we are seeing penal relief, and (given the Irish Catholic influence on the top echelons of local government and among the leading landowners), a form of Catholic resistance to the code.

There was more. Although it is never articulated on the island's statutes of the time, it is clear that a penal code related to the island government. The island government had been reorganized in 1668, and was tripartite: deputy governor (as monarchical representative), council (a mini-House of Lords, appointed by the deputy governor with the approval of the Lords of Trade and Plantations), and an assembly (a lower house, elected by freeholders and having less influence than the council). This was the common template on the Leeward Islands. That council and assembly, in its first year, passed an act respecting penal laws against "persons obedient to civil government" who "differ in judgement from the Church of England" meaning, effectively, Catholics and Quakers.[46] When, in 1671, the Leeward Islands were separated from Barbados and formed the Leeward Island Colony, a superordinate larger entity was created, but on the same pattern. This was the Governor of the Leeward Islands, the Council of the Islands, and an Assembly of the Islands. However, the key point is that the Toleration Act of 1672 became inoperative: council members had to take the oath of allegiance.[47] This was one of the oaths required by the English parliament of its governmental officers in 1672, when it introduced the Test Act. Later events make it clear that members of the assembly of the Leeward Islands also had to take the oath of allegiance. I think we can safely infer that the oath of allegiance was required by the London authorities not only of the assembly and council men of the Leeward Islands government, but of the local assemblies and councils of each island's government.

Does this mean, as Berleant-Schiller suggests, legal inhibitions "made it very difficult for the Irish Catholic freedmen of Montserrat to acquire significant property or political power"?[48] Yes; and no. Governmental provisions, with the locus of power being a London-appointed governor and a London-approved council, indeed shut out from power recent freedmen, small proprietors, and minor merchants. However, it was class discrimination, not religious, that locked them into a corner.

The real question is, did the attempted penal system keep *substantial* Catholics out of power? Absolutely not. Take an example: the petition of the Council of Montserrat to the Lords of Trade and Plantations of 13 July 1680 that, among other things, reported on ecclesiastical affairs on the Island,[49] and was signed by nine councillors. Four of these were of British extraction (John Symes, William Fox, John Bramley and Peter Cove). Three of them were "former Catholics" who, in later life, are known to have actually remained Catholics (James Cotter, David Gallway, and Redmond Stapleton), and two were of Irish Catholic extraction, but of unknown religious commitments at this time (Nicholas Meade and John Cormicke). And this at a time when James Cotter was acting as deputy governor of the island. Which is to say that out of the ten major posts on the island (nine councillorships and the deputy governorship), four of the slots were filled by Roman Catholics who were publicly willing to conform to the Anglican church, and two were filled by former Catholics who may, or may not, have been real adherents to the Established Church. Clearly, everyone involved had to know what was going on. It was a small society, and (as in the case of the crafting of the cleverly deceitful 1681 report about ecclesiastical affairs on the island), everyone was complicitous. The people at the top of Montserrat society – men of property and power – had decided that at their level the sectarian divisions engendered by a penal code could not be accepted. The solidarity of the rich overcame the divisiveness of the righteous. This was not resistance in the heroic mode that ecclesiastical historians prefer. These were not Christian martyrs in the making, just rich and ambitious men, doing what they had to do. The method they used was "occasional conformity," meaning the Catholics took the necessary oaths and then went on being Catholics.

This social system – involving simultaneously the public acceptance by the locals of penal measures dictated by the outside world in religious and civic matters, and the private circumventing of those same instructions – was inherently unstable. It worked so long as everybody knew how to wink. In 1685, however, a sincere man entered the picture and, as the earnest so often do, made the world worse, through trying to do good. This was Sir Nathaniel Johnson, an extreme royalist, who previously had been manager of the Hearth Tax.

When William Stapleton had gone to England in ill-health in 1685, he had arranged the appointment as acting governor of the Leeward Islands of Sir James Russel, a large landowner and, most importantly, one of Stapleton's relatives, and not one to upset the unspoken covenants of Leeward Islands life. Meanwhile, Johnson lobbied hard for the permanent appointment for himself, and was in good position when Stapleton died in Paris in August 1686. A new king, James II, a proto-absolutist and Catholic, was on the throne, and Johnson was a fervent royalist and a very keen high Anglican.[50] So, granted the appointment by the new monarch, Johnson arrived in the Leeward Islands and, by mid-1687, had begun making a great stir.

One might think that a strong royalist governor, devoted to a monarch who was a crypto-Catholic and on the verge of becoming an overt one, would have been a good thing for the Irish people of Montserrat, and thus it seemed. But, in an unstable social system, stir usually is trouble, and so it was now. Johnson thudded onto the local stage as a meddling outsider. He immediately moved the capital of the Leeward Islands from Nevis, where William Stapleton's chief estate had been, to Antigua. He then set about making alliances with the middling proprietors to topple the large plantation owners from their control of the legislative and judicial posts. This alienated most of the landlords on the various islands, Protestant and Catholic. Simultaneously, his overtly pro-Catholic and pro-French policies were almost perfectly (if unintentionally) designed to raise Protestant fears.[51] Stir.

Johnson's behaviour on Montserrat was immediately promising for the Catholics, especially those of the poorer sort, but ultimately disastrous. Soon after his arrival, the Catholics of the several islands petitioned him for the free exercise of their religion. This he quickly granted.[52] Thus, Catholic chapels could be built, without any danger of official interference, and these were begun in Montserrat and St Christopher, the two islands with the largest Catholic populations.[53] Next, the Catholics of Montserrat (and probably of St Christopher as well) petitioned Johnson to relieve them of the burden of paying for the ministers of the Established Church.[54] The rector on Montserrat, it will be recalled, was paid by Montserrat's governmental funds, there being no vestry system. Sir Nathaniel's response to the Catholic petition was to order a tiny civic revolution – namely, that in future the Protestant ministers should not be paid by the treasury but by their local vestry.[55] As he blandly explained to the home authorities, he made this ruling not only for Montserrat but for St Christopher because the Roman Catholics would have very heavy expenses in building and decorating their own chapels.[56]

Thus, the people of Montserrat had visible evidence of a new world a-borning: a Catholic chapel being started (one assumes at Kingsale), and the Anglican clergyman being thrown on the good will of his flock. Concerning the future, Catholic expectations inevitably must have been high, and Protestant apprehensions even higher.

In a related development, an amazingly bold-faced attempt at upsetting the fairly new freehold land system of Montserrat (and indeed, of all the Leeward Islands), was assayed by Johnson's royalist attorney-general for the islands, one Archibald Hutcheson. In 1688, Hutcheson put forward the argument that the freeholds granted under the 1668 Montserrat land law were valid, but that none of the patents granted since then were valid. This was because they were granted by the successive governors of the island and not with the consent of the king or of the Lords of Trade and Plantations acting in council. Therefore, he concluded, most land titles on Montserrat were void. He went further and suggested that the same was probably true of most of the holdings on Antigua and St Christopher. "Altogether, I believe that nearly all titles in the Leeward Islands are insecure, which is a hindrance to settlement and a loss to the King by the failure of escheats."[57]

The remedy? The king was to grant secure title to all proprietors (by surrender-and-regrant, yet again), but this time when the proprietors received a secure grant they would become subject to a rent of one-half to one percent on the annual produce of their estates. Or to put it another way: in order to make land titles secure, most land titles in the Leeward Islands would be declared to be invalid, and then the lands, which were now supposed to be freehold, would become perpetual leaseholds, subject to a very real annual tax. All this in order to encourage more white settlement! This particular scheme would have been especially noisome to settlers of Irish background because, as the attorney general noted, it was based on Lord Strafford's Act of Settlement in Ireland.[58] (He shrewdly failed to explain that the same act was a direct contributory cause of the Irish Civil War of the mid-seventeenth century.)

The conclusion of this modest proposal was a bit of further disinterested advice. "Finally, I would point out that it would be of great advantage to the islands to have a gentleman conversant with the laws and customs of England resident in them," Hutcheson noted, and quickly added, "and no one fitter than the Attorney General which is the title that I bear." And just in case anyone missed the point: "I give an outline of his duties. He might be allowed a percentage on the accidental revenues, fines, forfeitures, etc. of the Islands."[59] Fortunately for the peace of the Leeward Islands, the home countries were just then becoming distracted with a train of events that turned out to be a bloodless revolution in England and a bloody one in Ireland.[60]

That, however, was not clear at the moment. The sum total of all the changes begun, or contemplated, under Nathaniel Johnson's administration was to unsettle all the social concordats that made life on a place such as Montserrat tolerable. Johnson was threatening the entire ruling class (with his land legislation) and all Protestants in particular (by easing up on the Catholics). Neither of these policies may have been ethically wrong, but they certainly were socially destructive, for, among other things, they threatened the existence of an ecumenical ruling class, the capstone of Montserrat's social order.

How things would have worked out on Montserrat had James II kept his throne is difficult to conjecture: Catholic control of the island, meaning Irish Catholic control, in an overt and unashamed fashion, was probably the most likely outcome. That was not to be, for in early 1689, the islanders learned that a revolution had occurred in England the previous November. This revolution, called both "glorious" and "bloodless" in English historical writing, was neither in Ireland. There it took until October 1691 for the Williamites to crush the Jacobites, the adherents of the Stuart line, whom the majority of the Irish people manifestly favoured.

The accession of William of Orange and his wife Mary (as joint monarchs), in a context that was overtly anti-Catholic, forced the Irish at home, and the Irish in the various English colonies, to make the one decision that they had most wanted to avoid: choosing between loyalty to a royal line, and loyalty to the state. When the Stuarts were on the throne, Irish Catholics could give service to the state, while maintaining the fiction that they were only serving the monarch. Now, with the Stuarts ousted, they had to choose between the two. In the Leeward Islands, the task was made worse, for Nathaniel Johnson was "the stoutest Jacobite" in the Americas.[61] But he was an untrustworthy leader, the sort who got his followers in trouble. In May 1689, he informed William III that he could not accept the revolution.[62]

This helped to tip two local populations – the Irish Catholics on St Christopher and on Montserrat – towards the Jacobites. In June 1689, 130 armed Irishmen, apparently servants and wage labourers, absconded to the French side of St Christopher and the French refused to hand them back.[63] Worse, in late June when news reached St Christopher that a European war had broken out between England and France, the French on St Christopher, with the Irish in their vanguard, invaded the English district and burned and sacked it in a true jacquerie. Estimates were that they did £150,000 damage on their first onslaught.[64] They did so with "the Irish flying colours," which they called "King James's colours."[65] At this point, in mid-July, the leading colonists of the Leeward Islands asked Sir Nathaniel Johnson to resign as governor and he did so, appointing Christopher Codrington in his place. This personal appointment was later ratified by the London authorities.[66]

Would Montserrat follow St Christopher? And would the Irish Catholics on either Antigua or Nevis join in? Codrington, an old-time planter of great wealth garnered in Antigua and Barbados, was not interested in finding out. He possessed a superb tactical sense in military matters. Immediately he assumed power, he disarmed the Irish Catholics on Antigua (meaning the lower class Irish, not the members of the ruling elite) and did the same on Montserrat: this roughly between the fifteenth and eighteenth of July. Sixteen of the Irish Catholics of Montserrat were characterized by "insolent behaviour" and Codrington had them arrested and he shipped them to Jamaica for trial. He did the same on Nevis, disarming the potentially rebellious among the Catholics, arresting the hard cases, and sending them to Jamaica.[67] It worked. None of the other islands joined St Christopher in open rebellion.[68]

The situation in Montserrat stayed tense, however, and well into November, Governor Codrington still feared an Irish rebellion.[69] Therefore, near the end of the month, he visited the island (presumably with some troops), and talked directly to the Irish Catholic leaders. We do not know who they were, but they can scarcely be other than the leaders of the Kingsale community, the heartland of Catholic small proprietors and free wage labourers. (One can safely assume that the local Catholic large landowners were not involved; if they were to give their all for the Jacobite cause, it would not be at the head of a rag-tag band of small proprietors who were more apt to burn than follow them.) Codrington's facing them directly was the right approach. "I pointed out to the Irish the ruin they would bring on themselves if they proved treacherous, and the advantages of remaining faithful. They promised to be loyal and to work heartily with the English, and I do not hear the least occasion for suspicion against them."[70] The last phrase was part of a report Codrington made in 1690, and was written more in hope than in trust: for the rest of his career he was profoundly suspicious of all Irish Catholics.

To complete the story: Sir Nathaniel Johnson skived off to Carolina. He took 100 slaves with him and became a leading planter in America, serving as governor of South Carolina from 1703–09. Christopher Codrington was confirmed in office and served with rough distinction until his death in 1698, after which he was replaced by his son. The French, having captured St Christopher with the help of the local Irish in August 1689, were finally defeated by Codrington.[71] Local tradition on Montserrat holds that when the rebel Irish were cleared off St Christopher by Codrington, they were shipped to Montserrat.[72] If this is true, then the Irish Catholic rebels on Montserrat were considered to be broken indeed.

Thus, the first era of the "invisible" penal code, the years 1668–90, had ended badly for the Irish Catholics. Their bargaining position was greatly undercut. They would never again have the governmental leverage they had enjoyed in the Stapleton era or the briefer period of Sir Nathaniel Johnson's governorship of the Leeward Islands. They now entered an era, lasting from 1690 to roughly 1730, when they were much less able to resist penal enactments, and when, simultaneously, the more aggressive local Protestants were increasingly keen on anti-Catholic legislation. Once again, the evidence must be read, as on a brass rubbing, but it is there. The evolution of penal measures on Montserrat parallelled what happened in the home country, Ireland. Christopher Codrington, like William III of Orange, was not himself in favour of legislative persecution of Catholics; as a soldier, each man assumed that the battlefield had been the place of decision, and that everyone should be allowed to recover from his wounds without vexation. However, in the West Indies, as in England and Ireland, the Crown was pushed by outside forces to be hard on Catholics. Ireland came under an act of the English parliament of 1691 which introduced a new oath and an anti-Catholic declaration for membership in parliament and other public positions. Other acts followed, this time passed by the Irish parliament, such as a 1695 act which forbade Catholics to teach school and, simultaneously, forbade Catholic parents to send their children abroad for education. It was not until the early eighteenth century, however, that the anti-Catholic penal code was articulated fully. Similarly, on Montserrat, the 1690s were an unpleasant overture to the more virulent anti-Catholicism of the early 1700s. The deposing of the Stuarts meant that on Montserrat Catholic religious liberty was stopped: forget completing the Catholic chapel, and start paying taxes to the central treasury to support the good Rev. Mr. Molineux. That, though, was a return to the *status quo pro ante*. Soon, anti-Catholicism became more aggressive.[73]

To keep the development of the historically-obscured penal code in social perspective, for the 1690s and for the early eighteenth century, let us briefly look again at population trends, and do so in a bit more detail than previously. Table 6 gives the available census figures from the later seventeenth century to the mid-eighteenth. (Those for 1678 and 1729 are most trustworthy.)[74]

These figures indicate that the white population declined by a bit over 42 percent between 1678 and 1708. A reasonable supposition would be that most of that loss came after 1689. Further, since we know that the Irish population loss between 1678 and 1729 was roughly 3.8 times as great as the British population loss (1,204 Irish lost compared to 317 Britons), a reasonable inference is that most of the loss which we are inferring occurred after 1689, was overwhelmingly Irish and, indeed, Irish Catholic. Montserrat, as a result of the political whirl of 1685–90, was a much less hospitable place for Irish Catholics than it had been, especially for the Irish small holders, who did not have the financial resources to play politics among the emerging sugar plantocracy. Even for the better off, times were worrisome.

Now the second era of the largely-invisible penal code began: invisible because it has largely been scrubbed from the records. It was real. The Williamite Revolution of 1688–91 reversed the pro-Catholic measures of James II's reign. The most virulent act in the Leeward Islands was the statute of the Leeward Islands General Council and General Assembly, to prevent "Papists and reputed Papists" from settling in any of the islands. This incredibly short-sighted piece of legislation (short-sighted, given the desperate need for white settlers, especially indentured servants) soon became obsolete.[75] On Montserrat, this new anti-Catholicism meant that the requirement for oaths, repugnant to Catholics, as a prerequisite for council posts would be administered rigorously, and that Catholic freedom of worship, permitted as long as it was not ostentatious, would be reduced. Thus, in 1708, Daniel Parke, governor of the Leeward Islands, having heard that a Catholic priest was on Montserrat, gave orders "for taking him up."[76] The real question was whether or not the penal code would be

Table 6
Census Figures, 1678–1729

Year	*Black Population*	*White Population*	*Irish Component within White Population*
1678	1,894	2,676	1,845
1708	3,570	1,545	
1720	3,772	1,593	
1724	4,400	1,000	
1729	6,063	1,155	641

tightened legislatively. On Montserrat, the anti-Catholic pressure came from the assembly, which was elected by adult white freeholders, and, after 1690 was the place where aggrieved Protestant small- and medium-sized landholders could put pressure on the appointed council, which in the past had been strongly influenced by rich Catholic landowners. Thus, in 1698, the assembly demanded that the judges and justices of the island should be required to take strongly Protestant oaths. The council concurred, but it tried to sidestep a bit, by refusing to pass a special local law to this effect. "We think the laws of England sufficient without a local law to prevent Roman Catholics from holding [judicial] office."[77]

The local gentry may have wished to continue in the old ways, but they faced pressure not only from their own local assembly, but also from London and from the government of the Leeward Islands, and these pressures were all anti-Catholic. The assembly of the island of Nevis in 1701 passed "An Act to Prevent Papists and reputed Papists from settling in this Island for the future and for the better governance of those which are already settled."[78] This act was said merely to follow the policy of Great Britain with respect to papists[79] – that is, ban them from participation in government. Finally, in 1702, the Council of Montserrat gave in to local and external pressures and passed an explicitly anti-Catholic measure.

Unhappily, we know only its title directly, since the London authorities disallowed it for being too lenient and therefore it was never printed! It was "An Act determining the Setting of Assemblies, and regulating the Elections of the same," a nondescript title to be sure.[80] What its framers attempted, however, was very subtle, one infers, for it was both a penal law and a local bypass. What the London authorities clearly wanted was for the Montserrat legislature to take away the vote from Catholics for membership in the local assemblies. Instead, the Council of Trade and Plantations was distressed to learn, the Montserrat Act, while requiring the oaths of allegiance and supremacy of most voters, "does exempt the inhabitants of one part of the island from the obligation of taking the oaths … for which exemption there is no sufficient reason assigned."[81] The one-part of the island almost certainly was St Patrick's parish, where Kingsale and the Irish concentration were located. And the reason for exempting the inhabitants of this parish is that they had the potential of rebellion if pushed too hard and too unfairly.

Further, while the London authorities wanted the Montserrat legislature to enact stringent anti-Catholic oaths to be taken by assembly members, the locals wrote a new oath of their own. Presumably, Catholics could in good conscience take this and then assume assembly seats. This was another reason, the Council of Trade and Plantations advised the Crown, that the Montserrat act must be voided.[82]

Clearly the local elite – ecumenical as always, bent on continuing in power, also, as always – managed to beat back the local forces of the Protestant bourgeoisie. The issue now became whether or not the London authorities, having abrogated the Montserrat election act of 1702, would press harder. The London repeal of the 1702 act was supposed to be the prelude to Montserrat's introducing a vigorous anti-Catholic act, but the locals did no such thing. Instead, they ignored London and ignored the governor of the Leeward Islands (now Christopher Codrington the younger), and continued with the old "invisible" penal code. This at least had the virtue of permitting Roman Catholics to vote in assembly elections. In fact, an act of the Leeward Islands legislature of 1705 may have represented a direct victory for the Montserrat planters: it confirmed "all the laws and legal customs" in force on the various Leeward Islands, meaning, as far as Montserrat was concerned, that Catholics could continue to vote.[83]

However, the code, although no different in law than it had been in the era of Stapleton's governorship, was now in practice more effective and this despite the wishes of Montserrat's planter elite. Now, at London's direction, there was no more tip-of-the-wink to the requirement of oaths, particularly the oaths of supremacy and of allegiance which few Catholics would take since they affirmed the spiritual supremacy of the Crown as head of the church. And "occasional conformity" – the taking of the oaths while remaining Catholic – was now policed and prevented. This one infers from the buoyant report of the governor of the Leeward Islands in 1724, Col. John Hart, that concerning the population of Montserrat, two thirds of them were Irish papists, "who are justly excluded by Law from having any share in the Government."[84] The forcing out of Catholics from local government was reinforced in 1729, when the island's legislature set up a series of courts (King's bench, common pleas, and a court of errors), and required that the judges of these courts take the oaths of allegiance, supremacy and abjuration.[85] Thus, it appears that from approximately the beginning of the eighteenth century, Roman Catholics were locked out of local governmental office holding.

Indeed, at mid-century, an attempt was made by the local legislature, now acting in the spirit of British anti-Catholicism, to take away the Catholics' one governmental right, the exercise of the franchise; this was disallowed by the London authorities who now were beginning to have second thoughts about the wisdom of penal legislation.[86] From the early eighteenth century onward, any Roman Catholic who wished to participate in government had to give up his faith; no more local concordats for the rich, and no hope for the Catholic small holders of finding a co-religionist face on the local council.[87]

When this situation became clear during the first decade of the eighteenth century, it can only have increased alienation among Catholic small proprietors and thus speeded emigration. One is amazed at the impercipience of Christopher Codrington (the younger), governor of the Leeward Islands, who in 1701 tried to raise two companies of soldiers on Montserrat to come to the defence of St Christopher, at the time of its being threatened by French invasion. "Not one man of the Irish would enlist himself," he complained. He then wrote "a little warmly" about this to the governor and council of Montserrat and was told that they really could not help it. "They found the Irish resolved against assisting St Kitts: and the reason they gave was there had been several Acts made against Catholics at Nevis and St Kitt's." Indeed there had been and, understandably, the Irish Catholic small farmers and free labourers, the sort of hard men who made the best infantrymen, were not about to support an overtly anti-Catholic government in its fight against a Catholic power. The penal laws had soured them, surely. Yet, instead of accepting this obvious explanation, young Codrington opined that "the truth of the matter is, I believe, some Irish Priests from the French Islands in disguise have been amongst them to debauch them."[88] But, if disaffected, the Irish Catholics of Montserrat never again fought openly against the government of their own island. Those who truly hated the place left, and those who remained made their own kind of peace with the new order.

When Montserrat was thrice invaded by the French (on 28 June 1710, 14 June 1711, and 8 July 1712),[89] the Irish did not rush to join the French colours, but reported to their local militia units. These troops, though not notably efficient, were at least not disloyal. The

1710 French raid was of little consequence, and that of 1711 resulted in only the theft of fifty to sixty slaves, the burning of one house, and the death of one slave and two white inhabitants. The French lost an estimated sixty or seventy men (albeit only nineteen bodies were found). Considering that the invading force was 1,200, this was an acceptable result. The islanders were fortunate on this occasion that the warship HMS *Newcastle* was offshore and able to attack the French fleet and therefore cut short the assault on the island.[90]

The French invasion of 1712 was another matter entirely, a major disaster for the islanders. This time, an entire squadron of French warships, fresh from Toulon, took the island for twelve days of looting and burning.[91] When they left, the French took with them 1,200–1,400 of Montserrat's African slaves[92] – roughly one-third of the island's black population – and the most valuable form of moveable property. Other chattels, the French either removed or destroyed.

> The enemy overrun great part of the island, burnt our towns, destroyed our houses in the country, sugar works and plantations, carried away sundry of our slaves, killed and took with them most of our horses, cattle and small stock, broke, burnt and carried with them our household stuff, cloathing, and merchandizes, in so much that they left many of us destitute of the very necessaries of subsistence, food and raiment.

That is the summation by one of the island's leaders of what had occurred.[93] Once more, the white settlers of Montserrat were starting over, almost from scratch.

Therefore the picture which had seemed so clear – that the depletion of the white population in general and the Irish in particular was caused simply by the expansion of the sugar industry with its dependence on slave labour – was largely illusory. "Where the whites disappeared," Eric Williams believed, the cause was "the suppression of the small farm by the large plantation, with its consequent demand for a large and steady supply of labour."[94] That is a nice neat theory, but it is insensitive to reality.

Actually, a series of natural and military disasters made any sensible plantation owner, small proprietor, or free labourer consider that he might make a better and easier life elsewhere. And a shift in the political chemistry of the island after 1690 made Montserrat much less comfortable for many Irish Catholics. The waning of the political power of the Irish Catholic gentry, who in the Stapleton era had kept the worst aspects of the penal code from being enforced, left the Catholic small holders without protection. Large Catholic plantation owners were safe enough because of their economic power, but even they could not come forward and hold the reins of political power. It was a very good time for Irish Catholics to clear off.

That crucial point having been established, it is true that an economic revolution occurred on Montserrat in the 1680–1730 period. And it is precisely when one recognizes this point that the full ambiguity of Irish behaviour becomes apparent. Many Irish stayed (they still were the majority of the island population in 1729), and most of these persons were Catholics. As such they were living under a code that treated them as second-class human beings – papists, unworthy of full trust and banned from full civic participation and, therefore, full civil rights. Yet, these very same people, simultaneously and apparently without moral qualms, participated in the enslavement of another set of human beings.

The slave system on Montserrat was not in any fundamental way different from that elsewhere in the British West Indies, although it had its own barbarous touches, which I will mention in a moment. On almost every British West Indian island one finds the theme of labour-shortage running as a constant through the period. In the case of Montserrat in 1680, the council told the London authorities that "the great hindrance to the improvement of the island is the want of negroes."[95] In July 1688, a Dutch "interloper" was caught by Royal Africa Company officials landing fifty-six to sixty slaves on Montserrat. A riot by Montserrat whites ensued, and the local jury simply acquitted the rioters: slaves were desperately needed.[96] The same theme still resonated at the end of the period. In 1734 the governor of the Leeward Islands noted in his report on Montserrat that "as to its produce, it is stinted for want of negroes."[97] During the early eighteenth century, so short was the supply of labour, that it became common practice for planters to "delude away" from other owners' plantations their slaves, or to forcibly detain them or give them sanctuary as runaways and then keep them as their own slaves. (Again, Montserrat was not unique in having the problem.) An act of 1719 was passed by the Montserrat legislature to end this practice, invoking a fine of twenty shillings per day in each instance.[98] Not accidentally, this act provided the same penalties for the "deluding away" or harbouring or detaining indentured servants. Labour, white and black, was in very short supply on the island during the era of sugar's expansion, and this is yet another reason to reject the idea that black labour forced out white labour: chronic labour shortages of all sorts made such a forcing process impossible. So tight was the labour supply that in 1722, canoes were no longer permitted on the island, unless secured, as slaves frequently used them to escape.[99]

Most of the laws concerning slaves were routine matters, such as provisions against blacks being abroad at night without a pass from their owner. Or – a particular problem in Plymouth – against the serving of drink to slaves when they were on their Sunday holiday.[100] Still, there were severe penalties for slaves who broke fundamental rules, by stealing, by escaping, or by turning on their masters. These penalties, horrific as they are, must be kept in context. Seventeenth- and eighteenth-century penalties for theft by white people in the English legal tradition were horrific, as is well known. Running away was a severe crime even for white servants, but race differentials nevertheless existed. In 1698, the council of Montserrat ordered that two white women who were caught running away in a canoe be whipped on their bare backs for up to thirty-nine lashes and then were to have their labour contract extended for four additional years to compensate their master for his expense and loss caused by their levanting.[101] Had they been slaves, their penalty would have been much worse. (One notes with awe the mind set of the council of Barbados which in 1693 paid one Alice Mills ten guineas for castrating forty-two rebellious African slaves. The ghoulish rationality of this exercise in pre-decimal currency, was 2 shillings, sixpence per testicle.[102])

That is context. Montserrat, in 1693 enacted its own central slave-discipline measure, "An Act to restrain the Insolence of Slaves, and for preventing them from committing any Outrages, as also the better ordering such Slaves."[103] Any slave who stole anything worth twelve pence (one shilling) or more was to be put to death. If less, for the first offence, his or her ears were to be cut off and a severe whipping administered. A second offence was to be punished by death. Anyone who found a negro more than forty feet off the footpath had the right to shoot at and to kill the slave. Any slave found with meat in his house and not able to prove that it was come by honestly, was to have the "whole house" taken out and whipped, and also one of the house members was to have his or her ears cut off. The peculiar point was that, in 1714, the act had to be amended. The original measure had provided that whenever a slave acted in a criminal manner and was put to death for his or her crimes, the owner of the slave was to receive 3,500 pounds of muscovado sugar as recompense, from the public treasury, for the loss of the slave. It was discovered by experience, however, that this was not enough and that owners would hide the crimes of their African slaves, rather than lose their services. Therefore from 1714 onwards, the owner was to be paid the market value of the slave, as appraised by the deputy governor and council of the island, and this mordant appraisal to be made immediately after sentence was passed and before the judicial murder of the slave took place.[104] This is a nice instance of sensitivity to the laws of the capitalist marketplace.

Mostly, however, such market-sensitivity was not necessary. It was usually a matter of conducting only sufficient executions to encourage the others. Thus, in August 1693, the council and assembly ordered that a black man named Peter Boone, who had been convicted by them of the theft of nine pigs, be cut to pieces. His bowels were then to be burned and he was to be cut into four quarters and these were to be displayed on the most frequented of the public paths that adjoined the towns of Plymouth and Kingsale.[105] Another black, who had been found with fresh meat in his possession, for which he had no good explanation, was sentenced to have his right ear cut off. He was also to be branded on the breast with a hot iron, especially designed for marking thieves.[106]

Rather more creative was the punishment, carried out later in the same year, of a black who had almost beaten his overseer to death. He was to be suspended in chains and to be given no food or water, until he died.[107] For running away (and, really, for having been recaptured, after three months of freedom), an African slave was in 1698, hanged, drawn and quartered.[108] A year later, for stealing objects worth twelve pence, one "Coffee" was hanged and his severed body exhibited on poles in various separate public places.[109]

It profits no one to hear more of this vile litany. The point, which must be stressed, and stressed again, is that the Irish, overwhelmingly Catholic, bought into this system. The Irish Catholics, rich, middling, and just above white-trash-poor, they all did so. They did unto others even more than ever was done unto them.

This is the moment that the census of 1729 becomes invaluable. It is an extraordinary enumeration in its richness of detail. If interpreted with a sensitivity to what it says (and not with an anachronistic wrenching, making it out to carry a modern meaning which it cannot support: on this see Appendix B), it is a rare document. Its basic organizational principle is the organization: not the family; not the individual. It is a census of production units. Each unit is identified by its manager (to use a modern phrase that is not inappropriate) and, for our purposes that method is perfect. The ethnicity of the manager can be identified and the nature of the entrepreneurial unit (which usually was a family unit, plus servants and slaves), can be determined. Thus, we can virtually see the Irish in action, in their

Table 7
Ethnicity of Montserrat's White Population, 1678 and 1729

	1678 Calculated from All Adult White Males						*1729 Calculated from Adult White Males Who Were Heads of Enterprises*					
	Irish		*British*		*Total*		*Irish*		*British*		*Total*	
	No.	*%*	*No.*	*%*	*No.*	*%*	*No.*	*%*	*No.*	*%*	*No.*	*%*
St Peter's or "Northward" Division	81	45.3	98	54.7	179	100.0	24	42.1	33	57.9	57	100.0
St George's or "Windward" Division	52	51.0	50	49.0	102	100.0	12	67.6	11	32.4	34	100.0
St Anthony's Division	226	67.7	108	32.3	334	100.0	41	45.6	49	54.4	90	100.0
St Patrick's or "White River" Division	388	73.1	143	26.9	531	100.0	30	93.7	2	6.3	32	100.0
Total	747	65.2	399	34.8	1,146	100.0	118	55.4	95	44.6	213	100.0

Source: See Table 5 for 1678 data. On the 1729 data, see Appendix B.

Table 8
Montserrat, 1729: Number of White Persons (including Servants) in White Enterprises, according to Ethnicity of the Head of the Enterprise[1]

	Irish		*British*		*Total*	
	No.	*%*	*No.*	*%*	*No.*	*%*
St Peter's or "Northward" Division	77	37.7	127	62.3	204	100.0
St George's or "Windward" Division	141	66.8	70	33.2	211	100.0
St Anthony's Division	245	45.5	293	54.5	538	100.0
St Patrick's or "White River" Division	178	88.1	24	11.9	202	100.0
Total	641	55.5	514	44.5	1,155	100.0

Source: See Appendix B.
[1] Of the 245 heads of enterprises, 213 were male, 32 female.

Table 9
Average Number of White Persons (including Servants) in White Enterprises according to Ethnicity of the Head of the Enterprise

	Irish	*British*
St Peter's or "Northward" Division	3.1	3.6
St George's or "Windward" Division	5.6	4.7
St Anthony's Division	4.7	4.9
St Patrick's or "White River" Division	5.9	8.0
Total	4.9	4.5

Source: See Appendix B.
Note: N = 1,155 Average for combined total = 4.7
Total number of enterprises = 213 with male heads, 32 with female.

everyday economic life. And what the census reveals is that, if anything, the Irish were deeper into the slave system than were their British counterparts.

Tables 7, 8, 9, 10, and 11 provide the basic information on the interaction of persons of Irish ethnicity and the African-derived slave population of Montserrat. These tables make clear two salient facts. First, that the Irish were more apt to own slaves than were the British. Secondly, when they did own them, they on average owned more slaves than did their British counterparts. That is a contrast to the situation in 1678, when it was found that the Irish were more apt to have slaves than the British, but that the biggest slave holders were British. This no longer was true.

Something of an economic reconstruction had occurred along ethnic lines at exactly the same time that Montserrat's economy was

Table 10
Percentage of Enterprises Owning Slaves, by Ethnicity, 1729

	Irish	*British*	*Combined*
St Peter's or "Northward" Division	52.0	57.1	55.0
St George's or "Windward" Division	100.0	100.0	100.0
St Anthony's Division	100.0	100.0	100.0
St Patrick's or "White River" Division	100.0	100.0	100.0
Total	90.9	86.7	89.0

Source: See Appendix B.

Table 11
Number of Slaves per Enterprise, according to Ethnicity of the Head of the Enterprise, Montserrat, 1729

	Irish		*British*	
	Number of slaves	*Average number per enterprise*	*Number of slaves*	*Average number per enterprise*
St Peter's or "Northward" Division	171	6.8	511	14.6
St George's or "Windward" Division	1,005	40.2	218	14.5
St Anthony's Division	1,468	28.2	1,760	29.3
St Patrick's or "White River" Division	889	29.6	41	13.7
Total	3,533	26.8	2,530	22.4

Source: See Appendix B.
Note: The overall average number of slaves per enterprise on Montserrat in 1729 was 24.7; the total number of slaves was 6,063.

experiencing the sugar revolution; that is, the replacement of a mixed agriculture of tobacco, indigo and sugar, with a near-monoculture. This was not the simple blacks-forcing-out-the-Irish that is implied by Eric Williams' model of the introduction of sugar. There is no doubt that the number of Irish persons on the island dropped (by two-thirds between 1678 and 1729), but this does not prove either that they were forced off by slave labour or that they left penniless. The first condition, that their labour was simply replaced by cheaper slave labour, is incompatible with everything we know about the continual labour shortage on the island: witness the bonuses given for importing white servants and recall the complaints of the island's governors about the shortage, and consider the effects of the loss of blacks through French plunderings. No, the whites could have stayed as free labourers, in high demand.

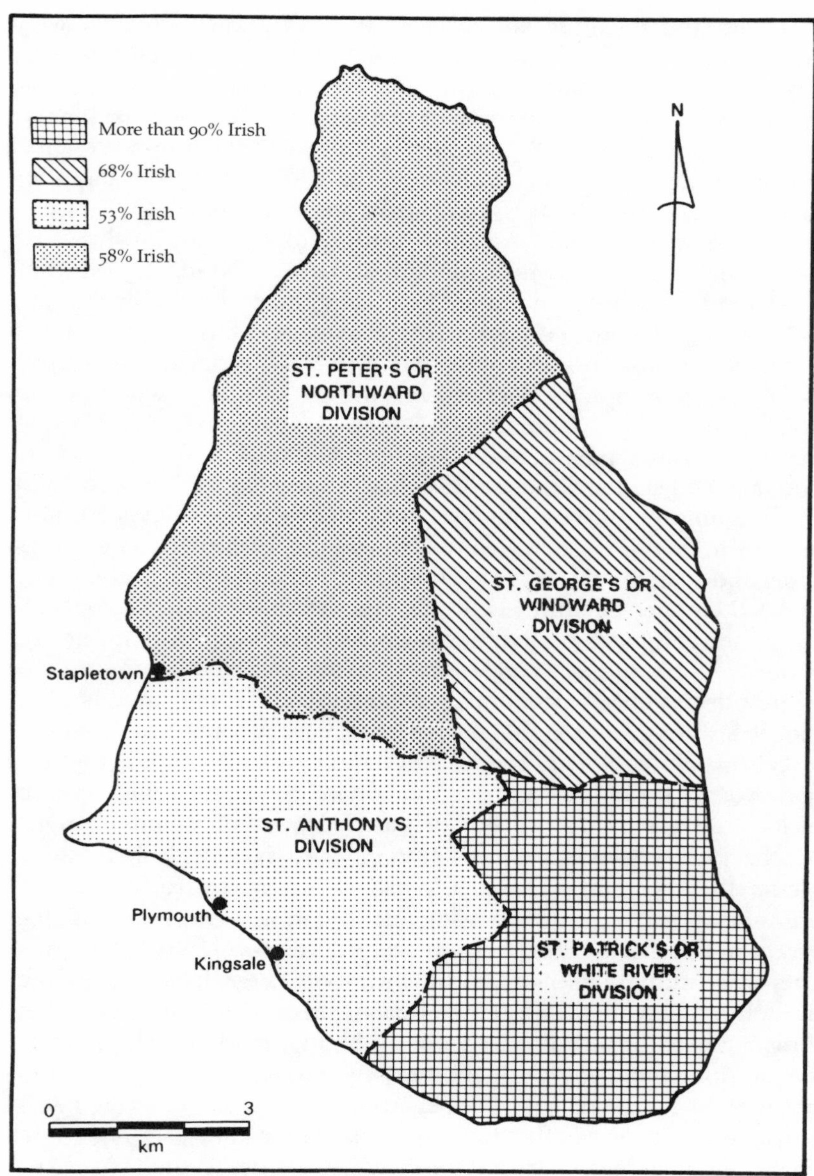

Map 6 Census divisions by ethnicity, 1729

Second, there is no reason to suppose that the Irish who left, went away broke, although one could apodictically assert that everyone who left was so deeply in debt as to have no positive equity to cash in. Given the lack of records, their exit-position can never be known. However, since it is clear that there were very strong non-economic reasons for Irish Catholics to clear off, this means that any suggestion that they left broke (that is, left for economic reasons) is not of probative value. They had been small proprietors, mostly in the "Irish horseshoe" around Kingsale, and they had something to sell: their household, their land and, most important, many (probably most by the early eighteenth century) owned slaves, and this at a time when the local rate for an adult slave was £30–35.[110] What the small proprietors did, I would conjecture, was to sell their land (whether freehold or tenancy), and either to sell their slaves or to take them with them to another part of the New World. Either way, they had the potential of leaving Montserrat with considerable resources in hand. The big holding of the Gallway family in St Patrick's Division (now, in 1729, in its third generation of Gallway ownership), had over 1,400 acres and was the third largest holding on the island, a cattle ranch. Lydia Pulsipher is almost certainly right in assuming that the Gallways bought most of that land from departing small farmers.[111] Where I think she is wrong is in seeing these small proprietors as being pushed out by economic forces. Rather, the Irish smallholders, like the shrewd and self-assertive men they always had been, followed their own best interests. After 1690, located on an island that had become hostile to their religion, where they were denied crumbs of local governmental patronage and which was becoming tougher on the kind of small-business traders that the law called "smugglers," they decided to make a living elsewhere. Instead of perceiving them as passive victims, I suggest that they were simply another group in the stream of active, self-seeking Irish emigrants. Their parents or grandparents had left Ireland, most often from Munster, as indentured servants, and this had given them a foothold in the New World. The family had carved out a holding, made a living, bought slaves, done modestly well, and now they moved on. The great Irish population loss was from the St Patrick's division, which is hardly surprising. Yet even after the depopulation of that division, it still was nearly 90 percent Irish. Significantly, the Irish who stayed consolidated control of St George's parish, on the windward side of the island, and this was an area of large plantations given over to sugar and slave labour.

Most crucial, however, was this change: whereas before the sugar-slave economic revolution, persons of Irish background were the largest ethnic group, but were, overall, less privileged economically than were the British, after this revolution, the Irish were still numerically dominant, and, crucially, they were now, on average, bigger planters, and owned more slaves, than did the British. This development is fascinating, because it runs in just the opposite direction of political developments: paradox indeed.

Just how well the Irish did can be graphically stated by using as a basis a detailed analysis conducted by Richard B. Sheridan. He sorted out the thirty leading sugar plantations on the island in 1729. A conservative estimate (that is, choosing "British" rather than "Irish" in ambiguous cases), is that eighteen of the thirty were of Irish background, which is 60 percent (as compared with the Irish being about 55 percent of the island's white population).[112]

Now, someone who wished to engage in special pleading for the virtue of the Irish might agree that, yes, at all levels of society the Irish were more apt to hold slaves than were the British, and yes, that the Irish were, on average, bigger slave holders than were the British, but that at the very top – the very largest plantations where the Irish were overrepresented – this social structure ensued because a bunch of apostate Irish had become Protestant (and, therefore, somehow become tinctured with vice). Lacking both a religious census and decent parish records, the next best thing one can do is to take the eighteen certainly Irish names on the list of the thirty largest sugar growers and compare them to all available lists of councils, acting governors, and holders of judicial office. This can be done because we know that Catholics were totally locked out of governmental posts after 1702, and that the old dodge of occasional conformity and false swearing did not play. Admittedly this is a far-from-perfect tool, even if improved by local genealogical information. That granted, the breakdown seems to have been as follows among large estate holders of Irish background (this ranking is by number of acres planted in sugar cane):[113]

Catholics (ranking on island)	*Protestants (ranking on island)*
Farrill, James (2)	Trant (3)
Roach (5)	Irish (10)
Dongan (6)	Meade (11)
Darcy (9)	Lee, Thomas (14)
Farrill, John (12)	Parsons (13)
Hussey (16)	Dyer (18)
Skerrett (17)	Daly (22)
Gallway (26)	Frye (23)
	Lee, Peter (25)
	FitzDennis (30)

Leaving aside the Parsons family (which always had been Protestant), it appears that eleven of the seventeen largest Irish landowning families on the island (roughly 53 percent) had, during the course of their family's history on the island, changed religion. One suspects that most of these cases had occurred after the Williamite Revolution of 1688–91. An apostasy rate of over 50 percent is significant but, like all dusty artifacts, it should be held up to the light. Actually, given the manifest advantages of turning Protestant, a religious-constancy rate of nearly 50 percent among the leading Catholics is remarkably high. Given that it was the richest people who were most hurt by being shut out of the local legislative council, and who were prevented from having their children vie for the plum jobs on the island, such as legal and administrative posts, this is no small indication of religious loyalty (not, emphatically, of religious practice, for there was very little of that on Montserrat: loyalty).

What one most wonders about the 53 percent who changed religion is, first, of course, how sincere was the change (and did the whole family change, or just the male head of the family?) and, second and more interesting, did the change of religion occur before or after these Irish landlords became rich? It would be easy to suggest that several of the leading Irish Catholics turned Protestant in order to obtain wealth. More likely, I think, is that they turned Protestant in order to keep it. We can never know. But if we cannot, they did: the one thing certain is that on such a small island, everyone knew what everybody had been for generations back. There are no secrets in large families or on small islands.

If we cannot unravel the religious history of each leading island family, we can at least chart the trajectory of a few of the major Irish landowning families. Take the Meades, for example. Nicholas Mead, an attorney, was in 1678 captain of the militia unit that included the commercial centre of the island, Plymouth. In 1729, the Meade family (the spelling evolved) were major plantation owners, operating the eleventh largest sugar plantation. They cultivated 200 acres of cane and owned 107 slaves. The then-head of the family, Thomas Meade, had made his fortune by first leasing land from absentee landlords and then buying his own. In addition, in 1724, he had married the daughter of a major Irish merchant and landowner, Peter Hussey. By 1745 Thomas Meade owned 340 slaves and three plantations. One of these that he acquired near mid-century was the "Waterwork," the most prestigious plantation on the island, having been the prize that William Stapleton had lifted in 1668 from the attainted estate of Anthony Briskett II.[114]

Other Irish families had more mixed results. Recall the Blake family. One of the brothers, Henry, who had arrived in late 1668, returned to Ireland and bought two significant estates in County Galway. The second, John – the one who brought a "whore" with him and freely used the word "neger" as a cattle-droving term – stayed on. The Blake line continued on Montserrat, though whether it was by virtue of John's descendants, or from a second generation sent out from Galway to the West Indies is unclear. In 1723 a Henry Blake, merchant of Montserrat (not to be confused with the Henry Blake who had been in Montserrat in the 1670s) left £10 sterling for the "Romish clergy of the town of Galway."[115] In the 1729 census, one finds various Blakes, widely separated on the socio-economic map. Two of them were déclassé, being labourers in the Northward division (that is, St Peter's parish). One of these men owned no land and the other held six acres of uncultivated bush. Between them they owned six slaves. Anthony Blake declared himself to be a "planter" in St Anthony's district, but he seems to have been more of a small merchant in Plymouth than a planter, for he owned no land. A fourth was a self-described merchant in Plymouth and doubtlessly a successful one, for his business employed twenty-one slaves. And, in 1729, the estate of one Thomas Blake was in the process of being probated. He had apparently been a merchant and owned fifteen slaves. Thereafter, the family dispersed. In 1783, the will of "Henry Blake, planter," was probated. He left three slaves, valued at £291, and just over £7 in other goods, and no land.[116]

The Gallway family, as already mentioned, quietly enlarged their estates in the Irish Catholic horseshoe around Kingsale. Gallway's plantation was situated at 1,100 feet above sea level and it was not easily accessible. It was, however, in an area that received a good deal of orographic rainfall, sometimes several times a day. Instead of farming sugar in the later part of the seventeenth and in the early eighteenth centuries, they mostly raised livestock, a shrewd decision, given the perpetual shortage of provisions on the island after sugar farming was introduced. The Gallways served in the militia, but other than that they remained in the background. Although earlier members of the family may have been occasional conformists (David Gallway had been a justice of the peace and a member of the legislative council), subsequent generations seem to have been silently recusant. How much land and how many slaves the Gallways held at the time of the 1678 census is unknown, because David Gallway was the enumerator of the district and he cannily kept himself out of the census. By 1729, the family held about 1,400 acres of land and sixty-two slaves. When he died in 1734, David Gallway (probably the grandson of the founder) left £20 to a Catholic church in Ireland. The Gallway estate kept expanding and by mid-eighteenth century had been converted into a major sugar plantation. At mid-century an impressive sugar processing complex was constructed. When the Gallway family left the island is unknown, but the sugar processing complex served as the basis of a settlement until at least the 1860s.[117]

The Trant family, which was a transatlantic group, with roots going back to the colony's earliest days, continued to prosper through most of the eighteenth century. The Catholic branch in the British Isles was briefly jolted by Sir Patrick Trant's embezzling of William Stapleton's funds and by his choosing the wrong side in the Williamite war. However, on the island, the Trants turned quietly Protestant and the estate named "Trants" was the third largest sugar-producing estate in 1729, with 155 African slaves working on this single enterprise. Dominic Trant, the third largest sugar planter in 1729, was also the island's only councillor-at-law, and on a litigious island, that was a licence to print money. The family seems to have come to an end in 1784. In that year the will of Edward Trant was probated and thereafter no more Trants are found on the island, although their estate remains a landmark to this day.[118]

The most pleasing career, however, was that of the Rev. Mr. Molineux and his descendants. Though not Irish, he might as well have been, for he and his descendants mined the formerly-Catholic among the Montserrat Irish with the touch of the born diamond merchant. The cleric himself married into the "Irish" family ("Irish" was both their name and their ethnicity), the tenth-largest sugar estate in 1729, who themselves were intermarried with the Wykes (of English origin and the largest estate holder on the island). In the next generation, the rector's second son, John, after having been educated at Trinity College, Oxford, married the daughter of Edward Buncombe (who, before his death in 1712, was one of the largest slave holders and the former speaker of the council). On the mother's side, the new Mrs Molineux was from landed people as well (the Sayers, medium-sized planters) and, more importantly, tied into the Trant connection. This John Molineux, in 1729, was the chief judge of Montserrat and the fifteenth largest sugar planter on the island. Meanwhile, his elder brother, Charles, also educated at Trinity College, Oxford, married a fortune on St Christopher. The result was that in the next generation (the third, counting the founding rector), one of the Molineux held plantations on St Christopher, married an English heiress, and was an MP in the London parliament for King's Lynn; another was speaker of Montserrat and a huge estate holder; and a third was also a large Montserrat planter, marrying into the Daly family, another group of formerly Catholic Irish. A more telling indication of the family's success, however, came when the MP for

King's Lynn mentioned above made his will. This he did in October 1791 (he died a year later). He passed on his estate, "Garboldisham Hall," Norfolk, in the usual manner, through primogeniture. But the seal of worldly success was that he was able to leave a bequest to the rector of Garboldisham, the advowson of which he undoubtedly owned. He had appointed this man and now rewarded him: for his faithful service, he left the rector all his firearms and wines. This was the Rev. Charles Sheard Molineux, "my natural son."[119]

5 The Long Wind-Down: After 1730

"The moral atmosphere of the British West Indies, in the first thirty years after the sugar cane was introduced was that of a gold-rush; the atmosphere of the next generation after that was that of a gold-rush when the gold is beginning to give out."[1] That syncline was reached later at Montserrat than on other islands. Roughly, 1730 is when the long downhill run began, not too quickly at first, barely noticeably, and then more swiftly and finally, as slave emancipation approached, a full, rude dash for the ports. Sugar production reached a high point on the island in 1735, and fluctuated thereafter, but in a downward direction. The years 1753 and 1761 and 1772 were excellent, but the trend line moved ever downward and on the eve of emancipation, output was less than one-third of what it had been a century earlier.[2]

Sugar production was a big casino. The investment in slaves was immense, much greater than in land or machinery. Montserrat in the mid-eighteenth century had approximately 250 slaves per square mile which, considering that two-thirds of the island was not suitable for sugar production, meant that the density per sugar acre was extremely high. To take the 1780s as an example, new slaves from Africa, untrained, cost about £70 in local currency for males and slightly less for females.[3] It was a huge gamble: high capital costs, wildly shifting annual production (due to weather, mostly), rapidly moving world prices – a recipe for debt and then bankruptcy. Montserrat planters took to laying off some of this risk by growing cotton. In 1789, it was estimated that about 6,000 acres were given over to growing sugar cane and 2,000 to cotton.[4] This was unusual – only the Virgin Islands at this time also exported cotton in quantity – and undoubtedly helped to keep many plantations afloat.

I have suggested that the white population was at its height in 1665, just before the French war that resulted in the pillaging of the island and the jacquerie of 1667. The decline of the white population, which had been so obvious from 1678 to 1729, continued unevenly for the remainder of the eighteenth century. This decline, which was documented in the censuses of 1678 and 1729, abated during the middle years of the century and then, near century's end, the white population tumbled.[5]

1729	1,155
1745	1,117
1756	1,430
1775	1,314
1788	880
1810–11	444

Against this one must balance the slave population and, in the last quarter of the eighteenth century, the emerging group of freed former slaves:[6]

	Slaves	*"Free Coloured"*
1729	6,063	N/A
1745	5,945	N/A
1756	8,853	N/A
1775	9,834	N/A
1788	8,310 (or) 8,285	260 (est)
1810–11	6,910	250 (est)

Behind these numbers were two social facts. The first of these is that the whites were, in their own view, dangerously thin on the ground. There was no equivalent on Montserrat of the poor white class that developed, for example, on Barbados. The Montserrat whites no longer did field work or manual labour, save for skilled (and expensive) artisans. Acting as an overseer of slave labourers was as close to field labour as they came.[7] But if the whites on Montserrat can be considered by mid-eighteenth century to have constituted a single ruling class (with caste divisions within that class), there existed a serious problem. The majority of white men – the people expected to perform all the civil functions – still were Irish Catholics. Thus, a House of Commons inquiry of 1788 revealed that there were on Montserrat only 290 adult white males.[8] Given that at least half were Catholics (see chapter 4), this meant that there were no more than 140–50 men for the management of the island's assembly, council, and law courts. And, assuming normal age profiles (some of the white males were doddering old men or otherwise incapacitated) and educational levels (not all white men could read and write), it becomes clear that the pool was very shallow indeed. Probably no more than 100 white men were available to run an island that had contained 100 times that number of blacks. Fear must have been the order of their day.

And well it should have been. Slave rebellions were in the air in the eighteenth century. Plans for a slave revolt were detected on St Christopher in 1725.[9] In Antigua in 1728, there occurred a rising that seems to have been the model for a later planned rising on Montserrat. In this case, the Antigua slaves planned a rising on the day of the king's birthday ball. The leading planters would have been in one building and they were to be locked inside and the building blown up. The plot was discovered and slave leaders were dealt with: three were burned alive, one hanged, drawn and quartered, and one transported to the "Spanish coast" and abandoned there. The governor of the Leeward Islands at the time, the first earl of Londonderry, reflected on these punishments and concluded that "considering the nature of the offence, [they] have been treated with much temper and moderation."[10]

The planned tactics of the Antiguan effort were replicated in tactics mooted on Montserrat in 1768. In that year, a black woman, who had heard two of the slave leaders arguing about a rising, told her master and the rebellion was prevented. The slaves had intended to use a St Patrick's Day soirée at Government House in Plymouth as the moment of opportunity. The domestic slaves who worked within Government House were to seize the weapons of the white men (swords, mostly, and probably a few fire arms), and then those outside were to have burned the building, with the slave owners inside.[11]

The context of this failed slave rising is not quite as transparent as later commentators have believed. Note the one group of slaveholders certain to be there: the Irish.[12] This bears comment because in the twentieth century another invented "tradition" has arisen: that the Irish were much kinder to their slaves than were the British.[13] If they were, then why were the slaves planning to toast them to a cinder? Third, involved in the conspiracy were not merely slaves, but "Mulattoes" and freed slaves. In any event, the aborted rising ended with a series of executions.[14] Fear of rebellion remained pervasive among the Leeward Island planters.[15]

Just how thin the white ruling class was is indicated by the fact that between 1728 and 1798 the legislature of the Leeward Islands did not meet.[16] On Montserrat itself, from the 1730s onwards, there was a constant shortage of whites to run local civic institutions. In

1734, a new governor of the Leeward Islands arrived with instructions from London as to whom to appoint to fill the Council of Montserrat. Of the four names given to him, he found that two were dead, one was returned to England with no intention of ever again setting foot on Montserrat, and the fourth "must be a misteake, there being no such person."[17] Two years later, the death of one council member and the absence of another, meant that even if every councillor attended, a quorum was impossible.[18]

The man mentioned in 1734 as being absent was Nathaniel Webb. He was a major merchant, planter, and collector of customs locally, and he served as MP for Taunton and Ilchester in the London parliament.[19] This raises the issue of absenteeism which, during the eighteenth century, certainly was common throughout the British West Indies. That granted, I question if absenteeism was really the fundamental problem: the white ruling class was numerically thin, and would have been so, even if, say, a dozen or more estate owners had lived on the island, rather than in the home country. The thinness of the white population was not just at the top of the white caste but, more importantly, at the lower end, where absenteeism was not even a possibility: small proprietors and overseers, if they left, went for good; their "estates" were not large enough to support them while abroad. In 1788, the island legislature implicitly recognized the weakness of the lower ranks of white society when it reduced the property qualification for voting for the Montserrat assembly from £10 to forty shillings.[20]

Obviously, the goal of maintaining a white ascendancy on Montserrat clashed with the maintenance of the anti-Catholic penal code: shutting out more than half the island's whites from civic office hardly strengthened the ruling class. In 1792, the first crack in the penal code appeared: Catholics on Montserrat were permitted to sit on juries. Then, in 1798, under the shadow of a full-scale European war impinging on their lives, the Leeward Islands legislature finally met. It passed an act declaring that white Roman Catholics should be freed from all civil disabilities. This was to be contingent upon their taking a form of the oath of allegiance, which most Catholics were willing to take. London disallowed the act.[21] Significantly, the 1798 attempt at "Catholic Emancipation" parallelled efforts in Ireland to provide civil liberties to Roman Catholics. Those efforts came unstuck in 1801 because of the determined opposition of King George III, who viewed such a measure as jacobinical, and its supporters as traitorous.

Therefore, during the eighteenth century, the position of the Catholics on Montserrat (meaning, effectively, Irish Catholics) did not improve in law. However, the second half of the century saw an improvement in informal matters. As mentioned in chapter 4, in February 1749, the Montserrat assembly had voted to deprive Catholics of their one remaining civil right, namely the franchise in local assembly elections. This measure was quashed in 1751, however, by the London authorities. That is one benchmark; the other, roughly fifty years later, is the attempt by the Leeward Islands legislature to grant full civil liberties to Roman Catholics. Clearly, in the half century between those two markers, a sea-change occurred in attitudes toward Irish Catholics.

I think we can see in Catholic religious affairs hints of the same move towards increasing toleration. (One says hints, because no Catholic ecclesiastical records for the island have survived for this period.) Aside from the brief heady days of 1685–88, when the Catholic church was freely tolerated and construction of a chapel was begun, the church on Montserrat operated under penalty. Catholics paid for support of the Anglican church, and had no cleric or chapel of their own. Priests from the French islands sometimes passed through Montserrat, but they did not have governmental approval and, as we saw in the early eighteenth century, were hunted by the local governors, so that they could be expelled.

However, sometime during the eighteenth century – I would suggest the middle of the century as a rough date – the Catholic church on the island came above ground and started providing divine service openly.[22] A Catholic cemetery had been established before 1710 (the exact date is unknown).[23] In 1756, the Vicar Apostolic of London (under whom the Leeward Islands fell) appointed the first parish priest, Father Dominic Lynch. In 1760, he was joined by Father Nicholas Crump and Father Patrick Dalton so, for a time, three Irish priests served the island. They were described by their ecclesiastical superiors as "missionaries" and this certainly must have been the case. The Catholic population of Montserrat in the mid-eighteenth century was virtually unchurched, there having been only fleeting visits from priests for the better part of a century. The missionary priests must have had to teach the people the basics of liturgy, and probably had a large backlog of baptisms and "subsequent marriages" to deal with. By 1777, Montserrat no longer was an emerging mission and a single secular priest, Father Patrick O'Brien, was placed in charge. He remained until his death in 1800 when, inexplicably, the island was left without a priest for the succeeding twenty-four years.[24]

If the Irish Catholics, at mid-eighteenth century, were beginning to put their heads above the hedge, part of it had to do with their reacquiring some powerful patronage. Again, we see only the shadows: but here the point is that the Catholics began to worship openly and did so in a large private residence, "Trescellian House," in Plymouth.[25] This was the property of the Hamilton family, who are memorialized as being devoted to the church, liberal in their gifts, and Irish.[26] Hamilton is hardly an Irish name, but I think local tradition is correct in seeing the family as having been Irish Catholic, although they arrived there by an unusual route. The key, I believe, was the extraordinary Walter Hamilton. Born in Germany of Scottish parents, he had been an adventurer and served on a privateering vessel in the West Indies before meeting and marrying a wealthy widow on the island of Nevis. Hamilton was accused of destabilizing (to use the modern word) the government of the Leeward Islands during a particularly unhappy period in the early eighteenth century, when the governor of the Leeward Islands, Daniel Parke, was murdered on Antigua: his killing by locals was partly on account of his arrogance and partly because of his cracking down on smuggling, which previous governors had tolerated. Eventually Walter Hamilton was cleared of being contumacious and was appointed governor. From 1715–21 he was an effective head of the Leeward Islands. He was a local man (as distinct from a stranger sent by London authorities), and he respected the local rules.[27]

Seemingly that has nothing to do with the Catholic worship on Montserrat. However, the key is that Hamilton married Frances Stapleton, the widow of the third son of Sir William Stapleton. She had large estates in her own right (she was a Russel), and she also inherited the bulk of the Stapleton fortune in the Leeward Islands. Thus Walter Hamilton came to hold considerable estates on Montserrat. Therefore, when this Scottish name, Hamilton, is associated with the Irish Catholics, it is not so strange after all. In the middle and late eighteenth century, we are seeing a son or, and probably, a grandson of Walter Hamilton acting as patron of the Irish Catholics on Montserrat. The money that was behind this generosity was that of the legendary Irishman William Stapleton, carried down now four generations, as had Stapleton's Irish Catholicism. As the writings of Robertson Davies so ably demonstrate, what's bred in the bone, comes out in the wash.

For Irish Catholics (and, one suspects, for almost everyone on Montserrat), probably the happiest year of the eighteenth century stretched from 22 February 1782 to 3 September 1783. During that period, the French occupied the island and installed a royal governor. Unlike previous French invasions of 1667 and 1712, this one involved no pillaging. Nor did the locals, Irish Catholic or others, openly rebel against the English when the French approached. They sat quietly. All that happened was that a French administration replaced the English one. People went about their business. The island legislature still passed its laws, and now a French royal governor approved them. When the locals wanted something special, they petitioned Louis XVI, instead of George III. The big change was that the Montserrat planters now were able to trade directly with French and Spanish merchants and with most of North America (which, during the period immediately after the American Revolution, had been off limits). So, the French conquest was a thoroughly good thing all around. Interestingly, the local legislature did not make any move to change the legal position of the Roman Catholics, although, undoubtedly, their religious practice was much less circumscribed under French Catholic rule than under an English Protestant administration. This brief idyll came to an end without bloodshed or destruction of property, through a peace treaty that followed George Brydges Rodney's epochal naval victory over Comte de Grasse in April 1783. Thereafter, Montserrat returned to dull and declining normal.[28]

For Montserrat, "emancipation" had two meanings: Catholic emancipation and the emancipation of the slaves – the same word, but very different implications. For the Irish Catholics, emancipation meant the restoration of their full civil liberties, and especially (as in the context of the Catholic emancipation in the British Isles), the right to sit in all legislative bodies. Thus occurred the great Daniel O'Connell's campaign, victorious in 1828–29, for Catholic emancipation in the homeland. Emancipation for the African-descended slaves was a bigger matter, meaning nothing less than recognition that they were full human beings, to whom inhered that most central of civil liberties, the right to ownership of one's own person. Still, Catholic emancipation and the emancipation of the slaves had something in common: each was the product of a vague, impossible-to-define, but undeniable gentling of the society of the British Isles. Ideas of what it was permissible to do to another member of the human species were sharply different in, say, 1830, than they had been in 1630. Montserrat changed because the culture to which it remained umbilically attached, that of the British Isles, forced it to change.

Expediency placed its part. On Montserrat, the practical effects of Catholic disabilities were clear to anyone engaged in civil affairs. The total white population in 1811 was 444 and only 154 of these were males above age sixteen.[29] Since more than half of these adult males were Irish Catholics, and thus disbarred from service, it is no wonder that the governor of the Leeward Islands wrote to London stating that "the present state of the decreased and decreasing, white population of this Island no longer furnishes a sufficient choice of men to fill the Legislature, the Law Offices, Juries, Militia, or any other public department."[30] The governor complained that in one parish (he obviously meant St Patrick's parish) which was supposed to send two representatives to Montserrat's legislative assembly, there were only six white males of legal age.[31]

There were only two ways out of this quandary: admit Catholics to full civil rights, and/or admit the free coloureds. The former path was the slightly less repugnant of the two in the opinion of most local planters. Catholics always had served in the militia and in 1792 they had been admitted to jury service. But the Protestants of Montserrat seem not to have shared the conviction of the Leeward Islands legislature, which had in 1798 unsuccessfully pushed for Catholic emancipation. (It did grant Catholics the right to vote in elections for the feeble Leeward Islands assembly, which had not met between 1728 and 1798, but for Montserrat, where Catholics had kept the vote for their own assembly, this gain was valueless.) And, equally, the tiny local Protestant band that controlled the government was loath to grant any civil rights to the free coloureds. In 1813, a general election for the general assembly of Montserrat was held (the first time one had been held in twenty-nine years!) and those free coloureds who possessed the property qualification tried to vote. They got so far as to have their votes recorded, but the island assembly refused to accept the votes. The free-coloured again tried to vote in 1820, and again were refused.[32] The closest the island's tiny ruling caste came to facing their basic problem was in 1822, when all white men and all free men of colour were permitted to serve as police officers.[33] Since this was the least attractive job in the island's government, it was not much of a concession to reality. In 1827, the legal system was in such tatters that it was necessary to fine jurors £5 in local currency for non-attendance at trials, and to reduce the number of jury challenges from twenty-three to twelve in contested cases, so shallow was the pool of potential jurors.[34]

Crumbling though local Montserrat white government was, it could not move. Only through external pressures did reform occur. The first external intervention was a major one: in 1807, the parliament of the United Kingdom of Great Britain and Ireland made the slave trade illegal within the empire. Effectively, this meant that no new slaves could be introduced legally into the system from Africa.

A decline in the number of slaves on Montserrat had begun even before this legislation, probably as early as the period of the French-English wars of the 1790s. The slave population and the white population, therefore, were declining simultaneously, but not in concert. The slave numbers dropped as follows:[35]

1775	9,834
1788	8,310 (or) 8,285
1810–11	6,910
1813	6,010
1817	6,340
1820	6,124
1823	5,835
1833	6,218

The entire system was characterized by intimations of entropy.

Significantly, the Irish slave holders stuck with the system right to the end. In fact, in the fifty years before emancipation (that is, roughly, the last two decades of the eighteenth century and the first three of the nineteenth), the Irish became, increasingly and unmistakeably, the dominant economic group on Montserrat and the big slave owners. In 1824, for example, nearly half of the slaves on the island belonged to nine owners; the largest of these (with 656 African slaves) was Queely Shiell, an Irish Catholic whose family had purchased property on Montserrat sometime after the 1729 enumeration. The sixth largest planter (with 286 slaves) was Henry Hamilton, of the Hamilton family, who were the patrons of the local Irish Catholic community. The seventh largest slaveholder was the joint venture of Clement and Matthew Kirwan (213 slaves). Clement Kirwan also held 71 slaves on his own account, making a family total of 284.[36]

Further to the point, if one recognizes that there were other Catholic families which, though not having an Irish name, were probably Irish on the distaff side, the picture becomes even more striking. That is, the third largest slave owner, Dudley Semper[37] (with 403 slaves) was known to have had his slaves baptized Catholic in 1824–28. And the Furlonge estate (the fifth largest, with 330 slaves) was the former Lee estate; the Furlonges were Catholics and their name is both a common name in England and a not-unusual Old English surname in Ireland. In 1920 their estate was left to the Catholic church. Thus, approximately one-third of the slaves on Montserrat in 1824 were owned by five Catholic families.[38]

If one examines the last enumeration of slaves before slave emancipation, and does so according to parish, the results are illuminating: the places where the ratio of slaves to owners was highest were the two parishes, St George's and St Patrick's, where Irish persons, and especially Irish Catholics, were predominant.[39]

Parish	*Ratio of slaves to slave owners*
St Peter's	24.6
St George's	161.9
St Anthony's	25.4
St Patrick's	84.8

So, on this most fundamental matter, nothing had changed during the eighteenth century: the Irish Catholics, though desirous of their own political emancipation, held on to the bitter end, investing heavily in slaves and praying that slave emancipation would not soon come.

In 1817 an act for establishing a registry of slaves was passed by the local legislature. This might be sold to the U.K. authorities as being a step towards amelioration but, if anything, it made the control of slaves more efficient.[40] In 1822, the notorious act of 1693 to restrain the insolence of slaves was repealed. Henceforth slaves accused of crimes were to be tried by the same evidentiary rules as whites and were to have legal counsel appointed for them, the attorney to be paid for out of the public treasury.[41] (One suspects outside pressures of being in play here, but the local documentation is lost.)

The Abolition of Slavery Act, passed in August 1833 by the United Kingdom parliament, set Emancipation Day as 1 August 1834: or, rather, semi-emancipation day. An "apprenticeship system" was to replace it, whereby for four to six years freed slaves were to work for their "former" masters without pay, but in return for food and lodging. If they worked more than forty-five hours a week they were to receive wages. (In the actual course of events, apprenticeship proved unsuccessful, and the date for full emancipation was moved up to 1 August 1838.) The key to this statute was that the acquiescence of the slave owners was purchased through compensation, paid by the United Kingdom exchequer, for their property loss. The Montserrat planters went along with this – they had little choice – and in return for the emancipation of 6,401 slaves, received £103,556 sterling, an average of £16 for every man, woman, and child they had owned.[42] This was below the market price but not very much below, if the probable return on the "apprenticeship" years was factored in. (One says "probable" because the boon to the slave owners depended on local conditions permitting the profitable usage of the "apprentices," and in Montserrat this turns out not to be the case.) Nevertheless, the arrangements permitted the planters to get out with something in their pockets.

By 1840, not only was slavery on Montserrat history, but the Irish were about to become history as well. Before their rapid exit from the island in the 1840s, however, they too had received emancipation in the political sense of the term. In 1826, the Montserrat legislature voted an annual grant of £100 to support a Roman Catholic clergyman and, "as a means of furnishing a convenient place of worship for the accommodation of his flock" – that is, to help the Catholics build a chapel, as they still were worshipping in Trescellian House. This grant was made, according to the Montserrat assembly, "with a conviction that it would be highly illiberal and unchristianlike to deny an adequate provision for such purposes, being aware that the portion of the Inhabitants in this Island professing the Roman Catholic religion is both numerous and respectable."[43] This local act followed British Isles precedents. It resembled the *Regium donum* which, in 1690, had been given to Presbyterian ministers in Ireland, and grants which the Catholic bishops of Ireland had demanded from the Irish government in the 1790s. The Montserrat Catholics took the money, and indeed, accepted it annually in subsequent years even when, for quite long periods, they had no priest. Thus, in 1874, the governor of Montserrat was to suggest that the money stop being paid unless a parish priest were permanently stationed on Montserrat.[44]

Finally, in 1832, the Montserrat legislature passed "An Act for the Relief of his majesty's Roman Catholic Subjects on this island."[45] They were to be allowed to hold all civil offices on the island upon their swearing an oath of allegiance to the monarch of the United Kingdom (William IV at the time of the act's passage). They did not have to repudiate any Catholic doctrines, such as transubstantiation. Essentially they were being given the same civil rights granted to Irish and British Catholics in 1829. One imagines that the governor received strong hints from London that it was time for the local legislature to do this. As in the case of slave emancipation, Catholic emancipation was dictated by outside events.

A seemingly germane question bedevils the religious history of Montserrat. This is well phrased by John C. Messenger: "Without doubt, the most intriguing of the many mysteries of Montserrat history is why, in the course of the last 130 years [meaning, from slave emancipation to the 1970s, the time he was writing], the number of Catholics has become reduced to 1,000, while the Anglican, Methodist and Seventh Day Adventist bodies combined have grown to

10,000 – the number once claimed by the Catholics."[46] It is an interesting question, and a good deal of ingenuity by ethnographers and anthropologists has been put into explaining the phenomenon. However, the situation is intellectually similar to that reputed to have occurred in the court of King Charles II. The monarch liked to pose hard questions to the savants of the Royal Society and one of these was why, when into a brimming fish bowl, a live minnow is introduced, the bowl runneth not over; but when a dead one is placed therein, it overspills. Indeed. The scholars worked out many ingenious explanations – of a non-existent phenomenon. And that is what is occurring here: *in fact, the allegedly historical situation that is being explained never occurred*.

Consider. Begin with the assertion that the Catholic church had 10,000 members at the time of emancipation. If so, it reflects a phenomenon that has to be viewed as excessively miraculous, given that the number of souls so enumerated exceeds the total number of physical bodies on the island by roughly 50 percent. Second, it is reported that "many local historians believe that following emancipation almost the entire slave population were baptized Catholic."[47] There is no record of this mass baptism of all the blacks having happened. What occurred was something different: the slaves belonging to the Sempers (403), the Hamiltons (286), the Kirwans (284), and the Canoniers (a smaller, unknown number) were in the years 1824–28 baptized by the Rev. Fr. O'Hannan.[48] Third, consider the explanation that at slave emancipation most former slaves chose to become Catholic "because most of the landowners belonged to the Established Church"[49] and the blacks had been better treated by Irish Catholic masters. As I have shown, most slaves were held by Catholics in the decades immediately preceding emancipation, not by Anglicans and, as far back as the 1720s, most slaves had been owned by Irish persons, most of whom were Catholic.

Thus, roughly 1,000 of the island's approximately 6,200 slaves were baptized Catholics. Therefore, over the past 150 years, there was no great loss of a previous Catholic faith: it never was there.

But like all legends, this one leads to some interesting, if less romantic, truths. The salient facts about the religious situation on Montserrat in the seventeenth through nineteenth centuries are fourfold. The first is that no denomination was notable either for the standard of its pastoral care or for the fervid allegiance of its flock. If the religious make-up of Montserrat was remarkably stable over time, this was because no one tried very hard to change it. Inertia rules.

Second, the Roman Catholic church was in no way distinguished by the level of religious service it provided for its people, and this judgment holds even when one takes into account the impediments the penal measures of the late seventeenth and early eighteenth centuries implied for the activities of the Catholic priesthood. Starting with the jurisdictional fight between the Irish Jesuits and the French Capuchins in the 1640s[50] (the result of which was that no cleric was sent to the Leeward Islands for a decade), only for relatively short periods of time were there priests resident on the island: the 1630s and 1660s being the major exception. There was thereafter no resident priest on the island until 1756. But even then, the line of succession was weak. From 1800–24 – the time of the run-up to emancipation and the era when Protestant missionaries were working among the slaves of Montserrat – there was no priest at all. Similarly, in the nineteenth century, resident priests were lacking between 1838–41, 1855–60, and 1871–81.[51] There was no Catholic church building on the island until well into the nineteenth century. The government's grant of 1826 was intended to start a church, and perhaps it was built: however, the first building that can be documented is an edifice begun in 1842 and completed in 1852.[52]

Thirdly, the Catholic church showed little interest in the black population. Whereas, in the British Isles, the leading campaigners for slave emancipation were Methodists, Quakers, and Anglicans, the Catholic church stayed away, concentrating its energies on prosecuting its own interests.[53] This was understandable, given the church's disadvantaged position, but had several effects: one of these was that until nearly the very last moment (1824), the Catholic church on Montserrat was for whites only, and whites meant Irish. In contrast, the pro-emancipation activities of some Anglicans, and, especially of the Wesleyan Methodists, became well known to the West Indies slave population. And the Methodists were active in sending missionaries to work among the slave population throughout the West Indies. A Wesleyan Methodist mission was started on Montserrat in 1820, and by 1824, a chapel was built, nearly thirty years ahead of the Catholics. The significant advantage the Methodists possessed was that their polity – unlike the Roman Catholics and the Anglicans – was organized from the bottom up, and was led by lay people. This gave the Wesleyans an immense advantage in the world of the slaves (and, later, of the former slaves), for local congregations could be formed by the initiative of the blacks themselves.[54]

Fourth, when Father O'Hannan baptized the slaves of the leading Catholic plantation owners in the years 1824–28, he was beginning a new practice for the Catholic church, but one that the Anglicans long had endorsed. No one would accuse the clerical representatives of the Established Church on Montserrat of being overly keen about their spiritual duties, but in the one period for which we possess baptismal records, they reveal an interesting pattern. Anglican baptism of slaves was frequent. Undoubtedly, these were favoured slaves, probably household servants, or trusted skilled artisans, but that helps to make the point. Not only were blacks frequently baptized in the state church, but this occurrence was a mark of special favour, and thus becoming a member of the Anglican communion was a step upwards in the status hierarchy of the black community. This contrasts sharply with Catholic practice, which ignored the slaves until 1824 and then enforced mass baptisms which, one suspects, were undergone with more confusion than enthusiasm.[55] Thus, the question of why the Catholic church declined so precipitously after slave emancipation is no question at all. It did not decline. In the early nineteenth century, it had been the church of the majority of the slave owners. It had been a whites-only, Irish-Catholic church, and the true miracle is that it did not disappear entirely when most of the former slave owners sailed away from Montserrat in the 1840s.

In the years 1845–48, John Davy, a medical doctor and Fellow of the Royal Society, resided in the Lesser Antilles and made detailed notes on several of the islands. Of Montserrat, he noted, "Agriculture is very striking and truly melancholy, and the more so, as its wretchedly depressed state appears to be more owing to mismanagement, carelessness, and neglect than to any incidental circumstances."[56] These were not just generalized impressions, for Davy had made statistical observations, in the way so beloved of nineteenth-century observers. "Of the 39 estates belonging to the island … four only are conducted by resident proprietors, eight by lessees, and the remaining 23 by attorneys acting for the absentee owners; and what is more remarkable, as many as twenty-three are, or were in 1847, under the charge of one individual, in his different capacities of owner, lessee, executor, attorney or receiver."[57] The effects on land usage were striking. "Of the whole number of estates twenty are reported as being in ordinary cultivation, ten as in imperfect or semi-cultivation, leaving nine, which it is believed, are abandoned."[58]

Perhaps the white population might have survived slave emancipation and adapted their estates to new forms of agriculture, but the island experienced one of those brutal body blows that have so often occurred in its history: on 8 February 1843, a severe earthquake hit Montserrat, wrecking homes and sugar manufactories. Bankruptcies and distress sales became the order of the 1840s and early fifties. Lady Cole's land in St Anthony's parish, 300 acres, was sold for £20 in back taxes in 1849. In 1852, the prized Tuite estate, now owned by the Shiell family, of 200 productive acres, was sold for £317 in cash and for £1,050 in loans owed to the government.[59]

The white population took to the boats. This was occurring elsewhere in the West Indies, albeit unevenly: Barbados, Antigua, and Trinidad did not experience the same exodus. For a time in the late 1830s and 1840s, the United Kingdom government tried to adjust matters by two special programs to send new migrants to the West Indies. A total of 4,029 white men and women had been sent to the West Indies by the mid 1840s, but the scheme was gravely mismanaged: mortality was high and those who survived either returned home or moved on to mainland North America.[60] The number of whites on Montserrat continually dropped. In the assembly election of 1838, there were only 144 eligible voters, and this despite the fact that Catholics and free coloured with the requisite property qualification now could vote.[61] In 1850, the total population of Montserrat was 7,053, of whom 150 were white.[62]

The government of the island virtually came apart. In 1848, the salaries of Montserrat's public officials were two years in arrears.[63] Given that the total number of persons on the island who were above twenty years of age and able to read was only eighty-five, it was amazing that in the late 1840s the total number of public offices – that is, the members of the two houses of the legislature and those in receipt of official salaries – was seventy-five.[64] The government, not surprisingly, was as bankrupt as was the economic system.

Some progress out of the governmental and economic swamp was made during the 1850s and sixties. In 1861, the size of government was reduced. The bicameral legislature was replaced by a single chamber consisting of four nominated members and four elected. This was changed in 1866, elections having been unsatisfactory, and the entire legislative council was made entirely appointive.[65] Montserrat became a crown colony in 1867. It was part of a confederation of the Leeward Islands (the members of which shifted over the years) until 1940. Basically, the English government, having adjudged that the local population was not capable of self-government, took over the administration.[66]

Sugar cane continued to be grown, but with the abandonment of protective legislation by Sir Robert Peel in 1846, the crop was only marginally profitable, until price rises in the 1860s resulted in Montserrat sugar production recovering to levels of 100 years previously.

Prices and production subsequently crashed near the end of the nineteenth century, never to recover.[67]

In the early 1840s, silkworms were introduced on the former Dwyer's estate, with the hope of establishing a silk industry. This failed.[68] More successful was the initiative of the Sturge family, Quakers from Gloucestershire, who had been active in the anti-slave movement. In 1837, the family purchased an estate on Montserrat, with the intention of operating a sugar works with freed slaves. This venture failed, but the family moved into lime production and this was noticeably successful. Production increased annually and, in 1885, the peak year, the company was growing 1,000 acres of limes and sending 180,000 gallons of lime juice to England.[69] So, slowly, the island worked its way out of the economic morass that had immediately engulfed it after slave emancipation.

It is axiomatic that the life of the former slaves had been improved by emancipation, for freedom is the one intangible that a person can touch. In terms of worldly comforts, however, the question is very much open as to whether or not they were better off before or after emancipation. By 1847, the number of abandoned or semi-abandoned sugar estates had risen to seventeen. Now that the former slaves were waged labour, a truck system (that is, the company-store system) which had recently been prohibited in England, sprang up on Montserrat, and those who worked were continually in debt. Living standards deteriorated. In 1849–50 a smallpox epidemic swept the island, with about a 3 percent mortality rate. This coincided with a drought of nine to ten months, which wiped out most sugar production.[70] The salvation of the black population probably was achieved by their own hands, through non-market incomes. In slave times, the blacks had been granted allotments for growing their own provisions, and now they worked these lands and probably also some of the lands abandoned by former estate owners. Given the steep and uneven topographical character of Montserrat, their farming was all done by hand, with rudimentary hoes. The use of horse or ox-drawn ploughs and harrows was rare, even on the largest estates. Hoes and other hand tools were the real tools, and human beings the draught animals.[71] In the 1970s, an historical geographer collected a living oral tradition that at the time of emancipation slaves were often allowed to continue to use the provision-growing land which their family had customarily cultivated, and this is what is today known as "family land."[72]

This was not largesse on the part of the former slave owners. They were a sour lot, and gave only what they could not withhold. This was well shown in early 1837, when a bill to release the apprentices early (that is, to end slavery entirely), passed Montserrat's council, but lost in the assembly by one vote: some of the assemblymen were proprietors of jobbing gangs that used the apprentices as roving labour squads.[73] If the apprentices were freed, then they would have to be paid for their labour.

That is not surprising: what is more revealing is that thereupon three members of the council and two other large proprietors individually released their apprentices from further servitude. Largesse? No. In the mid-1830s, Montserrat had experienced a vicious hurricane, followed by a severe drought (yet another body blow), and these planters were afraid that they would not have enough work for the apprentices to make it worthwhile giving them their rations.[74] The bill to end apprenticeship was reintroduced in November 1837 and this time it passed, albeit for the worst of reasons, to save money. From 1 August 1838, all forms of slavery were ended.[75] This coincided with empire-wide legislation passed in London.

The Irish connection with Montserrat effectively ended with the termination of slavery. It took a few years for the stragglers to clear off: the only surviving family of the great Irish slaveholders of the eighteenth century to make it into the twentieth under its own name were the Kirwans.[76] Through the distaff side, the Stapletons survived (as Hamiltons) and the Lees (as Furlonges). They remained as withered leaves in a harsh autumn wind.

At heart, the history of the Irish on Montserrat, from the 1630s onward, was a very simple one. They saw; they came; they used; they abused; they discarded; and they levanted.

6 Usable Traditions

These lectures have been directed for the most part toward depicting, in a laboratory setting, the social and cultural physiology of one portion of the great Irish diaspora. However, there may be points of interest to historians of the West Indies in particular, and to historians of the first English empire in general.

I hope it has been clearly implied that the concept of ethnicity – in the broad sense of national origin and cultural self-awareness – is necessary if the actions of the colonists in the first English empire are to make much sense to the historian. This point hardly bears mentioning to historians of the North American continent for, by 1700, representatives of several European cultural groups were strong and, often, strident. In the case of the West Indies, however, one notices an historical tendency to lump all white people together or, if they are distinguished, to do so either by stereotype or by socio-economic class. Granted, the West Indies' white population was overwhelmingly Anglo-Celtic in origin, but the constituent elements – Irish, English, Welsh, Scots – frequently acted differently and for reasons that were directly derivative from their cultural antecedents. The Montserrat Law of 1668 that forbade the inhabitants to call each other "English Dog, Scottish Dog, Tory, Irish Dog, Cavalier, and Roundhead, and many other opprobrious, scandalous, and Disgraceful Terms" is a reminder of that fact.[1]

What I suspect historians of the western hemisphere are less apt to take on board is this study's implication that during the seventeenth century one cannot use the concept of "the Irish" unless it is very clearly contextualized. They were not a single bunch. They came from a very complex cultural situation. Historians of seventeenth-century Ireland have found it necessary to distinguish four groups, three of which are important in the West Indies. These are the "native Irish," the "Old English," the "New English," and (a group important in North America) the Ulster-Scots. These groups held radically differing social, religious, and cultural views, and they cannot be lumped together, although at some moments they did, indeed, act as "the Irish." As was shown in this study, usually they acted quite distinctly (although not entirely differently) in their new colonial world. On Montserrat, by the early eighteenth century, the three Irish categories had lost their distinguishing power, and were replaced by the simple Protestant-Catholic distinction. But before then, these secondary signifiers are absolutely necessary. The worst thing one can do is to employ "the Irish" as some kind of racial cog in the machinery, characterizing them as a riotous, unruly, and contumacious lot, as if this was a universal characteristic and one which derived from Irishness. This kind of ethnic explanation unfortunately almost always becomes racist, unintentional though this usually is on the part of those who employ it. As the Montserrat laboratory showed, there were Irish who were rabblement, some who were members of the elite, and everything in between. "The Irish," in the general sense as it is often used by historians of the West Indies in the seventeenth century, did not exist.

That point is central. Less important are two other suggestions that derive from our examination of Montserrat. The first is that historians of the British West Indies might do well to revisit in detail the entire question of the relationship of white indentured labour and black slave labour. The relationship is too easily made the subject of a quick epigram, and then left unexamined. Montserrat may be an unusual case (but, unlike all the other islands, it is well documented by censuses), yet it at least raises the possibility that there is *no* direct relationship between white indentured labour and black slave labour. On Montserrat, black slave labour did not replace white indentured labour. If it replaced anything, African slave labour replaced free white labour and small proprietorships, but even then not by economic *force majeure*. The small proprietors and other free labourers left well before sugar plantations ingested all the usable land, and they left while there still was an acute labour shortage. They left, one infers, by economic and social choice and, probably, they cleared out with resources in hand, to prospect for their fortunes in other corners of the expanding New World.

The second matter that historians of the first English Empire may wish to re-examine is the issue of indentured labour. The topic has a large literature, and undeniably is very important. What needs reassessing, however, is the unexamined implication that, because indentured labour was important, it was dominant. Simple arithmetic would lead one to question whether on any of the islands of the British West Indies indentured labourers were the main form of labour (even the main form of white labour) for more than half a decade or so, in each case. It requires some quite supple gymnastics to present a set of assumptions concerning in-migration, out-migration, birth rates, death rates, and length of servitude that permit one to deduce that on any island most of the white labour force was held in bondage for as long as a decade. And such gymnastics trip on awkward matters of evidence.

In terms of the history of Ireland and of the Irish diaspora, these lectures have had a single primary purpose: to call into question something that is not a doctrine, but which is an assumption that has run through most historical writing about Ireland during the twentieth century: this is the assumption of Irish exceptionalism. This is seen most clearly in the Irish nationalist writings of the early twentieth century (one thinks of Eoin MacNeill and of Alice Stopford Green) and now, near century's end, of the vigorous "anti-revisionist" writings of those who believe that Irish history works differently from that of all the rest of the world. Of course, Ireland is an exceptional country (why else would one give one's life to studying it?), but it is not an exception to the patterns that have dominated western Europe since the end of the middle ages. Yet, with very rare exceptions, even the most rigorous historians of Ireland have refused to put the nation's history in international and comparative context; instead, it is studied in isolation, and therefore an unconscious acceptance of the attitude of Irish exceptionalism occurs – and frequently on the part of scholars who would be horrified to adopt the posture if it were consciously defined. Another way of stating the same mind-set is to suggest that it comprises a form of Irish essentialism: the belief that the Irish are essentially different from the rest of the European peoples, not in minor surface matters, but in their deep inner essence, a view that borders on racialism.

The point where the assumptions of Irish exceptionalism and Irish essentialism, conscious or unconscious, move from being an historical flaw to being a progenitor of moral amnesia is when imperialism enters the story. It is historically undeniable that throughout the last millennium the island of Ireland has experienced several forms of imperialism, none of them great blessings. The form which began in roughly the 1580s and continued throughout most of the seventeenth century involved several unconnected physical invasions of parts of Ireland by English and Scottish settlers, and, accompanying it, cultural anglicization, especially among the ruling classes and among those living in the penumbra of the seacoast towns. It was this imperialism that served as the background to Ireland's tiny empire in the West Indies, Montserrat. From the invaders, many Irish men and women learned how imperialists behaved. They acquired the English language, and they became part of the exponentially expanding web of knowledge (and thus, of opportunity) that linked the New World and the Irish ports, such as Kinsale. So, they were imperialized quickly and became expert imperialists themselves. This would not be a matter of note, save that the Irish have so rarely noticed it about themselves. The moral amnesia that runs through Irish historiography at home and abroad is a one-way system, when two-way is required. Seeing oneself as being imperialized should not blind one to also seeing oneself as an imperialist. The impact of the Irish as participants in the expansion of major empires – most notably, but not solely, those of the United Kingdom and of the United States of America in the nineteenth and twentieth centuries – is a phenomenon that is only beginning to be addressed directly,[2] and resistance to an assimilation of this historical reality is inevitable.

Montserrat, of course, is not "typical" of anything (no local history ever is), nor is its society presented as a representative random sample of a more general population. What it is for historians is the equivalent of the unusual environment of a physiology laboratory where, in artificial isolation, a section of tissue can be observed exhibiting certain physiological processes that are potentially ubiquitous in larger, uncontrolled experiments, but not directly observable. The admirable thing about a tight and early local observation point, such as Montserrat provides, is that it prevents those bent on denial through theoretical or abstract arguments from hiding from reality. Real human lives intervene. Thousands of African slaves on Montserrat (and, if one includes the British West Indies and American colonies), hundreds of thousands elsewhere, were during the course of the seventeenth, eighteenth, and part of the nineteenth centuries owned by Irish slaveholders, and still others experienced the fierceness of an Irish overseer. To focus again on Montserrat: Oliver Cromwell at his bloodiest did not indulge in the sadistic methods of torture through which we saw errant slaves being put to death for crimes as minor as stealing an item worth a single shilling.

None of this is pleasant to record. But if the self-replicating cycle of abuser-abused-abuser-abused is to be broken, the Irish polity, through the historians who are the keepers of its collective memory, must cease to view the emigrants from Ireland as forever-passive victims, and therefore as persons who were incapable of hard dealing. One of the fundamental stories of the Irish diaspora is of Irish emigrants choosing to do unto others what others had already done unto them. In neither case was that a matter of kind and tender mercies.

To take today's perspective, where did the intersection of the Irish imperialists and the African slaves leave the people of Montserrat? The answer is, adrift, in a rural backwater that is pleasant, clean, well-maintained and frequently charming, but a backwater nonetheless. The African-descended people of today's Montserrat are completely detribalized, having lost their African languages and all save the tiniest remnants of their own religions. How could it be otherwise? A primary method of the slave system was to dehumanize its victims and on Montserrat it succeeded terrifyingly.

Montserrat today is a crown colony of the United Kingdom, one of the few shards left of the English Empire. The island is heavily dependent upon the U.K. treasury for subventions. As of the 1970s, the island imported seventeen times more than it exported. At that time the agricultural sector produced less than 16 percent of the gross domestic product and the governmental bureaucracy 20 percent.[3] Enthusiasm for independence waxes and wanes. Spiritually, it sounds a good thing; economically, it would turn a poor islander poorer. During the 1950s and 60s, the British overcame much of the heavy loss entailed in running Montserrat by permitting the islanders to migrate (either seasonally or permanently) to the U.K. Montserrat had proportionately the highest rate of out-migration of any Caribbean territory during that period, and large amounts of remittances were sent back to relatives and friends on the island: a high of £616,800 in 1960.[4] However, when, in the 1960s, the U.K. introduced a policy of reducing to a trickle the number of non-white migrants from its former empire, Montserrat suffered greatly. The working class on the island, which had become dependent upon remittances, lapsed into chronic unemployment and poverty.[5] Thereafter, islanders had to go – often illegally – to other islands, or try to sneak into Canada or the United States. The official size of the population on the island in 1990 was 11,900 but, with various forms of temporary out-migration, mostly illegal, the actual population was suspected to be closer to 9,000.[6] This population is virtually entirely non-white: there are between fifty and 100 white residents, all of whom are expatriates from elsewhere.

At present, there is a struggle to create traditions that, while probably inaccurate in the strict historical sense, can be believed in, and can be passed on from one generation to the next, with the claim that they came from the far past. This is not a straightforward business, and the players are not all islanders. One vector comes from outside scholars, whose antecedents run back to the Jesuit historian of the 1920s and 1930s, the Rev. Aubrey Gwynn. Most notable in the present day is the American anthropologist John C. Messenger, a great enthusiast and promoter of the island: he has jocularly suggested in a letter to the editor of the local newspaper that the government strike a medal to him and his wife for economic service rendered.[7] Messenger is the proponent of a viewpoint that can best be labelled "Hibernicist." Basically, this view is that, although the Irish on the island had almost totally disappeared by 1850, the culture of the African-descended islanders was permanently etched with certain characteristics believed to be Irish in origin. Therefore, the history of Irish imperialism on the island is directly assimilable to the history of the population derived from former African slaves.

Messenger suggests that there are twelve residual effects from the former Irish domination of Montserrat.[8] These are (1) ubiquitous place names; (2) frequent Irish-derived family names; (3) language inheritance; (4) oral art, as in story-telling; (5) musical styles; (6) dance styles; (7) pieces of ancient mythology; (8) codes of etiquette and hospitality; (9) illegal distilling and drinking; (10) specific foods; (11) motor pattern and, perhaps (12) systems of values.

These can each be examined. Some of them certainly exist and some are problematic. The questions with those that do exist are, first, how important are they? and, secondly, how distinctively Irish are they? That is, some of the patterns may be of so little consequence as to be epiphenomenal and others may have been introduced by the Irish, but are not unequivocally Irish customs.

As for the first item on the list, there is no doubt that Montserrat is notable for its Irish-derived place names. Secondly, the prevalence of Irish surnames on the island is remarkable. Brian McGinn recently counted the ten most frequent names in the Montserrat phone book, and of these, seven undoubtedly are Irish (Ryan, Lee, Daley, Meade, Tuit, Fenton, and Farrell), two easily could be (Allen and White), leaving only Greenaway as an unambiguously English surname.[9] This occurs in a population that is almost totally non-white. Unlike many other black communities, neo-African or neo-Muslim names have not been introduced to shove aside the "slave names." The bulk of these names probably stem from the time of emancipation and the heavy loading towards Irish names is explained by the pattern we saw among the eighteenth- and early nineteenth-century slave owners: in the later days of slavery the Irish, and especially the Irish Catholic, slaveholders grew in power and became the dominant slave owners on the island. Hence the dominance of Irish names. Manifestly, both the frequency of Irish surnames and the ubiquity of Irish place names must have some influence in shaping the local sense of history, particularly as these matters are frequently called to the attention of outsiders – especially tourists who are told of the island's "Irish heritage."

Third, the jury still is out on the impact of the Irish settlers upon the linguistic character of the present-day Montserratian. The only professional linguist to test Messenger's assertion that an Irish accent and Irish speech patterns exist within the form of the English language spoken on Montserrat, or within the Creole of Montserrat, has arrived at strongly negative conclusions. This linguist, J.C. Wells, of University College, London, undertook a direct investigation of this Irish-brogue theory, and conducted field investigation on Montserrat and also collected data from Montserratians who lived in England. He came to the conclusion that most of the items that visitors attribute to Irish influence were shared with Caribbean English Creoles throughout the region and these are not especially Irish in origin. The accent system of Montserrat Creole and of standard English as spoken on the island was found to be mostly English, with elements of American and Scottish influence, but not of Irish. The phonological characteristics of Montserrat English and Creole developed independently of Irish, Wells concluded. With the exception of only a single word, *minnseach* (meaning female goat), there was no Gaelic language input into Montserrat Creole, and no morphological or syntactic influence whatsoever.[10]

The reason this still is an open issue is that if Montserrat's present population is not influenced by the island's three centuries of occupation by a dominant language group, then we are dealing with one of the most unusual cases of cultural resistance ever seen in the New World. Wells' claim of the total non-influence of the Irish on language is hard to square with reports of the members of the black population speaking Gaelic in the eighteenth and nineteenth centuries (see chapter 5, note 25). The matter requires further investigation. But that should perhaps be conducted within a larger linguistic context. The real effect of the Irish colonists upon the language of the slaves and of their descendants was that the Irish (along with the English planters) severed the African slaves from their African languages and replaced them with English. The Irish may have spoken some Gaelic, but the lingua franca of the island (and of the British West Indies in general) was English. So, the slave owners, having taught English to Montserratians, have largely determined the cultural world that the Montserratians today inhabit. They are tied to England, Canada, and the United States, not to Haiti, or to Cuba, places that though physically close are culturally far away indeed and, because of linguistic barriers, almost unapproachable.

Fourth, one has to be sceptical of claims that the Irish influenced greatly the oral art of the African-descended Montserratians. That there have been *senachaí* in Ireland in this century and storytellers on Montserrat is no great link: it would be hard to find a rural society that has not had its storytellers. The significant point is that the major collection of Montserratian folklore, collected during the 1930s, shows no indication whatsoever of Irish motifs. It employs the motifs of black culture and is entirely in the genres of folk story characteristic of African-derived cultures in the Caribbean and the southern United States.[11]

The fifth matter, musical styles, is unclear. One is not surprised to find that Messenger collected from an old woman the song "If I were a Blackbird." She had learned it from her grandmother. One is also not surprised by the observation of Howard Fergus, the island's main local historian, who replies, concerning Messenger: "He observes that Irish songs and airs are still heard, but this writer finds none except the Irish and Scottish airs which every English colonial schoolboy learnt in the twentieth century."[12] Messenger is on much more solid ground when he points to the structurally unique characteristics of the Irish drum, the *bodhran* (a flat instrument that employs the back of the hand for drumming), and the local drums, the jumbie drum and the *babala*.

Whether or not the Irish influenced the dance styles of Montserrat in any unique way, or merely passed on the common dance patterns of the British Isles, is uncertain. (Indeed, whether there was a distinct Irish dance tradition until the invention of Irish "traditional" dancing in the early twentieth century is still an open question.) "Set dancing," reels, quadrilles and the like, which also formed the basis (for example) of American square dancing, were common throughout the British Isles and would have been a standard at planters' galas, no matter what the national background. The only truly distinctive dance on Montserrat is (or was) the jombee dance. This was a form of ritual trance-dancing. It has been thoroughly studied and it shows no Irish provenance, but rather, generalized African origins.[13]

As for pieces of ancient mythology, Messenger points to a single instance, but it is compelling. Although there are no references to the classic Irish sagas or to the great mythic heroes, there is the "Chance Pond mermaid." She is said to be a white-skinned maiden who resides in a shallow lake at Chance's Peak. She has as her companion a diamond snake. And she has a pot of gold and a magic comb. If someone can steal the magic comb and make it to the sea without being caught by the diamond snake, the mermaid's buried pot of gold belongs to the adventurer.[14] These are fascinating elements. The mermaid is a fairly common figure in pre-Christian and early Christian tales. And the pot of gold is associated in Irish folklore not with a rainbow, but with a leprechaun who has to be snuck up on, caught, and then held. Usually, the creature tricks the adventurer who has caught him, and the gold is lost. (Never mind that the pot-of-gold and leprechaun have been horribly mutilated by the Walt Disney animators, and their like; the folk tales are very old, and have pre-Christian elements, particularly in the leprechaun or other-world creature, who is something to fear, as is the mermaid and her snake.) Messenger is convincing, therefore, in seeing this as an instance of the working out of very old Irish mythological elements in a West Indian environment.

The practice of keeping the coffee pot brewing and thus of hospitality to visitors, the practice of illegal brewing, and the cooking of goat stew are also said to be Irish. How one distinguishes those traits from general human ones (hospitality and illegal brewing are not exactly Irish in origin) is hard to say, and as for the island's famous goat stew recipe, a good case has been made that it can equally be interpreted as of Yoruba origin.[15] (This, however, leaves aside the fact that few Yoruba could have gone to Montserrat.)

And, it is suggested that the bodily postures, the motor habits, of the Montserratians are Irish-derived. In 1965, Messenger showed some of his slides of Montserrat islanders to some Dublin scholars. One of these said that the photographer might have been on the farms of Galway at the close of a dry summer day. According to Messenger, distinctly Irish motor habits are revealed in the films he took of several of the "black Irish." Perhaps: but if so, it will require documentation by another ethnographer, for Messenger found that "a detailed description of these and other cultural imponderables and of Irish phenotypic traits would require too much space."[16] Until someone actually tests these assertions by turning them into the form of disprovable hypotheses, a more realistic suggestion would be that, yes, tired old farmers look and move the same way, the world around.

As for the Irish influence on Montserratian value systems, Messenger suggests the possibility – he is careful to label it as only a possibility – that Montserratians are governed more by conscience than by external sanctions; that they are more receptive to Christian teaching than are other West Indians; and that they more frequently result to "blarney." This may be the case, but it certainly has not been demonstrated by any research. And why these would be "Irish" traits has not been specified. One remains sceptical.

If only a few of the alleged Irish influences posited by John Messenger have any demonstrable proof behind them, does this mean that his work is to be disregarded? Absolutely not. In fact, it is quite important. What Messenger is engaged in, however unintentionally, is the creation of historical traditions where none really exist. This is not a vicious or a mendacious activity but, indeed, is fundamental to holding any society together. This is especially important on a place such as Montserrat where, until recently, a strong negative attitude toward the past prevailed. Further, the local folk memory has been very limited and, in the case of the members of one village that was studied for nearly a year during the 1950s, had shrunk down to a period of thirty to forty years.[17] If ever there was a place that needed the invention of a robust historical tradition, it is Montserrat, and Messenger's Hibernicist vision is a valuable gift from outside, like the crashing of an overloaded cargo airplane on a remote island mountain top.

Europeans have always been good at inventing traditions. Witness: the invention of the Scottish tartan as an allegedly ancient form of clan identification; the introduction of the Red Dragon as an "ancient" symbol of Wales in 1807; the multiplication of rituals during the nineteenth and twentieth centuries that involved the English monarchy in ever-more baroque displays. Each new practice claimed to be from time immemorial, and most had no provenance farther back than the bright idea of some politician or functionary in the planning stages of an upcoming royal event.[18] An entire industry in "eighteenth-century" crystal that memorialized King William of Orange, or the Jacobites, or the Irish Volunteers, was founded in the early twentieth century and has, until recently, been taken as yielding enduring and treasured historical objects.[19] Indeed, it has been argued that the greatest, most wonderful, invented tradition in the British Isles was – Great Britain. Linda Colley has brilliantly argued that, at a level of national and of patriotic culture, Britishness was an invention of the period 1707–1837.[20] At a demotic and popular level, however, it has been pointed out that this union was much slower in coming, and the least keen upon being "British" were the English. Brian Deer has put it truculently, but well: "England was simply not big enough to satisfy new mass-production industries. The empire needed armies and administrators to sustain overseas profits. So the nation needed expansion – and the concept of 'being British' was born."[21] It was a long gestation, he suggests, and not until the 1940s, with the confluence of a war, of nationalized industries, and of a national health service, were the British peoples turned from an uneasy alliance into a unitary nation.[22] At its best, the Hibernicist invention has the potential of doing for Montserrat what the various invented traditions did for Great Britain: hold the people together until they find themselves and their own history.

The Hibernicist creation has special attraction to the black entrepreneurial class, which sees tourism as a major source of revenue. Playing up the Irish theme is worth money. From 1903–51, and again in 1982, a harp and Irish female harpist were found on the island postage stamps. The island's flag has a crest with the female harpist on it and a shamrock sits on the gable of Government House. The passport stamps bear Irish iconography, and government-financed tourist publications all are sure to include the Irish heritage aspect.[23]

The Hibernicist invention has also been useful to the Roman Catholic church. Given that this polity (in contrast, say, to the Pentecostals) values historical continuity, the imaginary connection of the now-black Catholic church with the then-Irish whites-only church of the seventeenth and eighteenth centuries is understandable. It provides a sense of continuity, a patina of age that is comforting. Further, the belief (shown to be fictitious in chapter 5) that most of the island's slaves were Catholic at the time of emancipation, sets up a past that is taken to be the natural future: the Catholic church should be the church of the island's people. Actually, the Catholic authorities began to serve the black population later than either the Anglicans or the Wesleyans, and during the nineteenth century left long gaps in their pastorates. In the 1860s, there were 500 or 600 black labourers attached to the Catholic church and "some very respectable families" (read: some white families), the priest reported.[24] Even with the local disestablishment of the Church of England in 1868, the Protestants did not lose ground dramatically. In 1922, of a total population of 12,120 (112 whites and 12,008 non-whites), the religious breakdown was as follows:[25]

Church of England	7,899
Roman Catholic	688
Methodist	3,144
Other denominations	389

The Irish tie with the Catholic church was cut in 1902. In that year the last Irish priest was replaced by a Belgian Redemptorist, and that order ran the parish until the early 1970s.[26] So, with the final link to Ireland severed, a convincing synthetic link was needed, if the church's continuity were to be credibly argued.[27]

To those of the Montserratians who went abroad, the Hibernicist tradition provided some comforts. It permitted them to explain easily to people in the British Isles or in North America, who they were: that they were Caribbeans, but that they were different, and that they would fit in better than most. This is shown clearly and engagingly in the reflection of one of Montserrat's most distinguished poets of this century, E.A. Markham. In 1992, after spending three years in Northern Ireland as writer-in-residence at the University of Ulster, he gave a revealing lecture concerning the relationship of Ireland and the Caribbean. Mostly he talked about international relationships between Joyce, Yeats, Synge, and, for example, Derek Walcott. He also discussed "my own personal engagement with all this, this Irishness, the culture emanating from Ireland," which, he said, "derives from the fact that I was, as I said, born in Montserrat." His feeling of selfhood was in part African Caribbean but, manifestly, Irish as well:

> In my own family, the story is that a great, great whatever, uncle worked on a farm of a couple of Irish sisters, as overseer [the sisters were the last of the Hamilton family]. He was, apparently, not paid, and when the sisters decided to sell up and return to Ireland, they gave him part of the estate (and the shop which they ran) in lieu of payment … The shop was called Trescellian House … It survives to this day, a general store, in Parliament St., Plymouth, Montserrat; and is owned by a first cousin of mine, Bertrand Osborne – Osborne being the name of the second governor of the island after Briskett and before Stapleton (names that populate my own fiction).[28]

Thus, the Hibernicist tradition provides a ready-made history that mediates, indeed serves as an analgesic, for African-Caribbeans who must confront Europe (and especially, the Anglo-Celtic world).[29]

In order for the Hibernicist tradition to work among the island population, one piece of sheer invention has to be maintained, namely that the Irish, though slave holders, were nicer than the other ones.[30] And, then, meaning inevitably slurs, and the comparative "nicer" unconsciously slides into the absolute "nice." Possibly the Irish slave owners actually were nicer but, if so, this is one of the few pieces of local historical memory that actually stretches back to even the mid-eighteenth century. The nice-Irish slaveholder idea curiously omits the fact that in 1768, it was a St Patrick's Day celebration that drew the island's only attempted slave rebellion; that in the second half of the eighteenth century, the expanding and successful slave owners were Irish Catholics; and that in the 1830s, the reason the local slaveholders (mostly Irish) ended slave "apprenticeship" early was that a drought was on and they did not want to be responsible for feeding blacks whom they could not work. No: though possible, I think there is no truth in the belief that the Irish were any less brutal or any more so than other slaveholders. And none were nice.

A threefold explanation for this belief in the nice-Irish-slaveholder seems reasonable. First, and most importantly, if the islanders are to embrace an Hibernicist tradition, then the dissonant elements in that myth must be sanded off: and for African-Caribbeans to embrace as a cultural progenitor a standard run-of-the-mill overseer or slave owner is just too much of a contradiction to their sense of integrity. So the Irish have to be made "nicer," if not explicitly nice. Secondly, the "nicening" was made easier by the fact that historically in Plymouth and in hamlets, the small shops, the legal drinking houses, and the shebeens were frequently owned by persons of Irish ancestry, so that in the slave era, the blacks had more frequent "normal" interaction with some Irish than with any other whites.[31] Thirdly, when the last of the descendants of the Irish slaveholders – the Mesdames Kirwan, Hamilton (descended from the Stapletons), and Furlonge (an English name, but also an Old English, Catholic, name common in the south of Ireland) – were coming to the end of their string, they were generous. As noted by E.A. Markham, above, Trescellian House, once the house of worship of the Catholic church, was given by the Hamiltons to a former employee, in lieu of salary owed. And these ladies, along with Mrs Kirwan (of one of the island's long-standing slaveowning families) and her daughter, and Miss Semper (daughter of great early nineteenth-century slave owners) assiduously collected money to rebuild the hurricane-damaged Catholic church in 1900–01.[32] Nice ladies, certainly. Eventually, in 1920, Miss Furlonge left to the Catholic church her family estate (it was the old Lee estate), and this legacy supported four teaching sisters who took charge of the local Catholic elementary school.[33] One can scarcely expect these teaching nuns to thank their benefactresses by describing the ultimate source of the bequest as brutish slave owners. So, for this and other reasons, in Hibernicist tradition, the Irish became "nice" slave owners.

Recently, John Messenger has been vexed by the appearance of a rival to his Hibernicist tradition. This he ascribed to "the influence of Afrocentric West Indian elitists," who are "Afrophiles, verging in some cases on counter-racism."[34] What particularly irritates Messenger was a metonymic event, a part of a larger change in the cultural viewpoint of many Montserratians. In this case, the annual St Patrick's Day celebrations were changed, in 1985, from a one-day religious-based, Irish-theme observance, to a six-day festival. That celebration had increasingly little to do with Ireland's St Patrick and instead became a celebration of African resistance to white domination. It was an apt occasion, for this was the anniversary of the unsuccessful attempt in 1768 of the slaves to incinerate their Irish masters at the annual St Patrick's Day ball.[35] An "Afrocentric bias" was shown in the Government Information Unit's handout:

> So today when we celebrate St Patrick's Day, we think not only of the Irish patron Saint, but more importantly to those first Montserratians – Negro slaves – who fought for the freedom of our people. They faced death to rid themselves of oppression and were brave enough to stand against the forces that sought to break the human spirit and create a society where freedom was for the few.[36]

Six days of the celebration of African resistance, and little about St Patrick, the Briton sold as a slave to the Irish, was an Hibernicist's nightmare. So too was the assertion by the island's leading local historian that "the day as celebrated now is a secular concept, the creation of local students of history blessed with national consciousness and insights into the role of development in history."[37]

Africanist traditions are no less invented than are Hibernicist. The attempt to rename the island of Montserrat, "Alliouagana" meaning either "island of the prickly bush" or "island of the aloe plant" in Carib, is a good example. The name comes not from any tradition or document preserved in African-Caribbean culture, but from the (probably inaccurate) report of a Dominican friar.[38] And, the implied brotherhood between the Carib and the blacks against the whites is hopelessly romantic. The Carib during the seventeenth century raided Montserrat several times, carrying off hundreds of African slaves whom they sold elsewhere. No more than a dozen African words are in modern usage on Montserrat, and these may have come from other islands, and quite recently, rather than from slave times.[39]

Among traditions praised in Africanist creations are the "maroon," which, on Montserrat, meant the coming together of neighbours to help each other in big tasks, such as moving house or harvesting a big crop, or putting up a new home. This is praised as being uniquely communal and "denotes a style of community living alien to the normal run of middle- and upper-class society; it relates to the regular concept of maroon as an assertion of freedom and escape from societal regimentation."[40] That it may be, but it is hardly uniquely and virtuously African: it replicates "cooring" in Ireland and the "bee" in North America, both of which were common from the sixteenth through nineteenth centuries. Similarly, an "African-based communistic practice" of the earlier twentieth century was that an individual who had a lot of cattle frequently had another individual raise a head or two or more of livestock for them and gave half the offspring as payment.[41] This is a practice which, far from being either communistic or singularly African, was practised commonly in virtually every western European country between the sixteenth and nineteenth centuries and was a stage in the development of market agriculture.

One could go on. The Africanist traditions are as creative as the Hibernicist. "These Africans brought with them a history and cultural heritage of moral and spiritual values, aesthetic sense of rhythm and music," one leading politician intoned, and continued breathlessly, "a thrilling art of story-telling, a cuisine, an inner strength of resistance to oppression, a burning desire for freedom, an amazing subtlety of language and communication skills as revealed in their proverbs, riddles and nancy stories, and a profound attachment to and understanding of nature, its curative herbs and its cyclical patterns."[42]

For two reasons, I suspect that the victory of the Africanist tradition over the Hibernicist tradition will take longer on Montserrat than in other, comparable situations. One of these reasons is the simple fact that most islanders have Irish surnames. These were chosen by them at emancipation, for the most part, and were taken not for any love of the Irish, but because at that time Irish slaveowners predominated. Irish place names also were adopted – Dublin, Kinsale, Cork – for the same reason. These surnames are not an indication of any positive relationships – quite the opposite, they indicate a particularly nasty form of human exploitation, slavery – but they are part of the personal identity of the people who bear the names, and are part of the collective history of the culture in which they predominate. Completely washing out the Irish background probably is not possible.

Secondly, there is the matter of the so-called "black Irish." According to both Messenger and Fergus (respectively Hibernicist and Africanist), these are a body of light-skinned individuals – they would have been called "coloured" on the ever-so-sensitive racial scale of apartheid South Africa[43] – who live on the northern part of the island and are (or at least, were, as of the 1960s and 1970s) extremely proud of their putative Irish background. This background, and their phenotype, is said to stem from legal marriages of the eighteenth century.[44] The predominant family names among these "black Irish" are Gibbons, Sweeney, and Allen, and Messenger noted that as of the 1960s there was a considerable degree of intermarriage, even between first cousins, in order, he suggested, to maintain the white physiognomy.[45]

Leaving aside the question of whether, in the eighteenth century, marital unions between African slaves and whites would have been permitted by the island's religious or civil authorities, we can take it as plausible that the offspring of these unions (licit or not) were baptized in the Church of England.[46] (In chapters 4 and 5, I referred to the baptism of slaves by Anglican slave owners, as indicated by parish registers.) In that case, the children would have had special status (being baptized at a time when few slaves of Protestant owners, and none of Catholic owners, were baptized) and they were half-white. Given the racism of the time (and, indeed, of our own), it is not surprising that the descendants kept alive their special distinction in Montserrat society. That the "black Irish" lived always in the north, which is and always was the most Protestant part of the island, and not the far south (the most Catholic part) is taken as a great mystery by students of ethnography. The answer probably lies in a very simple hypothesis: the slaveowners of the far south, in the "Irish horseshoe," were not as open in the eighteenth century to interracial relationships as were the Irish Protestants in the far north. In the eighteenth century, such openness, of course, would have been seen by most whites as a sign of moral dissoluteness. Thus, most likely, the "black Irish" live in the north because that is where their forebears lived; and they are Protestant because that is what their forebears were.

How Montserratians of the twenty-first century should invent their own history is no business of professional historians such as myself. We write for each other, and for a limited audience of the sympathetic. Professionally written history may be more accurate than are invented traditions, but usually it is less useful. The Montserratians have the right to create whatever fictions makes it easier for them to get through the day. One hopes that their inventions will be humane, generous, non-racist, and forgiving – for generous inventions of the past have the power of becoming self-fulfilling prophecies of the future.

For Montserratians contemplating their past, the task is not easy. An island with high unemployment and a low economic horizon is dotted with remnants of a busy, yet brutal past. One is reminded of the enigmatic verse penned by an anonymous Glasgow dweller:

The dark satanic mill
Still stands.
But stands
  so bleeding still.

APPENDIX A
The 1678 Census

Writing in 1734 to the Commissioners for Trade and Plantations, Governor Mathew of the Leeward Islands complained about the difficulty of doing even a rough census of Montserrat. "I cannot even yet tell you how to fill up the blanks of inhabitants in Montserat and Nevis," he wrote. "I have at last received lists from both those islands. But those from Montserat are one parish or division under one sort of denominations, another in another method, so that I cannot reduce them to one set." (14 Sept 1734, *CSPCS, 1734–1735*, 314). If the enumeration of the 1730s left Governor Mathew hopelessly distracted, those of the 1670s would have sent him into paroxysms of confusion. The enumerators of 1678 did not work to a standard set of rules, nor did they report in the same way. Some left out pieces of information that others provided.

The census of 1678 of Montserrat is found in the Public Record Office, London (C.O. 1/142). It is printed under the title "Montserrat, 1677–78," in V.L. Oliver (ed.), *Caribbeana*, vol. 2 (1912), 316–20 and 342–7. The transcription is quite accurate on names, but has significant copying errors on numerical matters.

The first thing that one must do with the 1678 enumeration is to retabulate the data from scratch. (I suspect that this should be done with the other censuses of the Leeward Islands as well, but that is at present beyond my brief.) The retabulation is necessary because the enumerators, local gentlemen of substance, were sometimes cavalier in totting up their tallies and, further, whoever did the summation of the district results had a fairly free idea of arithmetic. So one starts at ground level and works up. The changes are not major.

This sort of retabulation works well for the adult male portion of the white population. All of the adult males were enumerated by name (with the curious exception of three of the district administrators who left themselves off their own tallies and of the governor of the Leeward Islands, whose Montserrat address is not mentioned.)

All of the white women and white children were tallied collectively, but very few of the women were tallied by name, and none of the children. Therefore, although one can obtain reasonably accurate totals of white women and children, district by district, one is forced to work with the all-male adult cohort when one does secondary analysis of such things as ethnicity (the identification of which depends upon surname data).

It is absolutely crucial to understand that the 1678 census was *not* a household census. That is, it did not record the entire white population by household. We are given aggregate data on men, women, and children, from which it is possible to work out adult sex ratios, but that is all that can be done. There is no way legitimately to discuss average household size, because at no point is there any information on the actual number of households. We have to drop the idea of talking about household structure, except in the vague sense of noting that there were women on the island, and thus existed the possibility of conventional male-female households.

I emphasize this point because Robert V. Wells, in his authoritative book *The Population of the British Colonies in America before 1776* provides a discussion of household size on Montserrat (see, for example, 221 and 223 for data sets on Montserrat in 1678). This sort of discussion, unfortunately, was possible only by a misreading of the way the Montserrat census was compiled. In fact, in only three of the ten census districts was the enumeration done by households, a fact that Wells misses. (And, even were this noted, it would not help very much: the three enumeration districts cannot be used as a sample of the whole island, because the island varied so greatly in its social structure, a point elaborated in the text of the present study.)

Most of the census data (that in seven of the ten districts) was put together by an eccentric method that has misled successive historical commentators. The great bulk of white male inhabitants are enumerated not by household, but by pairs. And since, with only the rarest of exceptions, female names are not recorded, one is confronted with a set of lists, district by district, of paired male names. Lydia M. Pulsipher, the leading expert on seventeenth-century Montserrat called these "Male partner households," and worked out a set of possible explanations why these evolved. See her "The Cultural Landscape of Montserrat, West Indies, in the Seventeenth Century," 76.

Actually, though there may have been a few "male partner households" these were not what the census was reporting. To get an idea of what it was actually saying, we will take Captain Nicholas Mead's division as a good example. Mead listed himself "Captain Nicholas Mead" and "Captain Syms," both leaders of the local militia, separately. Then he listed in pairs 105 men (he made an error and tallied "Curnelius Newlas and a lady" as two men, but never mind), plus ten prisoners in the local lock-up. Were these 105 men, who are listed in pairs, actually fifty-two "male partner households?" Hardly, because in the same enumeration district are sixty adult white women, who are simply totalled at the end of the enumeration, but are not allocated to individual households. Thus, the census is not reporting that the listed pairs of men formed households. The theory that the island was dominated by male partnerships that were either economic or sexual (or both) misses the way the census worked (and also ignores the large number of women on the island).

Riva Berleant-Schiller ("Free Labor and the Economy in Seventeenth-Century Montserrat," 557–8) suggested that the apparently male-partner households were not male marriages or even male partnerships of convenience, but were more complicated. She expressed this and provided a range of explanations:

> More than seventy percent of households included two adult men, whomever else they might also have included. In a few cases, these housemates bear the same surname, but the census implies no kinship tie for the majority.... Did a married couple have a male boarder or servant? Did a single man have a servant of each sex, or a woman two manservants? Did one woman exchange domestic and sexual services with two men? Were three equal housemates cooperating? Were three servants billeted together? We do not know. Even without a woman, the two-man household offers possibilities for speculation.

Indeed it does, and most of it silly. Granted, any of the above combinations could have been possible on Montserrat; and granted, 70 percent of the listings of "households" involve the names of two males, but that misses the point: *in the 1678 census these were not households* and the pairing of the two male names was *not* intended to indicate that the two men (and, as Berleant-Schiller adds, their appurtenances) were a ménage. The men were listed in pairs simply because *that was a convenient method of counting*. Can we have become so lost in our own hermetic world that we forget that, for example, a farmer frequently counts a flock of sheep in twos, threes, or more, but almost never singly? Have we forgotten that certain species are counted only in pairs? The men doing the enumeration were rough, practical men, and most of them did not think like modern census takers.

That the pair-listing was merely a method of counting holds, whether or not one accepts my next suggestion on why they thought in pairs in this particular instance. Recall the example of Captain Nicholas Mead's division and note that the only men who are not enumerated in tandem were Captain Mead and Captain Syms, and ten prisoners in the local lock-up. Further, in each of the seven enumeration districts that used the pairs method of counting, the census was conducted by a captain or major in the militia. Each followed the same pattern of enumerating the commanding officers (and surgeon) separately. All the other males were listed in pairs. Clearly what we are seeing is a function of the way the militia worked. The white men of the island – every adult of whom was liable to militia service – were listed in double columns, a standard form of British militia organization and often part of a system where each member of a pair was responsible for being sure the other turned up. This militia-based system is hard to miss as the summation was entitled "The Several Companies or Divisions in this Island."

My interpretation is indirectly confirmed when one looks at the three enumeration districts where there were no paired males, but where, instead, each household was dealt with individually. There, two of the three enumerators were not ranking members of the militia. They did not think like militia leaders, so they did not list men in paired columns. Further, on the original of the census, but not on the printed copy, there are for some of the districts marginalia which indicate the lead officers and non-coms.

So, the method of counting by pairs was not an indication of household structure. That holds true, even if it had a different provenance than the one that I suggest. As a way of organizing how one thinks about people, the counting-in-pairs is an interesting piece of cultural history, but not a reflection of frontier demography.

A real difficulty inherent in the 1678 census (as distinct from those read into it by recent historians) involved the African slave population. Here, fortunately, the inconsistency of the enumeration methods is irritating, but not insurmountable. The problem is that the ten districts reported the African slave population in three different ways: some reported only the number of men; some reported the total number of slaves, meaning men, women, and children; and some reported a number, but did not say if it was the number of adult males or the total number of slaves. So, we have three sub-populations:

A. Adult males only reported	337
B. Entire slave population reported	212
C. Not specified	420

Another way of stating this is to say that "C" would have been either "A" or "B."

We can get out of this cul de sac by use of the old infantry method of bracketing fire, as follows. We first survey the structure of the slave population of the other three Leeward islands, Nevis, St. Christopher, and Antigua. These we use as a normal population from which to derive a "multiplier." The multiplier we need is one that, when applied to the number of males in a large slave population, gives a fairly accurate approximation of the total slave population. That number, in the Leeward Islands in 1678 is 2.69 (derived from Dunn, *Sugar and Slaves*, Table 12, 127). With it, we can now derive the notional boundaries of what the Montserrat slave population was in 1678. ("Notional" is an important word: this is not the same thing as actually counting people, for that is impossible. It is the best possible approximation of what an actual count would have shown, had it been done at the time.)

All that is necessary now is to do the bracketing figures. Estimate no. 1, below, assumes that item "C" was the same definitionally as item "B," namely, that it was meant to indicate all the blacks in the electoral districts where it was employed, women, children, and adult males. Thus:

A. Adult males.	
337 × 2.69 = total slave population of	907
B. Entire slave population reported.	
212 = total slave population of	212
C. Assume 420 is total slave population =	420
THEN, the total slave population for Montserrat was	1,539

Alternatively, in estimate no. 2 we assume item "C" was the same definitionally as item "A." That is, it includes adult males only:

A. Adult males.	
337 × 2.69 = total slave population of	907
B. Entire slave population reported.	
212 = total slave population of	212
C. Assume 420 is number of males only.	
420 × 2.69 = total slave population	1,130
THEN, the total slave population of Montserrat was	2,249

If one is willing to live with words, this is to say that the entire black population was between 1,500 and 2,250.

Where, between those bracketing figures, is the truth most apt to lie? My own view is that it lies closer to the higher than to the lower figure, but that a mid-point is not objectionable and is a good conservative choice.

For simplicity, let us say that we have three choices within the range of legitimate interpretation of the data: total slave population of 1,539, of 2,249, or of 1,894 (the mid-point between the bracketing figures). Now, those three numbers imply, respectively, an adult male component as follows (again, using the other Leeward Islands as a normal population): of 572, of 836, and of 704.

These inferred adult male numbers are useful because we have as a reference point the enumeration of 1672 (see text, Table 1) which showed that the island at that time had 523 adult male slaves. This means that the number 572 would be too low, because between the 1672 and the 1678 enumerations, (a) William Stapleton became governor of the Leeward Islands and pushed hard for slave augmentation; (b) on Montserrat, the sugar economy was advancing quickly, this being the decade which leads to its dominance and the importation of slaves (mostly via Nevis) was crucial to this process; and (c) over and above normal import of slaves, Montserrat made an effort to attract back from the French colonies the slaves who were stolen by the French in 1667 and were owed return. The Montserratians gave these slaves free choice of who their masters would be. Therefore, the suggestion that 704 is a more accurate notion for 1678 is dictated. (This number fits well with the later curve of the growth of the slave population.)

Therefore, the inferred (or notional) slave population that we use for Tables 2, 3 and 4 in the text is the moderate choice: 1,894. We should, however, realize that there is some possibility that the actual number was somewhat higher.

Now to the really interesting issue: ethnicity or, more accurately, land of origin.

There is no indication on the census of the ethnic origin of any specific individual. We are forced, therefore, to use as a surrogate the probable ethnic derivation of individual surnames.

This can be a very ropey process. The reader may be aware that I have argued that only in very tightly delimited cases are surnames a reliable indication of national background. In particular, I have suggested that the well-known efforts to determine the ethnic breakdown of the population of colonial America are totally flawed, and that this holds for recent as well as earlier efforts. I stand by that opinion. (See Akenson, "Why the Accepted Estimates of the Ethnicity of the American People, 1780, Are Unacceptable," 102–19, and 125–9.

However, I also argued that in certain tightly controlled conditions, ethnicity, or national background, can be determined for a given population, with an acceptable degree of accuracy. Montserrat in the seventeenth century is such a place, particularly in 1678. Why? First, because we have the surname of each adult male, in eight of ten census districts. Second, because we have an independent contemporary verification against which to check our own work. Whoever processed the manuscript census data provided his own estimate of what the national origins of the islanders were. These were (correcting for the inevitable arithmetic errors in the original MS):

	% of Adult Males	*% of Total Population*
Irish	67	70
English	30	28
Scottish	3	2

Third, this is a limited population in the sense that there really are only two ethnic categories: Irish and British (one lumps the Scots with the English, for they form too small a population to be meaningfully differentiated). This limits the possibility of error much more than in the colonial American case where, for example, someone with the name "Smith" could be any of half a dozen nationalities, "Smith" being a common anglicization of one of western Europe's most common names. With such a limited menu of choices on Montserrat, the chances of error drop dramatically. They decrease further when one notes that ethnically denotive first names often sort out ambiguities (were one to find a "Turlogh Oge Smith," he would not be an Englishman).

Fourth, Montserrat provides a controllable universe, for we know a good deal about its ethnicity independently of the 1678 census. There are large amounts of seemingly epiphenomenal information that help us to read the surnames correctly. (For instance, the seemingly fugitive pieces of information that the man who sometimes spelled his name Galloway and could have been Scots, was certainly Irish, and that the Blakes, who could have been English actually were Irish. And on and on.) None of these scraps of information themselves is crucial, but taken together they improve considerably one's statistical accuracy. Because one is dealing with such a small statistical universe, getting, say, 100 designations correct by nonlinguistic means, adds greatly to one's percent-of-accuracy. Fifth, it is of mild comfort to note the scores of contemporary observations which state that the Montserrat migrants came mostly from the south of Ireland, especially Munster, mesh exactly with the surname evidence. Perhaps 90 percent of the Irish names are associated with families whose locus was in Munster, and the additional counties of Wexford and Galway.

The messy (but very intriguing) point about the use of surnames is that Ireland in the seventeenth century was undergoing a complex and uneven process of anglicization and this is reflected in the names people applied to themselves. For example, sometimes "Smith" was used, other times "Gowan," or another time "MacGowan." And the orthography was amazingly inventive. "Donoghue," "Donohue," "Donohoo" (with variant prefixes as well) were the same name. Often members of the same family used widely variant spellings.

None of that is controversial, just technically interesting. What I have tried to do is to sort out the Irish names in a manner consonant with the way historians have come to describe seventeenth-century Irish history (the same vocabulary I have used in the text): namely, to distinguish between the two sorts of mostly-Catholic people, the "native Irish" and the "Old English," and between them and the mostly Protestant "New English" who came to Ireland in the later sixteenth and in the seventeenth centuries. (Anthony Briskett, founder of the colony, is an example of the last group, albeit an unusual one.) This is not as clear-cut a set of distinctions as is the Irish-British one, but it is consequential. As I argue in the text, lumping of all "the Irish" together in the seventeenth century destroys the reality of the social and economic structure of the island. The Montserrat rebellion of 1667, for example, was not a rising of "the Irish," but of a very specific subset of the entire Irish-descended group, both in social and cultural terms.

The sources that I have found most useful in dealing with the surnames of the island are Patrick Woulfe, *Sloinnte Gaedheal is Gall*; Edward MacLysaght, *A Guide to Irish Surnames*; P.H. Reaney, *A Dictionary of British Surnames*; Robert E. Matheson, *Special Report on Surnames in Ireland*.

At this point, an embarrassing, but necessary comment must be made. It is about the work on national origins (or, if one prefers, ethnicity) done by Lydia M. Pulsipher. Her pioneering work on seventeenth-century Montserrat is the plinth on which all later work is constructed. Her delineation of the probable outlines of the 1678 census districts is an achievement that borders on the heroic. I feel uncomfortable, and indeed ungrateful, in having to point out that her work on ethnicity is a bit beyond the pale, or at least the palings.

This is drawn to one's attention by something akin to Sherlock Holmes' famous dog-that-did-not-bark. Specifically, in neither her thesis, "The Cultural Landscape of Montserrat," nor her monograph, *Seventeenth-Century Montserrat: An Environmental Impact Statement* is there a single actual number referred to concerning the ethnic composition of the population, and this despite a very extensive discussion of the social stratigraphy and the geographical segregation of ethnic groups. Instead, one has only percentages, with no reference number being given. For example, see "The Cultural Landscape of Montserrat," Table 2, 66 and *Seventeenth-Century Montserrat*, Table 1, 27 which give the "ethnic and racial" characteristics of the island population. Not a single real number appears, not even a total population figure.

Why? because if one retrofits her work (the real total population figures for each census district for whites are indeed available), then one arrives at a reason. The ethnic distribution of the population that the contemporaries gave (that is, the reality-check) was as follows:

Adult white males	
Irish	67%
British	33%

But Pulsipher's figures work out as:

Irish	59%
British	41%

In fact, this divergence is never noted: the percentage ethnic breakdown of individual districts is given, but no ethnic breakdown for the entire population is provided. Had it been noted, the reader would have seen that the proportion of the Irish population was reduced by 11 percent from the census takers' determination, and that the British proportion of the population was increased by 23 percent of its real base. Errors of course occur in this sort of historical work, but they must be explicitly recognized.

Pulsipher was herself aware of the problem and, one infers, of its magnitude. In an appendix to "The Cultural Landscape of Montserrat," she suggested (174*n*2) that "my identifications probably erred in favour of English names. That is, in all likelihood, many of the English should actually have been classified as Irish." She also explains, slightly earlier, that "because of errors in the addition in the printed census and because of variance between me and the census taker in judging ethnic identity, neither my ethnic totals nor my general population figures agree with those included in the census" (ibid., 174). The arithmetic corrections are no great matter, but to imply that in ascertaining ethnicity, the judgment of a twentieth-century historian, working only on the basis of surname evidence, is somehow equally authoritative with that of the enumerator who lived among the people is intellectually nihilistic. (And the more so, given that we are dealing with a population that was highly sensitive on ethnic matters, and where national origin was a matter, at times, of virtual civil war.) If the two estimates disagree, the "variance" is not a matter of there being two equally valid opinions, but of the twentieth-century historian having made errors that are exposed by comparison to the observations of the seventeenth-century enumerator.

Finally, one must add that in two census districts (Devereaux and the Cove and Palmetto Point) a significant proportion of the male population (32 and 45 percent, respectively) was not named at all. Yet, the ethnic population of these areas is given in Pulsipher's tables in such a manner as to indicate 100 percent as being known (see tables cited previously). Now, there are perfectly reasonable ways of filling in blanks such as these, as long as one (a) admits that an "unknown" category exists and (b) specifies the methods one is using to fill in hypothetically the holes in the data. (The best way in such a case is simply to distribute the "unknown" or "no-information" category in each district according to the known distribution of data in that district.)

In sum, unhappily, and despite the valuable intuitions behind many of Pulsipher's observations on Montserrat, her actual data base has been too heavily bent to be of direct value.

How close are my own estimates to the contemporary reality-check? And, how did I deal with lacunae in the data?

As mentioned above, two of the ten census districts provided only an incomplete list of the adult males. (All men were counted in the totals, but some of their names were not listed). This occurred in the Devereaux division where thirty-two men were unnamed, and the Cove and Palmetto Point division where forty-five were unnamed. These I distributed among the ethnic categories in the same proportions as the ethnic distributions of those whose names were given in the respective divisions. (The men existed, after all, and had an ethnicity, so the norm by which to distribute that unknown cohort should be the population within which they lived.)

My final results yield:

Irish	65.2%
British	34.8%

As against the contemporary enumerators' standard of:

Irish	66.98%
British	33.02%

Because surnames are given for only a handful of adult white females, the ethnicity of white women cannot be dealt with in the same way as the men. (In any case, given the social rules of the time, many of the female names would merely be their husband's surname and thus not indicative of their own national background.)

We can infer the number of females of each ethnic group with reasonable accuracy, however, because we know the actual number of white women. And, from the contemporary collator of the census, we also have his indication of the percentage of women in the three main groups, Irish, English, and Scottish. (The ethnic tallies of women were done by the seventeenth-century enumerator, independently of his ethnicity estimates for men.) So, if one applies those proportions to the total number of white women, one infers their national background in the aggregate. (Interestingly, there was a fair difference between the proportion of women in the various groups and the men. The Irish had a higher proportion of women in their ethnic cohort. This is included in the census aggregates, so it is not a source of bias.)

As for children, one has parallel information and simply infers aggregate distributions in the same manner.

In sum, in the 1678 census gender-bias is not a source of potential error in ethnicity matters, so long as one is dealing with the Irish-English-Scottish set of distinctions. However, at the level of finer discriminations within the Irish group – Old English, native Irish, New English – gender matters may (or, equally, may not) involve some skewing. Given that we have confidence in the ethnicity of the adult male population, the question becomes: within the entire Irish cohort, are the adult males a representative sample of the larger Irish population? (Mind you, they are the largest group in that population, so the effect of any skewing is much more limited than if they were only a tiny minority: they are, undeniably, an accurate sample of themselves!) In practical terms, the potential skewing comes from the possibility that the women recruited to the West Indies from Ireland may have been more restricted in geographic locale than the men: especially, that they may have been more tightly localized in origin around Cork City. This possibility is raised by the only relevant study of female migration of which I am aware, that of Grainne Henry, who found that female migration in connection with the "Wild Geese" in the later sixteenth and early seventeenth centuries was highly localized and frequently involved kinship groups. See Grainne Henry, "Women 'Wild Geese,' 1585–1625," 23–40.

APPENDIX B
The Census of 1729

The Montserrat enumeration of 1729 is found in original in the Public Record Office, London (c.o. 152/18). An excellent transcript is found in V.L. Oliver (ed.), *Caribbeana*, 4: 302–11. Robert V. Wells, in his monograph on the population of the British Colonies before 1776, suggests that "the enumeration of Montserrat in 1729 is one of the most comprehensive ever made of a colonial population before the American Revolution," and his judgment has to be respected. The census is indeed a gold mine, but like all the Eldorados of the first British empire, it looks rather better, the farther away one is from it. See Wells, *The Population of the British Colonies in America Before 1776*, 229.

One minor problem is that the cross-tabulations done by the district compilers sometimes involved arithmetical errors. So the census-takers' totals cannot be taken for granted – the sums and cross-sums have to be redone.

More important is a conceptual matter and that is the concept of "family" (the enumerators' term) or "household," the term used by Wells. In each case the usage is somewhat misleading if taken literally. "Family" and "household" included everybody who worked within a given economic enterprise. This could range from a biological household (a family, say, of parents and two young children, working a tobacco farm), all the way to a plantation that included not only the master's biological family, but indentured servants, free labourers (especially slave overseers), and slaves. So, when Wells reports (*Population of the British Colonies*, Table VI-18, 221) that the mean household size was 28.2, he is correct in terms of how the census was composed, but unintentionally misleading. This is not "household" in the sense that later demographers use the term, and the number cannot be compared with that of, for example, nineteenth-century enumerations of the British Isles or the USA, or British North America. A better term than "family" or "household" would be "enterprise" or "economic unit."

Given that it would be useful to know not only the size of the economic units on the island, but what the actual household size was in conventional terms, one might think that it would be possible to get around the problem by simply subtracting the blacks from each enterprise (that would leave slave families undocumented, but the data preclude reconstructing slave families in any case). Yet this will not get us to the white biological family – the "household." Why not? Because of three anomalies in the way that the data for white persons were collected. As explained above, it was assembled according to economic enterprises. This meant that free white adult males were included within the number of men that were tallied for each family. Because only the name of the head is given for each economic unit, it is impossible to distinguish in the total number of adult males in any given family those who were the adult sons of the head of the enterprise and those (such as overseers and live-in free servants) who were not part of the biological family.*

Secondly, a similar problem existed with white females. Not only were wives and adult daughters included in "family" but so too were free white adult female servants.

Thirdly, the children of overseers and their wives (who, already, are included in the "family") are lumped into the "family" simply as white boys and girls.

---

* The fact that the reported number of adult males are an undifferentiated aggregate in each household is not immediately clear if one only looks at the overall totals and the column headings of the census. However, if one examines the line-by-line data, certain cases make clear the lumping that has taken place. For example, George Wyke, Sr, a planter of 700 acres in St Anthony's district, not only had 223 black slaves in his enterprise, but is listed as having sixteen persons in his white "family." That "family" includes three children, six adult women and six adult men. It would be stretching credulity to suggest that Wyke kept at home twelve adult children. His plantation staff is being enumerated as part of his family. Therefore, use of the term "family" or "household" is misleading. Several other cases could be put forward to make the same point.

In sum, it is impossible to talk of "family" or "household" in the sense used by demographers. One can think accurately only in terms of "economic units" or "enterprises."

I mentioned that various arithmetical corrections needed to be made in the cross-tabulations. These mistakes are random, and not technically difficult to fix.

However, there is a separate matter. In St Patrick's district, the enumerators included white male and female indentured servants in their subtotal for each enterprise. In the St Anthony's district they did not. In St Peter's district and in St George's, the enumerators were inconsistent, including these white servants in some economic units and not in others. And, in the St Peter's district, most single male heads of household were excluded from the population totals!

This means that before one can derive any totals for Montserrat, one has to disaggregate the data, meaning, take it apart and start over. The totals as they exist in the census summaries are not valid.

One sidebar appears that is culturally significant. Because the age for which children were tallied varied according to race and gender, one cannot do age distributions for children. However, the way that the enumerators worked bears notice. They tallied children as follows:

For whites: "Little girls under 8"
"Little boys under 9"
"Big girls under 14"
"Big boys under 15"
For blacks: "Negro girls under 13"
"Negro boys under 14"

One can parse these distinctions several ways. The unmistakeable point is that in the West Indies, nobody was equal.

On the matter of ethnicity, I have used the same surname distinguishers and sources for those as indicated in the discussion of the methods for analyzing the 1678 census (see Appendix A). However, for 1729, I have not distinguished between the three major sorts of Irish persons. That is because the categories "native Irish," "Old English," and "New English" are terms developed to fit the later sixteenth and the seventeenth centuries. They lose their analytic power in the eighteenth. This is especially true of an off-shore colony such as Montserrat, where, after nearly 100 years of Irish occupation, the Old World distinctions among the Irish become so blurred as to be of doubtful value.

What steps into its place, of course, on Montserrat, as in the homeland, is the Catholic-Protestant distinction, but even that is a variable matter.

Notes

CHAPTER ONE

1 For a convenient introduction to the history of the Irish in North America, see my *Irish Diaspora*, 217–69. Rather more readable is Wilson, *The Irish in Canada*.

2 For the full run of the relevant census data, see *Census of Canada, 1931*, vol. 1, 710ff.

3 Bridenbaugh, *No Peace Beyond the Line*, viii.

4 The issue is found most clearly in colonial American (mainland) historiography, in the polar views of Jack Greene who discounts ethnicity firmly, and David Hackett Fischer who sees it as central to the making of colonial America. Compare Greene, *Pursuits of Happiness* and Fischer, *Albion's Seed*. Neither author here deals with the British West Indies or with Irish Catholics.

5 The several works of Nicholas P. Canny have done the most to develop this theme. I have found most useful: *The Elizabethan Conquest of Ireland* and (ed.) *Europeans on the Move*. An especially penetrating essay is Canny's "Identity Formation in Ireland: The Emergence of the Anglo-Irish," in Canny and Pagden, *Colonial Identity in the Atlantic World, 1500–1800*, 159–212. Also valuable is Canny's essay, "The Permissive Frontier: Social Control in English Settlements in Ireland and Virginia, 1550–1640," in Andrews, Canny, and Hair (eds.), *The Westward Enterprise*, 17–44. Compare to Palmer, *Problem of Ireland in Tudor Foreign Policy, 1485–1603*.

6 Sheridan, *Sugar and Slavery*, 183.

7 Wells, *Population of the British Colonies in America before 1776*, 229.
8 Bridenbaugh, *No Peace Beyond the Line*, 15*n*15.
9 The copy of English's typescript in the public library, Plymouth, Montserrat, and the copy in the library of the Institute of Commonwealth Studies in London, have variant pagination, but the content is the same.
10 See Messenger, *Inis Beag* and Messenger, "Sex and Repression in an Irish Folk Community," in Marshall and Suggs (eds.), *Human Sexual Behavior*, 3–31. With characteristic generosity John Messenger sent to me a copy of T. Savage English's typescript. That it arrived after I had obtained a copy in London is not germane: his instinctive generosity to a fellow scholar is praiseworthy, and all too rare.
11 Fergus, "Montserrat, 'Colony of Ireland', 325–40.
12 Berleant-Schiller, *Montserrat*.
13 I hope that the following observation will not be taken as an indication of ingratitude by those on Montserrat who kindly helped me in my research when on the island: as far as conventional archival sources are concerned, the island possesses no original documents for the sixteenth and seventeenth centuries, and only a very few for the late eighteenth and nineteenth centuries. (This for reasons explained in the text, namely a series of military conquests, interspersed with natural disasters.) In Antiguan archives there is material that would be useful for the political historian of the Leeward Islands in their several political configurations, but not the sort of direct social information that is required for the present study.

I emphasize this point chiefly because I do not wish to be accused of assuming that everything comes from the imperial metropole and nothing from the peripheries. However, any Irish historian will understand this situation immediately: if one wishes to study the full range of early medieval Irish high material culture, one inevitably looks to Scandinavian museums, because conquering peoples send the local prizes home. Similarly, imperial regimes send records to the homeland. So, one uses the central sources to reconstruct the story of the hinterlands, all the time remaining aware that these records were generated with a certain imperial slant. That said, there really is no difference in the actual record in most cases – take, for example, the legal statutes of Montserrat, as collected by the London government during the eighteenth century – whether they were preserved in England or Ireland or (as, alas, was not the case) they were preserved in Montserrat: their content was not variable. Therefore, despite the lack of seventeenth- and early eighteenth-century records *in situ*, one can reconstruct seventeenth- and early eighteenth-century white society with a good deal of depth and accuracy.

What is most absent or, when present, most filtered, is material on the Amerindian population and on the African-derived population. This, however, is not a function of the loss of original records or of the remaining records being non-Caribbean in their present locale, but rather of the prevailing mind-set of the people who produced the original records. The elision of the historical record on these matters was accomplished by contemporaries. Archaeologists and anthropologists are trying to work their way past this mind barrier, but as yet for Montserrat their direct results are minimal.

For rigorous recent local studies of specific colonies which might profitably be compared to seventeenth-century Montserrat, see Kupperman, *Providence Island, 1630–1641* and Horn, *Adapting to a New World*.

The reader who is familiar with the West Indian historical literature may notice that I do not refer to Barbados as much as one might expect, despite its having a rich literature, and quite a number of references to "the Irish" in the seventeenth century. This is because (in my judgment) the position of the Irish on Barbados represented an extreme situation of ethnic dysfunction, not replicated elsewhere in the Caribbean.

That point implicitly raises a basic question concerning local histories: at what point, and at what level does one engage either in comparison or generalization? My focus is kept tightly on Montserrat, and my implicit comparisons and generalizations are confined to English colonization efforts in the Irish homeland and to the experience of the Irish diaspora worldwide. See my *Irish Diaspora*. Historians of the West Indies and of the English colonies in North America may find this disappointingly narrow. In such cases, they have my full licence (indeed encouragement) to use this small study in their own comparative work in any way that is helpful.

At a satellite-photograph level of generalization, there is nothing in the settlement of Montserrat that is not found in the Americas generally in the seventeenth century. This, basically, is ascribable to the English system of colonization in which (in comparison with the French and Spanish) the central power was so limited, the local so robust. That point accepted, one has in fact adduced a sound reason for looking closely at local colonial situations, and for letting each one speak for itself.

CHAPTER TWO

1 For background on the historiography of English activities in the West Indies, see Goveia, *Study on the Historiography of the British West Indies* and Williams, *British Historians and the West Indies*.

2 The classic, and still readable discussion of English privateering is Haring, *The Buccaneers in the West Indies in the XVII Century.*
3 Dunn, *Sugar and Slaves,* 10–11.
4 Ibid., 12.
5 Quinn, *Ireland and America,* 19.
6 The list is given in *Calendar of State Papers, Colonial Series, 1574–1660,* viii. (Hereafter, this series will be referred to as CSPCS and the date and page number will follow. The reader should be aware that CSPCS is just what the title implies: a calendar. Therefore quotations from it are sometimes in the form of indirect discourse.)
7 Basic to the following discussion is Quinn, *England and the Discovery of North America, 1481–1620.*
8 Quinn, *Ireland and America,* 11–17. On the military service of the Wild Geese, see Henry, *The Irish Military Community in Spanish Flanders, 1586–1621.*
9 The definition is that of Vincent T. Harlow, in "Introduction" to his edition *Colonising Expeditions,* lxvi *n*1.
10 Until recently, the most serviceable discussion of Irish colonization in the Amazon and Orinoco was Aubrey Gwynn's "Early Irish Emigration," 379–85; and "An Irish Settlement on the Amazon, 1612–1629." These have now been superseded by Joyce Lorimer's excellent *English and Irish Settlements.* Still useful as background is James A. Williamson, *English Colonies in Guiana and on the Amazon, 1604–1668.*
11 Harlow, *Colonising Expeditions,* lxxx-lxxxi; Lorimer, *English and Irish Settlements,* 43–59, 150–7; Quinn, *Ireland and America,* 40–3. Contemporary notice of the Tauregue settlement is found in de Forest, *A Walloon Family in America… together with a Voyage to Guiana being the Journal of Jesse de Forest and his colonists, 1623–1625.*
12 Quinn, *Ireland and America,* 28–33. See also Codignola, *The Coldest Harbour of the Land* and Cell, *Newfoundland Discovered.*
13 Quinn, *Ireland and America,* 21–2.
14 Gwynn, "Early Irish Emigration," 386–8; Gookin, *Daniel Gookin,* 32–47; Kingsbury (ed.), *The Records of the Virginia Company of London,* 1: 501–2, 554, 561–2, 618, 626, and 2: 75, 90, 93–4.
15 For example, the proposal to the Crown by Sir Pierce Crosby of 1628 (?) that he be granted £5,000 and two prize ships to transport ten companies of the Irish Regiment "into a rich and fruitful part of America, not inhabited by any Christians." He claimed that "the major part of the officers and many of the soldiers are Protestants," thus obscuring the fact that most of the settlers would in fact be Irish Catholics. Rather more honest was his suggestion that "a good proportion of land to be granted to the undertaker." CSPCS *1574–1660,* 95.
16 Smyth, "The Western Isle of Ireland," 8.

17 MacCarthy-Morrogh, *The Munster Plantation*, 244–84.
18 Smyth, "Western Isle of Ireland," 8.
19 Rolf Loeber and Magda Stouthamer-Loeber, "The lost architecture of the Wexford Plantation," in Whelan and Nolan (eds.), *Wexford*, 173–200. Rolf Loeber's *The Geography and Practice of English Colonisation in Ireland from 1534 to 1609* is an admirable and essential background study of the entire colonization process.
20 Gwynn, "Early Irish Emigration," 389. Virginia was not pleased to receive Catholics. Later, in 1630, when dispossessed Old English landlords from County Waterford were transported to Virginia, the colony refused to accept them (Quinn, *Ireland and America*, 26).
21 See the important essay by Nicholas Canny, "The Marginal Kingdom. Ireland in the First British Empire," in Bailyn and Morgan (eds.), *Strangers within the Realm*, esp. 42–8. See also McCavitt, "The Flight of the Earls, 1607," 159–73.
22 Smyth, "Western Isle of Ireland," 5.
23 Ibid., 9.
24 Ibid., 8, based on estimates made by Quinn. The regional concentration of various settlement groups can be inferred from Smyth, "Society and Settlement in Seventeenth Century Ireland: The Evidence of the '1659 Census,'" in Smyth and Whelan (eds.), *Common Ground*, 55–83.
25 Louis M. Cullen, "The Irish Diaspora," in Canny (ed.), *Europeans on the Move*, Table 6.1, 139. Cullen (138) estimates that seventeenth-century Irish out-migration annually was somewhere close to one per 1,000 of population. This compares to an eighteenth-century rate of one per 1,000 and a rate in the immediate pre-Famine decades of six per 1,000.
26 Cullen, "The Irish Diaspora," Table 6.1, 139.
27 The quotations that follow are from the pamphlet of 1623, *Advertisements for Ireland, being a description of the State of Ireland in the Reign of James I, contained in a manuscript in the Library of Trinity College Dublin*. The authorship of the publication was determined by George O'Brien, and he edited its publication in 1923 as an extra volume of the Royal Society of Antiquaries of Ireland. The passages cited are from 43–4.
28 At this point Gwynn, who quotes these pages ("Early Irish Emigration," 389–90) begins to edit the text as the subsequent passage implies more sexual promiscuity and economic idleness than Irish historians of the 1920s were willing to contemplate.
29 Gillespie, *The Transformation of the Irish Economy 1550–1700*, 15.
30 Higham, *Development of the Leeward Islands*, xii-xiii.
31 Ibid., x.
32 Dunn, *Sugar and Slaves*, 18.

33 West Indian data from Carl and Roberta Bridenbaugh, *No Peace Beyond the Line*, 19, and the *MacMillan Encyclopedia*. Trinidad is not here included, as it was not effectively colonized until the 1780s.

34 Henry A. Gemery, "Markets for migrants: English Indentured Servitude and Emigration in the Seventeenth and Eighteenth Centuries," in Emmer (ed.), *Colonialism and Migration*, Table II, 40.

35 Williamson, *Caribbee Islands*, 11–12.

36 Smith, *True Travels*, 50–2. Warner's priority as first colonizer was immediately recognized (see Commission reciting the discovery, 13 Sept. 1625, CSPCS 1574–1660, 75). Later versions varied slightly in detail from Smith's version (twenty-three men instead of fifteen) but in no way challenged Warner's priority (Deposition of James Astry, 2 Aug. 1660, ibid., 487).

The most important sources on the settlement of St Christopher and Nevis (in addition to Smith) are: "Relation of the First Settlement of St Christopher and Nevis by John Hilton, Storekeeper and Chief Gunner of Nevis," and "Narrative of the First Settlement of St Christopher and how it was taken from my Lord Willoughby's Deputy," reproduced in Harlow, *Colonising Expeditions*, 1–42.

37 Burns, *History of the British West Indies*, 190–5; Williamson, *Caribbee Islands*, 21–9. That more than three decades of litigation followed upon the Carlisle grant is not here important, for, whatever the legal difficulties, proprietary government operated on the ground.

38 Parry and Sherlock, *A Short History of the West Indies*, 53–4. Inferences on how the native Irish would adapt to the neo-feudal world are easily drawn from the groundbreaking article by Caball, "Providence and Exile."

39 Williamson, *Caribbee Islands*, 25–7.

40 On the general matter of the Stuart monarchs' attempts at instituting neo-feudal structures, see Michael Craton, "Reluctant Creoles. The Planters' World in the British West Indies" in Bailyn and Morgan, *Strangers Within the Realm*, 327–35.

41 Quinn, *Ireland and America*, 44.

42 "Relation of the First Settlement of St Christopher," in Harlow, *Colonising Expeditions*, 4–5.

43 Ibid., 6–7; Smith, *True Travels*, 57–8. An indication that there may have been a good deal of social tension on St Christopher is that after Hilton settled on Nevis, a Mr Asten, who was acting governor of St Christopher when Thomas Warner was in England, engaged one of Hilton's servants to murder him. The attempt was unsuccessful. ("Relation of the First Settlement of St. Christopher," in Harlow, *Colonising Expeditions*, 6–7.) Eventually Hilton, being in debt to an English merchant, Thomas Littleton (as were most of his settlers), resigned

the government of the island to Littleton and went off with his colonists to settle Tortuga (ibid., 14–16).

44 Harlow, *Colonising Expeditions*, xxiii; Quinn, *Ireland and America*, 44–5.

45 Hamshire, *The British in the Caribbean*, 30–8.

46 Bridenbaugh, *No Peace Beyond the Line*, 17.

47 Lorimer, *English and Irish Settlements*, 120–1.

48 "The Voyage of Sir Henry Colt," reproduced in Harlow, *Colonising Expeditions*, 87–8. Incidentally, two servants who expressed such views were placed on a wooden horse, with weights attached to the feet, and given a ride (88).

49 Winchester, *Outposts*, 232.

50 Fergus, *Alliouagana*, 5.

51 "The Voyage of Sir Henry Colt," in Harlow, *Colonising Expeditions*, 83.

52 Messenger, "The Influence of the Irish in Montserrat," 4.

53 Fergus, *Alliouagana*, 5.

54 English, "Records of Montserrat" (unpublished MS in the public library, Plymouth, Montserrat, and in the Institute of Commonwealth Studies, London), 47.

55 Pulsipher, "Cultural Landscape," 23–30.

56 Smith, *True Travels*, 52.

57 Pulsipher, "Cultural Landscape," 25–6.

58 Pulsipher (ibid., 30), says that: "It is evident from reports of Carib attacks on the early settlers in Montserrat that the island was highly valued by the Caribs" but she provides no evidence, save an attack of 1651 (discussed below in the text).

59 Anthony Bryskett [Briskett] to Charles II, 17 June 1669, *CSPCS 1669–1674*, 28.

60 For a sensible, document-based discussion of the Carib relations with the Anglo-Celts, see Higham, *Development of the Leeward Islands*, 122–42.

61 Jonathan Atkins to Commissioners of Trade and Plantations, 25 Sept 1676. *CSPCS, 1675–1676*, 349.

62 Arens, *Man-Eating Myth*, 10.

63 Thus, evidence of real cannibalism would need to come from within the culture in question. The one case that Arens misses is the New Zealand Maori, who have in their own folklore widespread reports of their own cannibalism as part of war rituals.

64 Arens, *Man-Eating Myth*, 14.

65 See ibid., 45.

66 Gwynn, "Documents Relating to the Irish," 209–10, reproducing the 1655 report of the Jesuit Father Pelleprat, as reprinted by his fellow Jesuit Father De Montezon in 1857.

One dates the incident as occurring in 1651, because Fr Stritch (who is the original witness to the event) did not sail from Bordeaux until September or October 1650, and spent at least three months on St Christopher before going to Montserrat (see Gwynn, "First Irish Priests," 227).

Two further points bear notice. The first is that in this French account of Carib behaviour there is no suggestion of cannibalism. Second, this account makes the Carib seem somewhat less formidable than do English accounts of their abilities. During the middle of the attack on Montserrat, some of the Carib broke into the Anglican church in Plymouth. One of the leaders put on a surplice (which was kept there for the convenience of the occasional visit by visiting clerics) and, screaming, jumped out to play a practical joke on his followers. They were so frightened that they fled and he chased after them, making them run away even faster. Finally, they were turned, and went back to their pillaging.

67 Hughes, *Society of Jesus*, 1: 279. For context, see Gwynn, "Documents Relating to the Irish," 184.

68 I am discounting as unreliable (though, given the narrowness of the time span involved, not necessarily inaccurate) the statement of the *Third Report of Commission of Inquiry into the Administration of Civil and Criminal Justice in the West Indies* of 1826 that Montserrat was first settled in 1632. This is because, in providing the settlement date of various West Indian colonies, the same report presented an impossibly early date for Nevis.

69 If we take the words "noble plantation" to imply that the settlement was well established, then some months earlier than the end of 1633 would be a necessary terminus.

70 Bernard O'Brien, the chronicler says: "and in the end they reached England," but since the men had split up, presumably he is speaking for himself and his own immediate companions. See "Bernard O'Brien's Account" in Lorimer, *English and Irish Settlements*, 415. See Lorimer's comments, 112–13.

71 Hughes, *Society of Jesus*, 279.

72 Ibid., 199–200.

73 That was the version sanctioned by the Maryland Historical Society in its edition of the Calvert Papers. Quoted in Gwynn, "Documents Relating to the Irish," 184.

74 Quinn, *Ireland and America*, 26.

75 It is a pleasure to commend to the reader's attention (that is, recommend that he or she read) *The Life and Correspondence of Lodowick Bryskett* by Henry R. Plomer and Tom Peete Cross. This book, small and graceful, is a joy to read, an example of old-fashioned historical scholarship at its best. It is thorough, wonderfully readable and wears its great learning unpretentiously. See also Loeber, "Lost Architecture," 44, 74.

76 Lodowick Briskett to Sir Francis Walsingham, 15 January 1682. Quoted in Plomer and Cross, *Lodowick Bryskett*, 33. I have modernized the spelling.

77 Gwynn, "Early Irish Emigration to the West Indies – Part II," 652.

78 Gwynn, "First Irish Priests," 220–1. The idea does not work, first, because there is no evidence for Gwynn's undocumented suggestion that Briskett "found his way to Virginia" implying that he did so on the way to the West Indies. Secondly, had Briskett been in possession of a grant from Carlisle, he would scarcely have gone to Virginia. Thirdly, even had he done so, taking with him as forced passengers the Old English landlords sent to Virginia in 1630, he would have arrived in Montserrat in any event before the year 1630 was out, much too early for the known time boundaries.

Gwynn's undocumented assertion that Anthony Briskett "found his way to Virginia" and the West Indies in consequence of the troubles which followed on the Wexford plantations under Chichester" (ibid., 221), is doubly curious because Gwynn's only documentation is a reference to his own work, which he considerably misinterprets. He tells the reader in this June 1932 article that he has already suggested (in December 1929) that Anthony Briskett made the trip to Virginia, thus implying that the case has been made earlier. In fact, in the earlier article, all that he says is, "Details we have none, but it seems fairly certain that Anthony, disappointed in his hopes of a comfortable establishment in Ireland, joined the large number of young adventurers who sought their fortune overseas" (Gwynn, "Early Irish Emigration – Part II," 652).

79 In an uncharacteristic lapse, Pulsipher ("Cultural Landscape," 33) states, without documentation, that "It is more likely that most of the earliest Irish in Montserrat came from the English settlement in St Christopher." In the monograph version of her work, this becomes the unequivocal statement that "most of the earlier Irish in Montserrat came from the English settlement in St Christopher; later Irish immigrants came from Virginia, New England, and the British Isles." There is no documentation for this new assertion save vague reference to an entire article of Aubrey Gwynn's (no page reference) which, as far as I can see, does not make the assertion which she endorses, much less document its accuracy (Pulsipher, *Seventeenth Century Montserrat*, 7.

80 This is suppositional, based on Canny's observation that at the tenant level English settlers were dominant in the more fertile parts of Munster. This held true generally not only on lands held by Protestant landlords, but also as tenants among Catholic landlords who held first class land, as in Limerick and Tipperary (see Canny in Bailyn

and Morgan, *Strangers Within the Realm*, 40–1 and see also Smyth in Smyth and Whelan, *Common Ground*, Fig. 4:2, 61).

81 Anthony Briskett to Charles I [1636], *CSPCS 1574–1660*, 240. The full petition is reproduced in Gwynn, "Documents Relating to the Irish," 184.

82 Ibid.

83 One would very much like to know what was meant in a memorial of 20 April 1638 transmitted by Malachy O'Queely, archbishop of Tuam to Francis Ingoli, secretary to the Sacred Congregation of Propaganda, stating that 600 Irish emigrants had sailed in March 1638 to the West Indies, "owing to the discovery of a new line of communication." (Gwynn, "First Irish Priests," 223). This may have meant, as Gwynn believed, that shipping had started directly from Galway. Alternately, it may have meant that one or several of the Leeward and Barbadian planters had begun a bigtime emigration business, but not necessarily from Galway.

84 Gwynn, "First Irish Priests," 219.

85 Bridenbaugh, *No Peace Beyond the Line*, 145; Harlow, *Colonising Expeditions*, xxviii.

86 Fergus, "Montserrat, 'Colony of Ireland,' 328.

87 English, "Records of Montserrat," 37 and 50.

88 Messenger, "Influence of the Irish," 8.

89 Gwynn, "First Irish Priests," 224. I take this reading "that three thousand Irish are at present living on St Christopher and the neighbouring islands" to be Gwynn's mature version. Earlier ("Early Irish Emigration – Part II," 656), he was somewhat more enthusiastic, stating that the number of Irish Catholics (not just Irish, but Irish Catholics) was "three thousand on St Christopher, and apparently as many more on Montserrat." For there to have been 3,000 Irish Catholics on Montserrat at the end of 1639 was patently impossible (given other evidence) and Gwynn wisely moderated his enthusiasm.

90 To keep this in context, the speculative, but very well informed, estimates of the Bridenbaughs on the total population of the Leeward Islands and Barbados are used (Bridenbaugh, *No Peace Beyond the Line*, 13). The figures are for 1650 and include all whites and blacks, but not indigenes:

St Christopher	20,000
Nevis	5,000
Montserrat	1,000
Antigua	900
(subtotal, Leeward Islands	26,900)
Barbados	30,000
Total	56,900

91 English, "Records of Montserrat," 50.
92 Fergus, "Montserrat, Colony of Ireland?" 329.
93 Williamson, *Caribbee Islands*, 31.
94 Harlow, *Colonising Expeditions*, xx.
95 On the size of Briskett's estate, see McGinn, "How Irish Is Montserrat?" Part 2, 15.

Thus, the modern estimate that, in 1650, 3 percent of Montserrat's population was black (roughly thirty persons), though speculative, is reasonable. See John J. McCusker, "The Rum Trade and the Balance of Payments of the Thirteen Continental Colonies, 1650–1775," (Ph.D., University of Pittsburgh, 1970), cited in Galenson, *White Servitude in Colonial America*, Table 8.2, 120. McCusker's doctoral thesis was published virtually unchanged in two volumes. It is a valuable compendium of demographic and economic data on the entire American colonial system.

96 Quinn, *Ireland and America*, 46–7.
97 Williamson, *Caribbee Islands*, 159–60.
98 Ibid., 160–1.
99 Bridenbaugh, *No Peace Beyond the Line*, 155.
100 Ibid., 156.
101 Ibid. Much the same thing happened on Nevis, where the governor avoided disorder by announcing that no rents due to Carlisle would be collected during the present emergency.
102 Higham, *Development of the Leeward Islands*, 2–3.
103 McGinn, "How Irish Is Montserrat?", 15.
104 A useful physical description of the island is found in Fergus, *Montserrat. Emerald Isle*, 1–4. For the historical geography of the island, the several works of Lydia M. Pulsipher are indispensable.
105 Waugh, *Love and the Caribbean*, 211.
106 Pulsipher, "Cultural Landscape," 15–23.
107 Pulsipher (ibid., 88) provides a table extremely useful to historians: a guide to the modern names of the major ghauts found on seventeenth-century maps and documents.
108 Fergus, *Rule Britannia*, 3.
109 Smith, *True Travels*, 53–4.
110 Williamson, *Caribbee Islands*, 96–7.
111 Hamshire, *British in the Caribbean*, 29.
112 See Bridenbaugh, *No Peace Beyond the Line*, 69; Pulsipher, "Cultural Landscape," 35–6.
113 Pulsipher, *Seventeenth-Century Montserrat*, 15.
114 Pulsipher, "Cultural Landscape," 99.
115 Higham, *Development of the Leeward Islands*, 186.
116 Bridenbaugh, *No Peace Beyond the Line*, 277.

117 *Acts of Assembly, passed in the Island of Montserrat; from 1668 to 1740, inclusive* (London: King's Printer, 1790). Law 14, 1669.

This collection is not to be confused with the *Abridgement* of the laws which was published in the same year.

Hereafter, reference to legal acts will be to the calendar year, and to the number of the law in the legal series that begins in 1668. Thus, for example, the law cited above will be referred to as *Laws* 1669: 14.

118 Higham, *Development of the Leeward Islands*, 190.

119 Pulsipher, "Cultural Landscape," 140.

120 Ibid., esp. 156–8.

121 For a summary of many of the ecological effects of the European invasion, see Merrill, "The Historical Record of Man as an Ecological Dominant in the Lesser Antilles," 17–22.

122 Gwynn, "Documents Relating to the Irish," 185.

123 John Davies (translation of Charles de Rochefort, *Histoire … Antilles …* (1666), 19, quoted in Pulsipher, "Cultural Landscape," 128.

124 William Stapleton to Lords of Trade and Plantations, 20 June 1676, CSPCS *1675–1676*, 500, 502.

125 Charles Wheeler to Council of Foreign Plantation, 9 Dec. 1671, quoted in Hughes, *Society of Jesus*, 282.

126 Gwynn, "First Irish Priests," 223–5.

127 Matthew O'Hartegan to Mutius Vitelleschi, 30 March 1643, reproduced in Gwynn, "Early Irish Emigration – Part II," 653–4. One must not read this letter literally. O'Hartegan claimed to have received "a petition from twenty thousand Irishmen who have been compelled by persecution and hardship to go into exile and to establish themselves on the island of St Christopher and neighbouring localities." The notion that Irish emigrants were all exiled, and often for their faith, is a literary conceit that runs strongly in Irish historiography and it has little relation to reality. One would indeed like to see the petition with names of 20,000 Irish settlers in the Leeward Islands, this being roughly six times the best estimate of total population.

128 Gwynn, "Early Irish Emigration – Part II," 655–6. It is perhaps as well for the Irish that Father O'Hartegan was not sent out to serve them. At the time of requesting the Leeward Islands mission, he was serving in Paris as an official agent of the Irish Confederation. For a man with such a connection to be attached to the Irish Catholics of the islands would have almost certainly brought the authorities down on the Irish, immediately and harshly.

129 Gwynn, "First Irish Priests," 226–7; extracts from Jean Baptiste du Tetre, *Histoire Generale des Antilles* (1654), in Gwynn, "Documents Relating to the Irish," 194–6; and extract from Pierre Pelleprat, *Relations des Missions* (1655) in Gwynn, ibid., 208–14. It was during one of

Father Stritch's pastoral visits that the Carib attack mentioned earlier occurred, probably in 1651.

130 Gwynn, "First Irish Priests," 228.

131 Depositions of Henry Ward, Richard Waad, and Henry Wheeler, 1 May 1654, and subsequent depositions of 9 October 1654, reproduced in Gwynn, "Documents Relating to the Irish," 224–8. Originals in PROL, CO 1/12.

132 Deposition of Henry Wheeler, ibid., 227.

133 Gwynn, "First Irish Priests," 228.

134 Demets, *The Catholic Church in Montserrat*, 22, 28.

135 Ibid., 27.

136 See chapter 5.

137 McGinn, "How Irish Is Montserrat?", 16.

138 Ibid.

139 Akenson, *The Irish Diaspora*, 244–50, based on the ethnicity and religion estimates of David Noel Doyle.

140 Patterson (ed.), *A Few Remains of the Rev. James MacGregor, D.D.*, 259. I am grateful to the late Professor George Rawlyk for this reference.

141 Gemery, "Markets for Migrants," 33.

142 Messenger, "Montserrat," 287.

143 Galenson, *White Servitude in Colonial America*, 3.

144 Eric Williams, "The Origin of Negro Slavery," reprinted from Williams, *Capitalism and Slavery* in Horowitz, *Peoples and Cultures of the Caribbean*, 63.

145 Ibid., 59. It may be relevant to point out that although Williams cites this quotation as an example that "the servants were regarded by the planters as 'white trash,' and were bracketed with the Negroes as laborers," in fact that petition from Montserrat had an entirely different meaning: namely, that the Council wanted slaves, never mind white servants. "The great hindrance to the improvement of the Island is the want of Negroes" was the council's main message. See Council of Montserrat to Lords of Trade and Plantations, 13 July 1680, *CSPCS 1677–1680*, 574–5.

146 As he does, for example (60), where he directly rejects Daniel Defoe's opinion that a white servant was a slave.

147 Eltis, "Europeans and the Rise and Fall of African Slavery," 1399–423.

148 Berleant-Schiller, "Free Labor," 539–64.

149 Beckles, *White Servitude*, 6.

150 Ibid., 8.

151 Ibid., 79.

152 Beckles, "'Black Men in White Skins,'" 5–21.

153 See also Sheppard, "An Historical Sketch of the Poor Whites of Barbados," 71–94.

154 Sheppard, *The "Redlegs" of Barbados*, 2.

155 See J. Michael Hill in *American Historical Review* (April 1994), 573 (rev. of Grainne Henry, *The Irish Military Community in Spanish Flanders, 1586–1621*).

156 Sheppard, *The "Redlegs" of Barbados*, 3.

157 Ibid.

158 On Scottish dress, which was the same as the Irish until the invention of the short kilt (in part as an attempt to escape from Irish influence), see Hugh Trevor-Roper, "The Invention of Tradition: The Highland Tradition of Scotland" in Hobsbawm and Ranger, *The Invention of Tradition*, 19–21.

159 An easily accessible example of such usage is Jeaffreson (ed.), *A Young Squire of the seventeenth century*, 2: 194–9. The date is late (1682) but one could put together literally sores of mss examples from before mid-century.

160 Galenson, *White Servitude in Colonial America*, 8–9.

161 Beckles, *White Servitude*, 75.

162 Patterson, *Slavery and Social Death*, 21–7.

163 Earl of Cork to Lord Dorchester, 6 May 1631, quoted in Gwynn, "Early Irish Emigration – Part II," 659. Recall here that substantially the same judgment had been made by Sir Henry Bourchier in 1623.

164 Gwynn, "Early Irish Emigration – Part II," 660–3.

165 Beckles, *White Servitude*, 61–3; Beckles, "A 'riotous and unruly lot'" 506; Dunn, *Sugar and Slaves*, 56–7.

166 Eltis, "Europeans and the Rise and Fall of African Slavery," (1413) points out that however severe these conditions may have been, the indentured servants travelled in ships with a great deal more amenities than on slave ships.

167 Beckles, *White Servitude*, 5.

168 Galenson, *White Servitude in Colonial America*, 102. The examples Gwynn provides ("Documents Relating to the Irish," 278) drawn from Kinsale indentures are most frequently for four years, with seven years being the maximum.

169 Gwynn, "Documents Relating to the Irish," 278.

170 Bridenbaugh, *No Peace Beyond the Line*, 113.

171 Based on Pulsipher, "Cultural Landscape," 99–100. The original estimates were by Governor William Stapleton.

172 As Bridenbaugh, *No Peace Beyond the Line*, 275. I will return to this point in the next chapter. The open purchase of freehold land was in fact unusual in the cultures from which most colonists originated.

173 Beckles, *White Servitude*, 122. Cf. Eltis, "Europeans and the Rise and Fall of African Slavery," 1405.

174 Another way of phrasing this is to say that an item which the employer conceives of as an input cost is, from the viewpoint of the labourer who controls it (as a free labourer), an endowment which he can sell. One way of conceiving of what the former indentured servant takes with him upon completion is to ask, What non-recoverable costs must the employer pay? These are (a) costs of transport, (b) profit and overhead to the servant transporter, and (c) freedom dues. Items "a" and "c" are taken away by the former servant upon completion of indenture. Thus, the average indentured servant, upon "freedom," receives a total package worth £15 to £18 sterling.

175 *CSPCS 1574–1660*, [n.d.] 1652, 374.

176 On the 1636 recruiting trip of Captain Anthony, mentioned earlier, the captain was imprisoned for two days by Kinsale's mayor when he was found to have kidnapped two servants (who were released) (Beckles, *White Servitude*, 62). In contrast, for English servants, kidnapping was more often necessary, especially to Barbados (thence the seventeenth-century term "Barbadosed" for being press-ganged or kidnapped). The kidnapping business in England was not ended until the 1680s. In 1682 the leading kidnapper was heavily fined by the Lord Chief Justice and, in 1686, an order in council, "checking the evil practices of people called 'spirits'" was framed, and its enforcement directed by King in Council on 26 March 1686 (Pares, *A West-India Fortune*, 8; Order of King in Council, 26 March 1686, *CSPCS 1685–1688*, 166).

177 Bridenbaugh, *No Peace Beyond the Line*, 15; Beckles, "A Riotous and Unruly Lot," 505–6. Barbados was most extreme in the West Indies in its anti-Irish valence. Why this should be the case, I do not know, but it does make one leery of uncritically using Barbados (which has a richly documented history) as a source of analogies for the much less well documented history of Montserrat.

178 Charles de Rochefort, *Histoire naturelle et moralle des Isles Antilles de l'Amerique* (1658), quoted in Bridenbaugh, *No Peace Beyond the Line*, 37. This description agrees with the observations of Ligon (cited below) concerning Barbados.

179 Ligon, *A True and Exact History*, 44–5, 109, 113.

180 For instance, the well-known mid-1660s observations that on Barbados the indentured servants, "a very great part Irish, [are] derided by the Negroes and branded with the epithet of white slaves" should not be transferred to Montserrat and certainly not the Montserrat of the pre-1650 era: the less so because there were so few slaves on early Montserrat as to make such a comparison unlikely. Source C.O. 1/XXI, no. 170, reproduced in Gwynn, "Documents Relating to the Irish," 250.

Incidentally, this same document (which Gwynn [ibid., 249] attributes to John Scott, a Restoration adventurer), is the source of the frequently quoted statement that the observer has seen "English, Scotch and Irish at work in the parching sun without shirt, shoe or stocking," while Negroes work at their respective trades "in a good condition." This has sometimes been seen as one of the sources of the "Redleg" condition. (Sheppard [*The "Redlegs" of Barbados*, 3] relies on it, albeit without citation.)

The interesting point, however, is that historians have taken the document's claim that such a condition represented obvious oppression of the labourers. Actually, it indicates one of the rare times when we see settlers from the British Isles who are not dressed in the tropics as if they were in Munster or in the Home Counties.

181 Bridenbaugh, *No Peace Beyond the Line*, 160.

182 Dunn, "The English Sugar Islands and the Founding of South Carolina," 87.

183 Ligon, *A True and Exact History*, 45–6, quoted in Sheppard, *The "Redlegs" of Barbados*, 23.

184 See Beckles, "A Riotous and Unruly Lot," 517–20.

185 Beckles, *White Servitude*, 82.

CHAPTER THREE

1 Thornton, *West-India Policy under the Restoration*, 22.

2 Hamshire, *The British in the Caribbean*, 53–64.

3 The 1650 appointment is referred to in Francis Lord Willoughby to Roger Osborne, 19 Feb. 1660, reproduced in Gwynn, "Documents Relating to the Irish in the West Indies," 242–3.

4 Williamson, *The Caribbee Islands under the Proprietary Patents*, 178 *n* 1.

5 Two small Dutch vessels tried to provision themselves from Montserrat in mid-1652, but were denied. (Daniel Searle to Council of State, 30 June 1652, *CSPCS 1574–1660*, 383.)

6 McGinn, "How Irish Is Montserrat?," 15; English, "Records of Montserrat," 59–61.

7 The primary documentation for the story here being told is reproduced in Gwynn, "Documents Relating to the Irish," 221–8, with additional information from *CSPCS 1574–1660*, 419–20, 434. The originals are in PROL, CO 1/12.

8 McGinn, "How Irish Is Montserrat?", 15.

9 The entire deed of transfer is reproduced in English, "Records of Montserrat," 59–61.

10 *CSPCS 1574–1660*, 31 Dec. [?] 1655, 434.

11 See Anthony Briskett II to the king, 17 June 1669, *CSPCS 1669–1675*, 28.

12 Unfortunately, the standard literature on the subject deals almost entirely with England and mostly with the eighteenth century. See, for example, Coldham, *Emigrants in Chains* and Ekirch, *Bound for America.*

13 Eltis, "Europeans and the Rise and Fall of African Slavery in the Americas, 1407–8.

14 In any case, under Irish statutes, it was only in 1707 that vagrants could be banished. Even non-capital felons could not be banished before the 1660s (Ekirch, *Bound for America*, 24). The Cromwellian era of course is the great exception to those limitations.

15 Gwynn, "Cromwell's Policy of Transportation – Part I," 611.

16 Ibid., 614.

17 Ibid., 615.

18 Instructions to Commissioners of Ireland, 24 August 1652, reproduced ibid., 615.

19 Order in Council of State, 19 Oct. 1654, *CSPCS 1574–1660*, 419.

20 Order of the Council of State, 22 May 1656, ibid., 441. One should note that the Commonwealth did not forget the spiritual needs of the forces of order in the West Indies. On 9 June 1655 the Council of State ordered that 2,000 bibles be sent to the soldiers in the West Indies.

21 Instructions to Commissioners of Ireland, 12 May 1653, reproduced in Gwynn, "Cromwell's Policy," 616.

22 Minutes of Council of State, 26 Sept. 1655 and Order of Council of State, 3 Oct. 1655, *CSPCS 1574–1660*, 430, 431. For the conditions of several instances of transportation of Irish vagrants see Gwynn, "Cromwell's Policy," 616–22.

23 See Patrick J. Corish, "The Cromwellian Conquest, 1649–53," in Moody, Martin, and Byrne (eds.), *A New History of Ireland*, 3:363.

24 Ibid., 623.

25 Gwynn, "Cromwell's Policy of Transportation – Part II," 291–9.

26 Extract from Minutes of the Council of Barbados, 21 May 1656, reproduced in Gwynn, "Documents Relating to the Irish," 235.

27 "There are several Irish Servants and Negroes out in Rebellion in the thicketts and thereabouts," Extract from Minutes of the Council of Barbados, 6 Nov. 1655, reproduced ibid., 234.

28 Gwynn, "Cromwell's Policy – Part II," 301, quoting *Persecution of the Irish Catholics* by Cardinal Moran.

29 Ibid.

30 Corish, "Cromwellian Conquests," in Moody, Martin, and Byrne (eds.), *A New History of Ireland*, judges that 34,000 of the exiles went voluntarily to serve in continental European armies. This, if accurate, reduces even further the number that we may infer landed in the West Indies.

31 Sheppard, "A Historical Sketch of the Poor Whites of Barbados," 73.

32 My estimate, made independently of Corish's, should be compared to his. He concludes that 8,000 Irish were forcibly sent to Barbados and another 4,000 to other West Indian islands (Corish, "Cromwellian Conquest," in Moody, Martin and Byrne [eds.], *A New History of Ireland*, 364).

33 The Navigation Acts of 1651, 1660, and 1663 still permitted the direct servant trade from Ireland.

The attitude of Cromwellians to the land of Ireland is indicated in an anonymous Puritan pamphlet of 1652, which celebrated Cromwell's 1649 victory in Ireland. It stated, "War is never its own end … Fighting and planting are inseparable." It asserted that Ireland was worth more by far than was Scotland: "in the rich soil of Ireland we aim at founding of new English colonies, and thereby of enlarging England." Anon., *The Present Posture and Condition of Ireland* (London: n.p. 1652), 7 and 12.

34 Return by Governor William Stapleton, July 1672, CSPCS *1669–1674*, 394.

35 A census of 1678 enumerated not only adult males but women and children as well. By applying the ratio of adult males to women and children of that census, to the 1672 enumeration, one acquires a reasonable notional total figure for the total white population in 1672.

36 Higham (*The Development of the Leeward Islands under the Restoration, 1660–1688*, 143) states that the French war of 1666–67 marked a turning point in the history of the Leeward Islands. He also points out that "It is quite impossible to say what was the population of the islands before the war, records of immigration were never kept, and such records as did exist were mostly destroyed in the fighting" (143–4).

37 Beckles, *White Servitude and Black Slavery in Barbados, 1627–1715*, 60–1.

38 I am concerned that the reader will encounter the argument in the influential *William and Mary Quarterly* of Riva Berleant-Schiller that the economy of Montserrat "evolved from a tobacco economy worked mainly by the European indentured servants into a sugar economy worked by African slaves" (Berleant-Schiller, "Free Labor and the Economy in Seventeenth-Century Montserrat," 540). This is based on a seemingly authoritative table in which it is stated that there were in 1678, 2,682 white in-arrivals on the island and that 1,644 of these were bound, 1,038 free (ibid., Table 1, 541). This requires comment in detail because the figures are the basis for an interpretation of Montserrat as a white bound-worker economy, which is certainly not the historical case.

Berleant-Schiller's figures on the bound-free breakdown are quite literally impossible. The 1678 census with which Berleant-Schiller works showed that there were 943 children included in the total white population, children being by definition below the age when they could be indentured. Now, even if one takes Berleant-Schiller's total population figure of 2,682 whites, and removes from it the 943 children, one has a total adult white population of 1,739, of which she says 1,644 (94.5 percent) are indentured servants! For this to be the case, it would mean that (a) 94.5 percent of the white adult population had come to the island since 1671, assuming a six-year indentureship; and (b) given the inhibitions on indentured servants marrying and having children, it would mean that the remaining 6 percent of adult whites – ninety-five persons, meaning, say, fifty households – had over 900 children, or, roughly eighteen children per household.

Not only is "b" a demographic improbability of some proportion, but condition "a" does not seem any more likely, given that in December 1671 we find Sir Charles Wheeler, governor of the Leeward Islands, reporting that since his arrival (he had been there well over a year, probably closer to two years), though there had been forty ships come and go in the islands, there had "not been six … English, Scotch, and Irish" newcomers, and no blacks or slaves (Charles Wheeler to Council for Foreign Plantations, 9 December 1671, *CSPCS 1669–1674*, 289). Wheeler was a notorious blowhard, and, further, wanted increased labour shipped to the islands, so one should not take his assessment as literally true, but rather as indicative that, from the end of the French War, 1667, to at least the close of 1671, there was no significant white in-migration. Therefore, were most of the white population of Montserrat to be, in 1678, bound labourers, as Berleant-Schiller believes, there would have had to have been a massive immigration to Montserrat of indentured servants in 1672–77, inclusive, one which somehow passed the notice of the authorities both in London and in the Leeward Islands. This is not to mention a concurrent massive, and slightly larger, out-migration from Montserrat of free adult whites – which would have had to have occurred, since, between 1672 and 1678, the total white population of the island actually dropped.

The reader also may be aware of David W. Galenson's table of net migration figures for the British West Indies in his book on white servitude in colonial America (Table H.4, 218). I have no opinion about how good the estimates are for other islands, but for Montserrat they are wholly untenable. To take the troubled decade of 1670–80, for example, he infers that Montserrat had a net in-migration of 2,259 white persons. (For his assumptions and methods, see David W. Galenson, *White Servitude in Colonial America*, 212–17. Considering that the white population in 1672 was about 2,835, and that the population in 1678 was somewhat less, 2,676, then for the net in-migration to have been 2,259 in the 1670s (that is, for the number of people coming in, to exceed the number leaving by 2,259), one has to posit

(a) a total in-migration of roughly 5,200 persons, combined with an out-migration of roughly 2,875; or
(b) an in-migration of 2,259 and a death toll in the same period of approximately 2,420; or
(c) any combination of gross immigration and of out-migration and deaths that equalled the suggested net in-migration (2,259) and the decrease in population between 1672 and 1678 (159), and leaves, in 1678, a population of 2,676.

Now, in fact, both local and London authorities were unaware either of (a) any unusual white migration into Montserrat; (b) any great out-migration, though there was a steady and normal leakage; (c) or any plague or other cause of widespread death, which would have made Galenson's figures possible. Galenson's figures of the 1670s are all the more impossible because, as we know from Governor Wheeler's testimony, the two years 1670–71, inclusive, were a complete washout as far as white in-migration was concerned.

The manifest impossibility of Galenson's estimates concerning in-migration to Montserrat in the 1670s does not necessarily invalidate his estimates for any of the other islands. That is for historians of those jurisdictions to evaluate.

In the case of Berleant-Schiller's work, however, it is important to go somewhat further. I think the arguments already adduced indicate that she is wrong about the white indentured servants being the majority of the work force in the 1670s. Therefore, her whole discussion of the economy of Montserrat in the later 1670s is untenable.

However, the real question is, how did she get things so wrong? for she is a very good scholar and if she has been misled, other, less talented scholars will be totally flummoxed. I think the problem originated as follows. Berleant-Schiller (557) refers to a poll tax list of 1678 which shows tax payments on 2,636 bondspeople, both white and black. She reasons that "if 992 of these are known to be slaves, there remained 1,644 servants and therefore 1,038 free whites." That would mean that 61.3 percent of the white population of all ages were indentured servants and that (as mentioned above) 94.5 percent of the adult whites were indentured.

But the "if" in her calculation is inaccurate. The number 992 for African slaves comes not from a delineation of bondspeople but from the usually repeated version of the 1678 census of Montserrat. (The island accounts for 1678, 1679, and 1680 do the poll tax "by the severall lists." This refers to the enumeration lists of 1678, as the numbers of negroes referred to – 993 in 1680 – make clear. John Rylands Library, Manchester, Stapleton MSS 2/3). However (as discussed in detail in Appendix A), this number is inaccurate, and is a considerable underestimate of the black population. This occurs because of the eccentric methods of enumeration employed in 1678: in only three of the ten enumeration districts were all of the slaves reported. As detailed in Appendix A, instead of 992 black slaves, a much more realistic (but still conservative) estimate of blacks on the island is 1,894.

Therefore, the basic arithmetic, the foundation of Berleant-Schiller's views on the economy of Montserrat, might be corrected as follows:

1 There were, indeed, 2,636 bondspeople.
2 1,894 of these were, by corrected estimates, black.
3 Therefore an estimated 742 white indentured servants were living on Montserrat in 1678.
4 This is 27.6 percent (742 of 2,682) of the white population.

Actually, however, even that revision is highly questionable. I suspect that the meaning of the original data has been misread. That is, the poll tax – the "levy imposed on Christians … and Negroes" – was just that: a poll tax, district by district, on what was believed to be (a) the black population as set down by the same methods: the 1678 census had reported in its eccentric accounting 989 blacks, and in 1680 the poll taxes required payment for 993 blacks; and (b) on all adult whites. The 1678 census had enumerated 1,735 adult whites and the 1680 poll tax required the several districts to pay headage for 1,680 "Christians." Given that the line between childhood and adulthood was not numerically defined, it is probable that the reason there were slightly fewer people caught by the 1680 poll tax than were enumerated in the 1678 census, was that, given it was tax time, children of ambiguous years were not counted as adults. Also, the white population of the island had begun to decline. (Cf 1678 census data in the text and the account books, Stapleton Papers 2/3.)

The sum of this discussion is that, for whatever reason (I think basic misreading of the primary data, confounding a poll tax with a tax on indentured servants), a conclusion was drawn concerning the indentured population that, from other demographic data, we know to be totally impossible.

39 See the depositions reproduced in Gwynn, "Documents Relating to the Irish," 225–8.

40 Translated and reproduced, ibid., 214–19.

41 Pulsipher, "Cultural Landscape," Table 1, 40.

42 Higham, *Development of the Leeward Islands*, 139. The governor, Lord Willoughby, passed the petition on to the king with favourable comment.

43 Parry and Sherlock, *A Short History of the West Indies*, 58.

44 Higham, *Development of the Leeward Islands*, 198. One suspects that the glut was in large part caused by the Navigation Acts of 1660 and 1663. Colonies where the acts could easily be enforced (unlike Montserrat) suddenly were forced to switch from selling to Europe, via the Dutch, to selling into England.

45 Pulsipher, "Cultural Landscape," 45.

46 Ibid., 38.

47 For background on Irish trading patterns in this period: see Cullen, *Anglo-Irish Trade*; Nash, "Irish Atlantic Trade"; and Truxes, *Irish-American Trade*.

48 The discussion of the Blake family which follows is based on Blake (ed.), *Blake Family Records*. This is a collection of transcriptions of contemporary documents. Except in the case of direct quotations, I shall not cite specific documents, since the content of the entire volume is relevant to the discussion.

49 Petition of John Blake to Commissioners for the plantation of the County of Galway, 30 April 1640, reproduced ibid., 50–1. The spelling in this and subsequent Blake documents quoted is modernized.

50 He was allowed to operate within Galway as a merchant under the terms of a 1671 proclamation of the Lord Lieutenant of Ireland permitting Roman Catholics to hire and purchase premises in the corporate towns of Ireland. One suspects that, as usually was the case in these penal matters, the Catholic occupancy in places like Galway preceded the official permission.

51 At some point before this final transaction, John had become a partner with Henry in the Montserrat estate.

52 Henry Blake to Thomas Blake, 29 May 1675, reproduced in Blake (ed.), *Blake Family Records*, 112.

53 John Blake to Thomas Blake, 5 Nov. 1675, reproduced ibid., 112–13. Spelling and punctuation modernized.

54 The Blake line continued on Montserrat, however. See text below.

55 Trevor Burnard reminds me that Montserrat was one of the least auspicious places in the Caribbean to plant sugar, and, hence, it was late in starting sugar cultivation and early to move away from sugar, and even when sugar was central, other crops were significant. I am grateful to Dr Burnard for this and other comments on an earlier version of this study.

56 Eric Williams, "The Origin of Negro Slavery," reprinted from Williams, *Capitalism and Slavery*, in Horowitz (ed.), *Peoples and Cultures of the Caribbean*, 63.

57 See Eltis, "Europeans and the Rise and Fall of African Slavery," and also Eltis, "Labour and Coercion."

58 Galeano, *Memory of Fire*, 244.

59 Bridenbaugh, *No Peace Beyond the Line*, 106–7.

60 Warrant to Samuel Atkins, 3 July 1649, CSPCS *1574–1660*, 330.

61 Deposition of 2 April 1654, reproduced in Gwynn, "Documents Relating to the Irish," 223.

62 Fergus, "Montserrat, 'Colony of Ireland,'" 329.

63 This statement is based on the 1678 census. See Appendix "A." This corrects Galenson (*White Servitude in Colonial America*, Table 8.2, 120) who, based on McCusker (*Rum and the American Revolution*, Table B-49, 637) states that the blacks comprised in 1678 51 percent of the island's population. This comes from McCusker's deriving an inferred black population that totalled 2,681. This, however, is based on a misreading of the 1678 census by McCusker. The 992 slaves reported in that document were not (as McCusker believed) all adult males: in some districts women and children were included in the total. Thus McCusker, and Galenson after him, over-estimated the total number of blacks in Montserrat.

64 William Stapleton to Council for Trade and Foreign Plantations, 17 July 1672, CSPCS *1669–1674*, 392–3.

65 Council of Montserrat to Lords of Trade and Plantations, 13 July 1680, CSPCS *1677–1680*, 574.

66 Ibid., 574–5. Incidentally, complaints about the paucity of white servants confirm what I suggested earlier: Berleant-Schiller and Galenson each is wrong in presenting arguments that are based on the assumption that there was a big influx of white indentured labour in the 1670s.

67 In fact, in August 1679, the Montserratians had received a full cargo of 117 slaves (which they are conveniently ignoring in their 1680 petition). That lot in the records of the Royal African Company, however, was described as a "very mean parcel" (Higham, *Development of the Leeward Islands*, Table VI, 161).

68 *Acts of Assembly, passed in the Island of Montserrat; from 1668 to 1740, inclusive* (London: King's Printer, 1790). Law 9, 1668.

This collection is not to be confused with the *Abridgement* of the laws which was published in the same year.

Hereafter, reference to legal acts will be to the calendar year, and to the number of the law in the legal series that begins in 1668. Thus, for example, the law cited above will be referred to as *Laws* 1668: 9.

69 Abstract of article concerning St Christopher and elsewhere, Dec. 1675, CSPCS *1675–76*, 327.

70 Berleant-Schiller, "Free Labour," Table II, 549.

71 Caulfield (ed.), *The Council Book of the Corporation of Kinsale*, Appendix B, 335.

72 McGinn, "How Irish Is Montserrat?", 17.

73 Deposition of January 1668, reproduced in Gwynn, "Documents Relating to the Irish," 259–61.

74 Truxes, *Irish-American Trade*, 101.

75 Pulsipher and Goodwin, "A Sugar Boiling House," 25–6.

76 McGinn, "How Irish Is Montserrat?", 17.

77 For a succinct discussion of seventeenth-century Irish land law changes and their effects, see Gillespie, *Transformation of the Irish Economy*, 19–24. For the economic and social context, see Cullen, *An Economic History of Ireland since 1660*, 7–25, and his *Emergence of Modern Ireland*, 25–60.

78 I am not here denying the fundamental insight of Macfarlane in *Origins of English Individualism* that the ownership of land as an economic good developed much earlier in England than in most continental European countries (and one should add, ahead of Scotland and Ireland). Nor is one inclined to disagree with the notion that most land was held freehold (that is, non-feudally), nor that a lively market in English tenancies developed in the early modern period.

However, this is easily confused with a mistaken set of ideas: (a) that most occupiers were freeholders. They were not, even in England; (b) that tenancies traded as pure economic entities without inhibitions of law and custom; (c) that the situation in southern and central England was the same as that for the most of the land area of the British Isles. Indeed, in Ulster, rundale communal holdings were the basis of the agrarian organization of much of the province as late as the 1750s. See Desmond McCourt, "The Decline of Rundale, 1750–1850," in Roebuck (ed.), *Plantation to Partition*, 119–39.

79 Fergus, *Montserrat*, 18.

80 Charles II to Francis Lord Willoughby, 9 July 1660, *CSPCS 1574–1660*, 483. The various entails on the Carlisle patent as of 1660 are discussed in Thornton, *West-India Policy*, 22.

81 Document lodged against Willoughby, concerning Surinam, 16 July 1660, *CSPCS 1574–1660*, 483.

82 Smith, *True Travels*, 53.

83 Thornton, *West-India Policy*, 36–8. Though surrendering the lease, Willoughby did not surrender any right he had to the renewal of the patent (which might someday become valuable). That right of renewal was quashed by the Committee of Plantation in 1669, when Francis Lord Willoughby was dead, and his brother William was holding the governorship of Barbados and the Leeward Islands. See 131–3.

84 Miscellaneous paper, West Indies, 1674–76, *CSPCS 1574–1676*, 155; "An Account of His Majestys Island of Barbados and the Government

thereof, 1676," ibid., 348; Michael Craton, "Reluctant Creoles. The Planters' World in the British West Indies," in Bailyn and Morgan, *Strangers Within the Realm*, 329; Dunn, *Sugar and Slaves*, 122.

85 Higham, *Development of the Leeward Islands*, 182.

86 In the case of the process in Ireland, the landholders always seem to have got back less than they surrendered, or were lumbered with new charges and fines. This was not, however, the case in this process in Montserrat.

87 *Laws* 1668: nos. 1, 2, and 3.

88 *Laws* 1668: 4.

89 *Laws* 1668: 5. One of these fallow plantations to which title was not granted at this time was that of "Mr. Irish," the property being 160 acres "sometimes called the cow pasture." This bears note because the earliest document of individual freehold possession anyone has yet found, was a fragment that T. Savage English discovered, saying "Lord Willoughby to Bridget Irish and William Irish, Patent of Estate." (English, "Records of Montserrat," 59). This well may have been the 150 acre "Cow Pasture," which they subsequently were able to put into production, and thereby escape its permanent confiscation.

90 *Laws* 1670: 21.

91 Francis Lord Willoughby to Roger Osborne, 19 Feb. 1660, reproduced in Gwynn, "Documents Relating to the Irish," 242–3.

92 A letter from Osborne to Willoughby of 20 September 1659, providing "a verie acceptable account" of Osborne's governorship, is referred to ibid.

93 The pre-1668 structure (which dates from 1638) can be glimpsed in a series of ten laws, of the neo-feudal council and governor, that were re-enacted by the new government in 1668. (See *Laws*: 26–31.)

Pulsipher, "Cultural Landscape," 42 *n* 5) states that a council existed "at least by 1659," but the citation she provides is inaccurate. Even if there was an assembly, it probably was an *ad hoc* affair, designed to express grievance, and not part of the formal governmental structure. That said, there is one piece of opposite evidence. One of the depositions against Roger Osborne in 1654 referred to "A Common Council and Assembly" (Gwynn, "Documents Relating to the Irish," 223).

94 See the description of the systems of government which prevailed in the Leeward Islands, as of 1671. They all followed the Westminster pattern. Sir Charles Wheeler to Council for Foreign Plantations, 9 Dec. 1671, CSPCS *1669–1674*, 287.

95 Fergus, *Montserrat*, 28. The right of all freeholders to vote for assembly members was confirmed for all the Leeward Island assemblies by an act of the Leeward Island General Council and General Assembly of 1694 (no. 14). *Acts of Assembly passed in the Charibbee Leeward Islands*

from 1690 to 1730 (London: Lords Commissioners of Trade and Plantations, 1734. Hereafter cited as *Leeward Acts.*

96 The individual who experienced this ambiguity most intensively was the deputy-governor, for he was expected to be simultaneously monarch-surrogate and errand boy for the Lords of Trade and Plantations. As William Laws observes, "It is necessary to stress this role of go-between for it could be decisive in colonial administration." Earlier Laws noted, "The record shows too that in no sugar colony was the role of go-between more marked than in the Leeward Islands" (Laws, *Distinction, Death and Disgrace*, 1).

97 *Leeward Acts* 1705: 31.

98 Minute of 3 Dec. 1751, *Journal of the Commissioners for Trade and Plantations from January 1749–1750 to December 1753*, 234. For an indication that Barbados suffered from the same ambiguity, see Thornton, *West-India Policy*, 190–1.

99 Gwynn, "Documents Relating to the Irish," (245–9) reproduces very useful extracts from the contemporary account, Du Tertre's *Histoire Generale des Antilles* (1667).

100 Petition of William Stapleton and Council and Assembly of Montserrat to Council for Foreign Plantations, 19 Jun. 1672, CSPCS *1669–1674*, 373.

101 Richard Carey to William People, 26 July 1697, CSPCS *1696–1697*, 565–6.

102 "Account of the Island of Montserrat [Census of 1672]," CSPCS *1669–1674*, 394.

103 Thomas Modyford to Lord Arlington, 4 April 1667, CSPCS *1661–1668*, 459.

104 William Lord Willoughby to Lord Arlington, 11 Feb. 1668, CSPCS *1661–1668*, 547.

105 Thomas Lynch to Lord Arlington, 15 Jun 1671, CSPCS *1669–1674*, 227.

106 William Lord Willoughby to Lords of the Council, 9 July 1668, CSPCS *1661–1668*, 587.

107 Du Tertre, *Histoire Generale des Antilles*, 203–4, reproduced in Gwynn, "Documents Relating to the Irish," 247.

108 Remonstrance Declaration and Petition of Inhabitants of Montserrat to William Lord Willoughby [Jan. 1668], reproduced in Gwynn, ibid., 259. Abstract in CSPCS *1661–1668*, 540. Spelling has been modernized.

109 William Lord Willoughby to Charles II, 11 February 1668, ibid., 547.

110 Ibid.

111 William Lord Willoughby to Joseph Williamson, 3 April 1668, ibid., 556.

112 Gwynn, "Documents Relating to the Irish," 259–61.

113 William Lord Willoughby to Charles II, ——— 1669, reproduced in Gwynn, ibid., 264–5. Abstract in CSPCS *1669–1674*, 29.

114 Ibid., 264.

115 *Laws*, 1668: 5. Technically, this was not quite the same as attainder for treason. Everyone on the island had his or her lands surrendered to the English Crown and then all had them regranted, except certain individuals, of whom Briskett was the first named. He was not charged with any crime.

(Note that this act of April 1668 was the last to be dealt with directly by Willoughby. Act No. 6 was approved by Stapleton's authority, which implies that he arrived to take control of Montserrat in late April 1668.)

116 Anthony Briskett to Charles II, 17 June 1669, *CSPCS 1669–1674*, 28.

117 Anthony Briskett to Charles II, ——— 1669, ibid., 28–9.

118 Willoughby to Charles II, in Gwynn, "Documents Relating to the Irish," 264–5. My inference that it was Stanley who received the land comes from Willoughby's reporting that he had allocated the residual of the Forthouse plantation to support and maintain the deputy governor for the time being (ibid., 265); and from Willoughby's report to the Lords of Council, 9 July 1668, that Stanley had temporarily been appointed deputy governor. Stapleton soon replaced him.

119 Willoughby to Charles II, 1669, in Gwynn, "Documents Relating to the Irish," 265.

120 Thomas Borhall Jr to Joseph Williamson, 28 Nov. 1670, *CSPCS 1669–1674*, 139.

121 Pulsipher, "The Cultural Landscape of Montserrat," 129.

122 William Stapleton to Council for Trade and Plantations, 1673, *CSPCS 1669–1674*, 501.

123 Higham, *Development of the Leeward Islands*, 99.

124 William Stapleton to Lords of Trade and Plantations, 18 Dec. 1679, *CSPCS 1667–1680*, 458.

125 Higham, *Development of the Leeward Islands*, 118.

126 Extract from Du Tertre, *Histoire Générale des Antilles*, in Gwynn, "Documents Relating to the Irish," 246.

127 Pulsipher, "The Cultural Landscape of Montserrat," 135; *Laws* 1668: 8.

128 William Stapleton to Council for Plantation, 27 May 1672, *CSPCS 1669–1674*, 364.

129 Burns, *History of the British West Indies*, 343–5; thirteen depositions of 1676 on the Indian Warner case, *CSPCS 1675–1676*, 382–5.

130 William Stapleton to Lords of Trade and Plantations, 20 June 1676, *CSPCS 1675–1676*, 410.

131 Ibid.

132 In 1683, after yet another set of Carib raids on Montserrat and Antigua, he took a small fleet to Dominica where he destroyed eleven war canoes. He got thirty-five more at St Vincent. (Bridenbaugh, *No Peace Beyond the Line*, 173).

133 Pulsipher, *Seventeenth-Century Montserrat*, 46.
134 Lord Carlisle to Lord Secretary Coventry, 24 February 1679, CSPCS *1677–1680*, 333. Even though he had moved most of his establishment to Jamaica, Carroll was enumerated in the 1678 census as having a domicile on Montserrat, with no slaves, one male servant, a wife and four children.
135 Bridenbaugh, *No Peace Beyond the Line*, (224) dates the law as "sometime before 1678" but provides no citation. Pulsipher, "The Cultural Landscape of Montserrat," (47) cites Carroll's complaint but does not cite a law. I can find no such law in the Montserrat statutes. I suspect that the statute was one affecting the entire Leeward Islands, not just Montserrat, and was made by the Leeward Islands council and assembly, a body that met only irregularly.
136 *Laws* 1668: 10.
137 *Laws* 1669: 14. The law provided for a fine of 1,000 pounds in sugar for each violation of the over-charging clause. One-half of the fine was to go to the informer, which opens up a whole new branch of the informing trade. For provisions against shebeens see *Laws* 1670: 13.
138 *Laws*, p. 28. (Confusingly called 1668:5, a number that is also used for an Act of 1668).
139 *Laws* 1669: 14.
140 *Laws* 1670: 20.
141 *Laws* 1670: 16, sect. I.
142 *Laws* 1673: 24. Notice (1) that this applies to free labourers and was limited to amounts of 1,000 pounds sugar, (2) one may infer that non-payment of the wages of freed labourers was an inflammatory practice, and if that was so in 1673, it well may have been so in 1667, the year of the jacquerie; and (3) that the fine was specified in sugar, not tobacco. From the 1670s onwards, sugar becomes the chief commodity-currency, thus indicating that it is becoming ascendant on the island.
143 *Laws* 1670: 16, sects. II and III.
144 *Laws* 1669: 15.
145 William Stapleton to Council for Trade and Plantations, 17 July 1672, CSPCS *1669–1674*, 393.
146 *Laws* 1668: 11, sect. I.
147 Ibid.
148 Ibid., Section II.
149 Ibid.
150 Johnston, "The Stapleton Sugar Plantations in the Leeward Islands," 177. With correction from *Laws* 1679: 30.
151 See for example, depositions taken by John Carrill (var: Carroll) in CSPCS *1675–1676*, 382.
152 *Laws* 1680: 31.

153 *Laws* 1680: 32; McGinn, "How Irish Is Montserrat?" 16, has Cotter returning to settle in Ballinsperrig in County Cork in 1682. That did not keep him from continuing to receive the fees from his lifetime offices (held in addition to his Montserrat position) of secretary and marshal of the Leeward Islands.

The Calendar of State Papers for this period, 1681–85, is quite comprehensive and well indexed, and he is the only deputy governor Montserrat documented in that period. I suspect that he had the job done for him by someone who was acceptable to his friend William Stapleton. A reasonable guess would be that the surrogate was Redmond Stapleton, who becomes deputy governor of Montserrat in his own right in 1685. That, however, is surmise.

154 McGinn, "How Irish Is Montserrat?", 15–16; Higham, "The Accounts of a Colonial Governor's Agent in the Seventeenth Century," 264, 268; O'Cuiv, "James Cotter," 135–9.

155 McGinn, "How Irish Is Montserrat?", 16. In addition to no longer hiding his Catholicism once he had returned to Ireland, Cotter supported James II in 1688–91, and was made governor of the city of Cork. He survived the defeat of the Jacobites (being protected under the Treaty of Limerick) and remained a major figure in County Cork until his death in 1705. His eldest son was executed in 1720 for abducting and ravishing a Quaker woman, but this was held in popular opinion to have been merely the excuse for a political execution. See Breandan O'Buachalla, "The Making of a Cork Jacobite," in O'Flanagan and Buttimer (eds.), *Cork History and Society*. Cullen (*The Emergence of Modern Ireland*, 198–200), adjudges this execution to have been easily the most traumatic political event of the first half of the eighteenth century.

156 Johnston, "Stapleton Sugar Plantations," 176; Cullen, *The Emergence of Modern Ireland*, 118 and 126.

157 Burns, *British West Indies*, 341–2; Higham, "Accounts," 264.

158 Johnston, "Stapleton Sugar Plantations," 177, and see Higham, "Some Treasurers Accounts of Montserrat," 87–90, and his "Accounts," 263–85.

159 William Lord Willoughby to Charles II, ——— 1669, reproduced in Gwynn, "Documents Relating to the Irish," 264–5.

160 Johnston, "Stapleton Sugar Plantations," 176–8; Thomas Lynch to Lord Arlington, 15 June 1671, *CSPCS 1669–1674*, 226.

161 Johnston, "Stapleton Sugar Plantations," 177–8.

162 The documents, quoted ibid., 177–8, are very confusing. Stapleton talks of owning two plantations, the Waterwork and the Windward Plantations (plural). From comparison with a map, they seem to comprise 1,200 to 1,500 acres, roughly two square miles. That, however, is a very rough estimate indeed.

163 Johnston, "Stapleton Sugar Plantations," 178.
164 Ibid., 178–9.
165 In 1682, Stapleton's agent paid a £50 bill drawn on behalf of Pim (Higham, "Accounts," 278).
166 Petition of William Stapleton to Charles II, enclosed in Stapleton to Lord Arlington 13 July 1672, *CSPCS 1669–1674*, 389–90.
167 Johnston, "Stapleton Sugar Plantations," 179.
168 Ibid., 178. It may be relevant that a John Nagle acted as an Irish agent for Stapleton. See Higham, "Accounts," 283, 285. The Nagles were a distinguished County Cork family and were part of the same social network as the Cotter family. In the early eighteenth century they became in-laws when the ill-fated James Cotter and Garret Nagle of Ballygriffin married two sisters. It is more than a sidebar to the interrelatedness of their society that Richard Burke, the lawyer for James Cotter in his capital case, married a Nagle: these were the parents of the great Edmund Burke. See O'Brien, *The Great Melody*, 3–9.
169 Higham, *Development of the Leeward Islands*, 217.
170 The size of the final testamentary estate is unknown. To give an idea of the scale: his two best plantations on Nevis were a total of 794 acres and had 183 African slaves attached (Sheridan, *Sugar and Slavery*).
171 Higham, "Accounts," 264–6; Johnston, "Stapleton Sugar Plantations," 180; Cullen, *Emergence of Modern Ireland*, 118. At least one branch of the Irish side of the Trant family did well in the homeland in the eighteenth century (even as the Montserrat branch was prospering). This is indicated by Dominick Trant's being elected member of the Irish parliament for Kilkenny in 1781. He was, of course, a Protestant. His brother-in-law was John Fitzgibbon who became Earl of Clare and Lord Chancellor of Ireland. His sister-in-law married into the powerful Beresford clan, through an alliance with William Beresford, who became the Protestant bishop of Ossory. See Thomas P. Power, "Parliamentary Representation in County Kilkenny in the eighteenth century," in Nolan and Whelan (eds.), *Kilkenny*, 318.
172 Higham, "Accounts," 268–9. On the division of the estate, see Johnston, "Stapleton Sugar Plantations," 180–5.

The Antigua estates went to the youngest son, Miles, and the Nevis estates to Anne, Stapleton's wife (a half interest originally had been intended for James, the oldest, but he died).

The Montserrat estate went to the second son, William (b. 1674), who, after the brief term of his elder brother as second baronet, became the third baronet. While in his early twenties, William married his first cousin, Frances Russel, who was the co-heir to two Russel estates on Nevis (to which she had become heir through a series of fortunate deaths).

The De Nogle plantation on St Christopher, which had been intended by William Stapleton to be sold to buy an Irish estate for his eldest son, was not immediately sold and eventually formed part of the inheritance of Miles.

Young Sir William (the third baronet) decided to live on Nevis and to rent his Montserrat plantations to tenants. He died in 1699, leaving two infant sons, who were taken to England by their mother. Thereafter the Montserrat estates were under absentee management and were finally sold in 1727 (Johnston, "Stapleton Sugar Plantations," 180–5).

173 Johnston (ibid.,180), based on contemporary records, suggests the former. McGinn ("How Irish Is Montserrat?" 15), working from age data (one assumes), suggests the latter: age data in the sense that Mary Stapleton predeceased William, her alleged father.

I think Johnston is correct, as in Stapleton's personal accounts there is a payment to James Cotter by agent, "per your order for your daughter's legacy left per Mr. Rookby." (Higham, "Accounts," 217).

174 Burns, *British West Indies*, 340–2; "Revocation of the commission of Sir Charles Wheeler," February 1672, CSPCS *1669–1674*, 328. This was the second time the Great Seal had been lost. The first was in 1665, when Francis Lord Willoughby drowned.

175 William Stapleton to Council for Trade and Plantations, 23 July 1674, CSPCS *1669–1674*, 599.

176 William Stapleton to Council for Trade and Plantations, 23 July 1674, reproduced in Higham, *Development of the Leeward Islands*, 213. An abstract is in CSPCS *1669–1674*, 599.

177 Hughes, "Landholding of Gaelic Poets."

178 Michelle O'Riordan has documented in detail the change of patrons and the change of subjects of praise by the Gaelic poets, while arguing that these changes were essentially conservative. One can grant her argument that the world view of the Gaelic poets hardly changed, while accepting simultaneously that they were willing to change patrons, attest to new loyalties, and, in sum, constantly look out for their own welfare. See O'Riordan, *The Gaelic Mind*.

179 Hughes, "Landholding of Gaelic Poets."

180 William Lord Willoughby to Lords of Trade and Plantation, ——— 1669, CSPCS *1669–1674*, 29.

181 Jeannette D. Black, *The Blathwayt Atlas*.

182 Pulsipher, *Seventeenth-Century Montserrat*, 79–84; Pulsipher, "Assessing the usefulness of a Cartographic Curiosity."

183 Pulsipher, *Seventeenth-Century Montserrat*, Figure 2, 18.

184 The reader who has studied Appendix A may ask why I do not reconstitute the female population district-by-district, employing the same

methods by which I reconstituted the aggregate totals. The answer is that although this would not be technically difficult, the individual cells become so small as to be unreliable.

The same point holds for the African slave population. Although I have no trouble defending my notional accounting of the aggregate number of blacks on the island, I would not feel confident in forcing the analysis down to a district level. An accurate set of procedures for an entire population becomes potentially unreliable for small segments of that same population, unless the characteristics of the smaller cells are the same as the aggregate. And for Montserrat, the one thing certain is that it was a very uneven place indeed.

185 Incidentally, there was a tiny "ghetto" of Scots – really, a concentration – of about eighteen men and their families in Andrew Booth's division. I suspect that this was the result of chain migration.

186 Pulsipher, "The Cultural Landscape of Montserrat," (68, Table 3) presents a set of data on the ratio of white males to white women. (The higher the ratio of males to women, the less "normal" the district will be in terms of community life: think of a lumber camp, or an overseas military unit, as an example.)

The key point is that when one juxtaposes Pulsipher's data on male: female ratios with my Table 5, an almost perfect correlation appears between the normalcy of the sex ratio and the proportion of Irish persons in the census district. The most normal district (that is, the one with the most even sex ratio) was the Cove and Palmetto Point district, of the far south, and the least normal was the Northward division, which was predominantly British. Of course, in the absence of census data on individual households, this situation is suggestive, rather than conclusive. However, unless one suggests that most of the women lived in some form of segregation from the men, the sex-ratio should be accepted as indicative of the most basic contours of the familial structure, and Pulsipher's general correlation is directly confirmed in the three districts for which we have direct data on households.

187 One well might ask what light is cast back upon the migration process by the knowledge that the place where the poorest Irish settlers lived (and, these were the most "native Irish" of the Irish on the island) apparently had the most normal family structure? I could speculate that this is related to (a) anecdotal evidence on the early servant-traders' activities which indicated that significant numbers of young Irish women emigrated, and (b) our certain knowledge from 1815 onwards that, uniquely among European nations, Irish women emigrated in numbers equal to Irish men. I suspect that we are here observing the beginning of that unique pattern. This is not to suggest

that in this early period Irish women migrated as frequently as did men, but that the pattern was beginning and that relative to the English and Scots, there were more women in the migrant flow, especially among the servant class.

CHAPTER FOUR

1 See Appendix A on the nature of this construction of the black population, and Appendices A and B on Irish ethnicity.
2 Berleant-Schiller, "Free Labor," 550 cites a transaction wherein, in 1678, 640 acres were sold for £417 sterling. This was a consolidated parcel of good land. Small parcels of bush would have been much cheaper.
3 William Stapleton to Lords of Trade and Plantations, 20 Dec. 1682, *CSPCS 1681–1685*, 359.
4 Bridenbaugh, *No Peace Beyond the Line*, 173.
5 Ibid.
6 Journal of the General Assembly of Nevis, 17 March 1684, *CSPCS 1681–1685*, 609.
7 Daniel Parke to Council for Trade and Plantations, 8 Oct. 1707, *CSPCS 1706–1709*, 558.
8 Haring, *Buccaneers in the West Indies*, 200.
9 Thornton, *West-India Policy*, 243–4.
10 Jonathan Atkins to Lords of Trade and Plantations, 25 April 1678, *CSPCS 1677–1680*, 246.
11 Christopher Codrington to Lords of Trade and Plantations, 17 October 1693, *CSPCS 1693–1696*, 183.
12 *Acts of Assembly, passed in the Island of Montserrat; from 1668 to 1740, inclusive* (London: King's Printer, 1790). Law 38, 1693.

This collection is not to be confused with the *Abridgement* of the laws which was published in the same year.

Hereafter, reference to legal acts will be to the calendar year, and to the number of the law in the legal series that begins in 1668. Thus, for example, the law cited above will be referred to as *Laws* 1693: 38.
13 Minutes of council and assembly of Montserrat, 5 Nov. 1693, *CSPCS 1693–1696*, 202; Christopher Codrington to Lords of Trade and Plantations, 6 Nov. 1693, ibid., 202; Minutes of council and assembly of Montserrat, 20 Nov. 1693, ibid., 209; Minutes of Council and assembly of Montserrat, 25 Nov. 1693, ibid., 212.
14 Joseph Crispe to Governor Russel, 16 July 1695, ibid., 530.
15 Ibid.
16 English, "Records of Montserrat," 95.
17 Petition of Edward Buncombe to H.M. in Council, 24 March 1711, *CSPCS 1710–1711*, 437.

18 Burns, *British West Indies*, 425; English, "Records of Montserrat," 95.
19 Burns, *British West Indies*, 42 *n* 5.
20 *Laws* 1693: 37.
21 Note that this term, which is the statutory norm, four years, is markedly shorter than the 6.5 years that Beckles found prevailed on Barbados near mid-century.
22 Walter Hamilton to Council of Trade and Plantations, 14 Dec. 1716, *CSPCS 1716–1717*, 230.
23 Walter Hamilton to Council of Trade and Plantations, 26 August 1717, and enclosure, *CSPCS 1717–1718*, 13–14.

When Crabb Island turned out not to be hospitable, in part by reason of Spanish invasion, the settlers dispersed, some returning to their home islands, others going to various small islands. Walter Hamilton to Council of Trade and Plantations, 8 Aug. 1718, *CSPCS 1719–1720*, 167.

24 Governor Hart to Council of Trade and Plantations, ——— 1724, *CSPCS 1724–1725*, 151. The former French lands were attractive to the kind of solid small proprietors Montserrat wanted to hold. The St Christopher grants, instead of going to big planters, were limited to lots of no more than 200 acres. See H.M. Commission to William Mathew et al., 4 June 1726, *CSPCS 1726–1727*, 130.
25 Daniel Parke to Council of Trade and Plantations, 1 Oct. 1708, *CSPCS 1708–1709*, 105.
26 William Stapleton to Lords of Trade and Plantations, 20 June 1676, *CSPCS 1675–1676*, 500. See also 502.
27 Ibid., 502.
28 Governor Mathew to Lords Commissioners of Trade and Plantations, 18 April 1734, *CSPCS 1734–1735*, 84.
29 *Laws* 1734: 101.
30 *Laws* 1734: 105.
31 *Laws* 1668: 6. In 1705 the stipends of clergymen on all the main Leeward Islands were raised to 16,000 pounds of Muscovado sugar. *Leeward Acts* 1705:33.
32 Actually, the entire Leeward Islands must have been hell for a serious cleric. In 1681 the Lords of Trade and Plantations wrote to Stapleton that "we have been informed for some time past that the ministers sent by the Bishop of London to the Leeward Islands have not been so well used there as they ought, especially in Montserrat." Lords of Trade and Plantations to William Stapleton, 12 March 1681, *CSPCS 1681–1685*, 21. By 1681, however, Stapleton was immune to criticism, being one of the few truly competent colonial governors.
33 Minutes of Council and Assembly of Montserrat, 27 February 1699, *CSPCS 1699*, 81.

Molineux's curate and eventual successor, the Rev. James Cruickshank, was also suitably civic. He stayed on at his charge until old age. One finds him in 1734 sitting as a member of the legislative council, "very old and infirm." (Gov. Matthew to Commissioners of Trade and Plantations, 18 April 1734, *CSPCS 1734–1735*, 85).

The last of the eighteenth-century Anglican curates was the Rev. Howel Powell, who died in 1811, leaving an estate of £560 in cash, plus forty-one bottles of Malmsey, 101 bottles of Madeira, 10 bottles of porter, 72 bottles of Old Rumm, and 111 gallons of other rum, plus, among other things, thirteen silk handkerchiefs, thirteen waistcoats, and twenty-eight cravats (English, "Records of Montserrat," 180).

34 This, incidentally, is a useful clue as to where the second Anglican church on the island was located: St Peter's parish, most probably in Stapleton, the only settlement of any size in the parish.

35 Governor Mathew to Commissioners of Trade and Plantations, 18 April 1734, *CSPCS 1734–1735*, 85.

36 Council of Montserrat to Commissioners of Trade and Plantations, 13 July 1680, *CSPCS 1677–1680*, 574.

37 William Stapleton to Lords of Trade and Plantations, 20 June 1676, *CSPCS 1675–1676*, 502.

38 Ibid.

39 Col. Fox to Council of Trade and Plantations, 11 July 1701, *CSPCS 1701*, 349.

40 Gwynn, "Documents Relating to the Irish," 279.

41 John Hart to Lords of Trade and Plantations, 16 March 1724, *CSPCS 1724–1725*, 65.

42 Burns, *British West Indies*, 457.

43 Governor Mathew to Commissioners of Trade and Plantations, 18 April 1734, *CSPCS 1734–1735*, 85.

44 William Stapleton to Lords of Trade and Plantations, 20 June 1676, *CSPCS 1675–1676*, 502.

45 *Laws* 1678: 29.

46 *Leeward Acts* 1668: 31. The act was officially obsolete by 1730, but, in fact, it must have become inoperative by virtue of the oaths required in 1672 (see text).

47 Berleant-Schiller, "Free Labour," 545–6.

48 Ibid., 546.

49 *CSPCS 1677–1680*, 574–5.

50 On Johnson's lobbying, see Higham, *Development of the Leeward Islands*, 218.

51 Dunn, *Sugar and Slaves*, 133.

52 Nathaniel Johnson to Lords of Trade and Plantations, 3 March 1688, *CSPCS 1685–1688*, 513.

53 Ibid.
54 Petition of Nicholas Lynch and others to Nathaniel Johnson, 23 Nov. 1687, *CSPCS 1685–1688*, 470.
55 Copy of Order of Sir Nathaniel Johnson, attached ibid.
56 Nathaniel Johnson to Lords of Trade and Plantations, 3 March 1688, ibid., 513.
57 Report of Archibald Hutcheson to Lords of Trade and Plantations, 25 July 1688, *CSPCS 1685–1688*, 531.
58 Ibid., 532.
59 Ibid.
60 Though the attack on the freehold system of landholding on Montserrat was stopped by political events in the British Isles, there remained, however, real problems with the fee-simple system of landholding, matters that were unique to Montserrat. In 1705 the assembly found it necessary to pass an act "for quieting the Inhabitants of this island in the Possession of their respective estates." This was because of "several Hurricanes, Fires, Invasions by the French and Indians, Insurrections of Negroes, and other unforeseen Accidents," the result of which was that "most of the Records of this Island, together with several Patents, Deeds, and Evidence, whereupon the greater Part of the Titles of this Island depended, were lost and destroyed." (*Laws*, 1705: 54).

What the Montserrat settlers were discovering was a basic fact of freehold (fee-simple) ownership: that although it claimed to provide ownership of lands to individuals and their heirs in perpetuity, such permanency was only as good as the records which recorded the freeholds. If land records did not exist independent of the actual occupancy of the soil, then the freehold system quickly collapsed into a system of customary law (disguised though that may have been by modern language), in which the rights to the land were dependent upon the collective memory. And that was what happened on Montserrat. Therefore, in 1705, occupiers of lands and "tenements" in the towns who had held the parcels for ten years and who had a claim (however undocumented) to fee-simple ownership were confirmed in ownership in fee simple. Further, persons who occupied lands, but could not (or dared not) claim them in fee simple, but rented them under various tenancies ("in Fee-tail…for Life, for Years, or as Tenant at Will, or Sufferance,") had their tenancy rights confirmed. *Laws* 1705: 54. (This provision confirms what I suggested earlier concerning the availability of various tenancies which would be especially useful to previously indentured servants as a step towards ownership of their own land.)

Actually, the problem became worse. Just as the records were being put in order, the French, in 1712–13, pillaged Montserrat yet again.

Scarcely a piece of paper was left. As late as 1729, the island's assembly was still making legal provision to straighten out the land title problem stemming from that invasion. (*Laws*, 1729: 90).

61 Dunn, *Sugar and Slaves*, 134.

62 Ibid.

63 Gwynn, "Documents Relating to the Irish," 279); Archibald Hutcheson to Lords of Trade and Plantations, 27 June 1689, CSPCS *1689–1692*, 74.

64 Remonstrance of the sufferings of St Christopher, 9 July 1689, ibid., 79. See also Gov. Stede to Earl of Shrewsbury, 16 July 1689, ibid., 95 and also Christopher Codrington to Lords of Trade and Plantations, 31 July 1689, ibid., 111.

65 Deposition of Darby Considine, 29 June 1689, ibid., 79.

66 Harlow, *Christopher Codrington*, 16.

67 Christopher Codrington to Lords of Trade and Plantations, 31 July 1689, CSPCS *1689–1692*, 112; same to same, 15 Aug. 1689, ibid., 123; Henry Carpenter and Thomas Belchamber to Commissioners of Customs, 19 August 1689, ibid., 129; Christopher Codrington to Lords of Trade and Plantations, 19 Sept. 1689, ibid., 147.

68 Christopher Codrington (the younger) in a letter of 18 August 1701 to the Council of Trade and Plantations (*CSPCS, 1701*, 417) claimed that "in the beginning of the last war the Irish of Montserrat rose in rebellion, [and] my father sent down some companies from hence to quell them." This was an overstatement of the case, made as part of some special pleading for his own purposes, by the younger Codrington. "Rebellion," in the sense of the jacquerie carried on St Christopher, did not occur on Montserrat, although the threat was always there. Codrington (the elder) did not describe the situation as being one of rebellion.

69 Harlow, *Christopher Codrington*, 17.

70 Christopher Codrington to Lords of Trade and Plantations, 1 March 1690, CSPCS *1689–1692*, 225.

71 Dunn, *Sugar and Slaves*, 134–5; Harlow, *Christopher Codrington*, 13, 17–37. St Christopher, which was now solely in English hands, was once again partitioned in 1697, under the treaty of Ryswick.

72 Demets, *The Catholic Church in Montserrat*, 25; Fergus, *Alliouagana*, 26. Neither assertion is documented.

73 For recent scholarship on the penal laws, see Bartlett, *The Fall and Rise of the Irish Nation*; Connolly, *Religion, Law and Power*; and McGrath, "Securing the Protestant Interest."

74 Sources: Retabulated census of 1678 and 1729 (see Appendices A and B); Pitman, *The Development of the British West Indies*, 378–82; CSPCS *1706–1708*, 706; CSPCS *1720–1721*, 115; CSPCS *1724–1725*, 151.

75 *Leeward Acts* 1701: 22.

76 Daniel Parke to Council of Trade and Plantations, 1 Oct. 1708, *CSPCS 1708–1709*, 105. To Parke's vexation, the priest proved elusive.
77 Minutes of Council of Montserrat, 20 Dec. 1698, *CSPCS 1697–1698*, 580.
78 Referred to in a case reported in *Journal of the Commissioner for Trade and Plantations from January 1749–50 to December 1753*, 5 Dec. 1751, 237.
79 Ibid.
80 *Laws* 1702: 49. Because it was inoperative, the law was not printed in the collection of Montserrat statutes for 1668–1740 compiled by the London authorities.
81 Council of Trade and Plantations to the Queen, 7 May 1703, *CSPCS 1702–1703*, 402.
82 Ibid.
83 *Leeward Acts* 1705: 28.
84 John Hart to Council of Trade and Plantations, 16 March 1724, *CSPCS 1724–1725*, 65.
85 *Laws* 1729: 89.
86 The legal proceedings on the case are one of the few windows that open on the way the penal code actually worked on Montserrat. See *Journal of the Commissioners for Trade and Plantations from January 1749–50 to December 1753*, 234–43.
87 This means that in the first half of the eighteenth century (but not in the seventeenth), one can use lists of membership on the island's governing council to distinguish those large landowners of Irish Catholic background who permanently turned Anglican (as distinct from the occasional conformists of the earlier period).
88 Christopher Codrington (the younger) to Council of Trade and Plantations, 18 August 1701, *CSPCS 1701*, 417.
89 Address of Governor Douglas and the President, Council and Assembly of Montserrat to the Queen, 7 January 1713, *CSPCS 1714–1715*, 2.
90 William Hamilton to Lord Dartmouth, 25 June 1711, *CSPCS 1710–1711*, 566–8; Council of Trade and Plantations to Governor Lowther, 26 October 1711, *CSPCS 1711–1712*, 118.
91 Laws, *Distinction, Death, and Disgrace*, 22.
92 Deposition of William Bevell and James Brookes, 9 August 1712, *CSPCS 1712–1714*, 23.
93 Address of Governor Douglas and the President, Council and Assembly of Montserrat to the Queen, 7 January 1713, *CSPCS 1714–1715*, 2.
94 Eric Williams, "The Origin of Negro Slavery," reprinted from Williams, *Capitalism and Slavery* in Horowitz (ed.), *People and Cultures in the Caribbean*, 63.
95 Council of Montserrat to Lords of Trade and Plantations, 13 July 1680, *CSPCS 1677–1680*, 574.
96 I am grateful to David Eltis for calling this episode to my attention.

97 Governor Mathew to Mr. Popple, 31 August 1734, CSPCS *1734–1735*, 218.

98 *Laws* 1719: 75. Historians of Ireland and of Africa will doubtlessly appreciate the implications of judgment being obtained before the council and assembly of Montserrat on behalf of Isabel Scheurman (née Marrow) against Thomas Pakenham for one negro woman and two negro children.

99 *Laws* 1722: 9.

100 *Laws* 1724: 85.

101 Minutes of Council of Montserrat, 16 Sept. 1698, CSPCS *1697–1698*, 444.

102 Minutes of Council of Barbados, 24 January 1693, CSPCS *1693–1694*, 5. A hideous pun – half-a-crown for a bob – probably was behind this grisly rate of punishment.

103 *Laws* 1693: 36.

104 *Laws* 1714: 62.

105 Minutes of Council and Assembly of Montserrat, 22 August 1693, CSPCS *1693–1696*, 150.

106 Ibid.

107 Minutes of Council and Assembly of Montserrat, 19 Dec. 1693, CSPCS *1693–1696*, 219.

108 Minutes of the Council of Montserrat, 15 Nov. 1698, CSPCS *1697–1698*, 558.

109 Minutes of the Council of Montserrat, 14 June 1699, CSPCS *1699*, 284.

110 "Separate Traders" to the Council of Trade and Plantation, 11 Dec. 1710, CSPCS *1710–1711*, 311.

111 Pulsipher and Goodwin, "A Sugar Boiling House," 26.

112 Sheridan, *Sugar and Slavery*, Table 8.4, 175. The Irish were as follows: James Farrill, Trant, Roach, Dongan, Darcy, Irish, Meade, John Farrill, Thomas Lee, Hussey, Skerrett, Dyer, Parson ("New English," that is, Irish Protestant, long resident in the island), Frye (identified by Sheridan, 180, as being a Devonshire "New English" family in Ireland), Daly, Peter Lee, Gallway, and Fitz Denis.

Non-Irish names, therefore: Wyke, White (a Protestant who easily could be Irish), Liddell, Hodges, Brambley, Molineux (the family of which was now heavily intermarried with the Irish), Daniell, Roynan (which may be variant of a common County Cork name), Cooke, Bevrone, Bramley, and Fox.

113 Actually, the largest source of error is that it was easy (and quite sensible) for the male of a household to take the required oaths, but for the rest of the household to remain Catholic.

Sources of information on largest sugar planters and on whether or not they held offices requiring Protestant oaths: *The Journals of the Commissioners for Trade and Plantations*, from 1714–28; information contained on the 1729 census sheets; *CSPCS 1717–1718*, 408; *CSPCS 1726–1727*, 99; *CSPCS 1733*, 334; *CSPCS 1734–1735*, 532; *CSPCS 1735–1736*, 449.

In addition to using the oaths of office as an indication of conformity to the Anglican church, I have also compared the list of landowners to the available Anglican parish registers of births, baptisms, marriages, and burials for the 1720s (PROL, CO 152/18). This is a tool that has to be used with judgment, for merely because someone is entered in the book does not mean that the family was committed to the Established Church. For example, one of the daughters of the Gallway family had a bastard son in 1724. The child was baptised in the Established Church, but this indicates nothing about the rest of the family, with whom, presumably, she was at odds because of her unchaste behaviour. Similarly, because large landowners will frequently feel insecure about the hereditability of their lands, I do not believe that having one child – particularly a male – baptised by the Church of England clergy was necessarily a sign of religious conversion to that church. Thus, the baptising of a child of Nicholas Kirwan (whose family we know from other sources was one of the most staunch Catholic families on the island). However, there are two instances recorded in the registers wherein an Irish landowner acted in such a way as to lead one to infer real adherence to the Church of England, and both of these are cases that one does not pick up in the other public records. One of these is the Dyer family, of St Anthony's parish. Captain John Dyer and his wife Margaret had two of their children baptized as Anglican, and nine of their slaves as well. The other is the Fitz Denis family, who had several children baptized.

I do not take as definite sign of conversion, the burial of the wife of John Farrill in an Anglican graveyard, nor James Farrill's having his son baptized. These are judgment calls. One thing one learns when observing how people on a frontier acted in religious matters is that later standards of canonical behaviour cannot be imposed on them. Simple people, superstitious people, even well-read people, frequently felt a need for some basic religious services at major moments in their lives, and if a Catholic priest was not available (as one rarely was on Montserrat), then they frequently accepted whatever service was offered, in this case, Anglican.

The context of the Irish homeland is here relevant. Thomas P. Power has argued that in eighteenth-century Ireland most conversions to Protestantism were nominal in nature and were largely a response to legal requirements. Thomas P. Power, "Converts," in Power and Whelan (eds.), *Endurance and Emergence*, 101–27.

114 On the post-1729 history of the Meades, see Sheridan, *Sugar and Slavery*, 177–8.

115 McGinn, "How Irish is Montserrat?", 17.
116 English, "Records of Montserrat," 174.
117 McGinn, "How Irish Is Montserrat?", 17; Pulsipher and Goodwin, "A Sugar Boiling House," 243.
118 English, "Records of Montserrat," 176.
119 In addition to the 1729 census, see "Molineux of Montserrat," Sheridan, *Sugar and Slavery*, 180–1.

CHAPTER FIVE

1 Pares, *A West-India Fortune*, 25.
2 The production series for the years 1697–1927 is found in Deerr, *The History of Sugar*, 2: 196.
3 Goveia, *Slave Society*, 122.
4 Ibid., 103.
5 Sources: Pitman, *Development of the British West Indies*, 378–82; Sheridan, *Sugar and Slavery*, 150; and Hugh Elliot to earl of Liverpool, 14 March 1811, cited in Ragatz, *Fall of the Planter Class*, 47.
6 Ibid. Davy, *The West Indies*, p. 412 has for 1787 and 1805 clearly estimates, not the results of enumerations, of 10,000 and 9,500, respectively. The latter number is suspect.
7 Goveia, *Slave Society*, 206–7.
8 Ibid., 88.
9 Burns, *British West Indies*, 460.
10 Ibid.
11 English, "Records of Montserrat," 150.
12 On St Christopher in 1785, Horatio Nelson was vexed to find that "Yesterday being St Patrick's Day, the Irish Colours with thirteen stripes in them was hoisted all over the Town" (Burns, *British West Indies*, 545).
13 This idea is virtually part of the official tourist guide's kit, which is hardly surprising, given that the island's tourism authorities have done well out of emphasizing the allegedly Irish aspects of present-day Montserrat, and therefore the island attracts considerable numbers of visitors of Irish extraction: insulting the visitors would hardly be good business. However, the oral-tradition predates the last two decades' development of the tourist industry, and rests, I think, on two artifacts of social psychology: the need of the Roman Catholic church to rationalize the fact that it was, until well into the nineteenth century, an entirely white church (overwhelmingly Irish) and one whose constituency was made up almost entirely of slave-holders and their families; and the need of those of African descent, who today bear Irish-origin surnames to rationalize their wearing of the

names of their onetime oppressors. The belief that the Irish were somehow nicer slave owners than the British, helps in both these regards. As a social analgesic, this nice-slave-owner belief is useful, but it should not be introduced into historical discussions as if it were an accurate description of the situation in the seventeenth, eighteenth and nineteenth century.

John Messenger states that "it is a widely held view in Montserrat that Irish landowners treated their slaves with more care and kindness than did their English and Scottish counterparts; they also were more prone to have their slaves baptized and to free them, especially between 1807 and 1834" (Messenger, "The 'Black Irish' of Montserrat," 31, repeated in "Montserrat," 290). As a statement of the oral tradition on the island, as it had developed by roughly mid-twentieth century, this is a valuable report. However, the problem is that local historians have assimilated these oral traditions as if they were historical facts. Thus, we have the factual assertions that (1) the Irish were kinder to their slaves than were the British; (2) they were more apt to have them baptized, and (3) were more apt to free the slaves in the pre-emancipation era. As historical assertions, each of these statements is demonstrably false, as my discussion in the text and in the notes indicates.

However, the naive acceptance of oral tradition also results, through the process of displacement, in certain other historical problems: (4) an attempt to wish away the distance between the Irish population and the African-descended population. For example, Fergus (*Montserrat*, 52–3) asserts that in the later seventeenth century "social and economic rejection by the English and Anglo-Irish elite led the white servant wage-owners to liaise closely with the slaves for mutual succour. One in wretchedness, it was natural that both ethnic groups would wish to formulate common strategies for survival." John Messenger goes even farther along this romantic path that erases the line between the Irish and the blacks in the mid-seventeenth century: "Among the slaves were compulsory indentured servants, exiled political agitators and priests (after 1655) and prison inmates, vagrants, and beggars from both Ireland and England. Neither legendary nor historical sources reveal the conditions of servitude experienced by *Irish slaves* [emphasis added] in Montserrat before 1664 and their position vis-à-vis African slaves thereafter until freed." The text discusses the reasons why this narrowing (or even erasing) of the distance between portions of the Irish population and the slaves is completely inaccurate.

14 English, "Records of Montserrat," 150; Fergus, *Alliouagana*, 17. Fergus, in *Montserrat*, states that nine of the ringleaders were executed and

thirty more were banished. Though Fergus gives no documentation for this statement the numbers are reasonable, given the size of Montserrat's slave population.

15 In March 1770, a false alarm arose on Montserrat over an apprehended slave rising. Sixteen Africans were arrested, but they were declared innocent after trial (Fergus, *Montserrat*, 75, citing PROL, CO 153/22). In 1778 a conspiracy to murder the whites and deliver the island to the French was discovered on St Christopher. In 1790 a rising began on Tortola, but was suppressed (Goveia, *Slave Society*, 95).

16 Philpott, *West Indian Migration*, 17.

17 Governor Mathew to Council of Trade and Plantations, 19 March 1734, *CSPCS 1734–1735*, 58.

18 Governor Mathew to Mr Popple, 16 Sept. 1734, *CSPCS 1735–1736*, 274.

19 Sheridan, *Sugar and Slavery*, 65.

20 Goveia, *Slave Society*, 93–4.

21 Ibid., 92–3.

22 This is pure speculation; however, I would suggest the strong possibility that the attempt in 1749 to take away the vote from Irish Catholics was a response to their already having begun to assert themselves openly in religious matters.

23 Demets, *The Catholic Church in Montserrat*, 33.

24 Ibid., 28, 30, 34; English, "Records of Montserrat," 214–15.

25 Demets, *The Catholic Church in Montserrat*, 26–7. The house still exists.

Fergus, *Alliouagana*, 11, says that "Trescellian" is the only remaining evidence of Gaelic on Montserrat. Whatever language it is, the word certainly is not Gaelic. Conceivably it could be Cornish. More likely, given that the name of the building in English was "Shamrock House," is that the word was an attempt by eighteenth-century English speakers, who had learned a bit of frontier French, to find a French word for "shamrock."

The question of how much the Irish language was spoken on the island is one that I have intentionally ignored. I have found only one seventeenth-century reference to the language, and that was by a Jesuit priest who had never been to the West Indies, and who was touting his own credentials in the hope of being appointed to serve the islands (see chapter 2).

That said, it is hard to conceive of the Irish language not having been used extensively in the first two or three generations. The bulk of the indentured servants had come from Irish-speaking areas in Munster, and most of their social superiors were from Munster or Connaught and must have at least understood the language, even if they habitually used English as the language of government and commerce. The "Irish horseshoe" in the far south of the island was exactly the sort of compact and isolated community that would have preserved the language. It was, however, sharply depopulated after 1690.

A direct reference to the use of Irish was published in 1780 in Jeffreys' *The West-Indian Atlas* which stated that "the use of the Irish language is preserved on the island, even among the Negroes" (Jeffreys, 22, quoted in Truxes, *Irish-American Trade*, 100.)

The best direct evidence, however, comes from the testimony of one John Donovan, a merchant sailor, and a native of Ring, and consequently a fluent Irish speaker. In 1852 he was mate of the brig "Kaloolah" and he went ashore on Montserrat. There he was surprised to hear the blacks speaking Irish among themselves, and he joined in conversation with them. This is reported by W.F. Butler, and is a note in Tomas De Bhaldraithe's translation of *The Diary of Humphrey O'Sullivan, 1827–1835* (Cork: Mercier Press, 1979, 104).

Humphrey O'Sullivan is the English name of an accomplished Irish language poet and, also, a diarist. In an entry for early April 1831, he had noted, concerning Montserrat, that "Irish is spoken commonly there by both whites and blacks. My heart goes out to the poor Irish deportees. Be they black or white I love the Irish people" (ibid., 104). That O'Sullivan had never been near the West Indies means that his own diary entry is not direct evidence; however, it is an indication that in rural Ireland (which was remarkably well-informed about the places around the world where Irish emigrants had gone), it was believed that the Irish language still was spoken.

26 See Fergus, *Alliouagana*, 11.

27 Laws, *Distinction, Death, and Disgrace*, 4–13.

28 English, "Records of Montserrat," 165–75.

29 Goveia, *Slave Society*, 98.

30 Hugh Elliott to earl of Liverpool, 8 Sept. 1810, quoted in Ragatz, *Fall of the Planter Class*, 47.

31 Ibid., quoted in Goveia, *Slave Society*, 98.

32 Goveia, *Slave Society*, 98–9; Fergus, *Montserrat*, 79.

33 English, "Records of Montserrat," 184.

34 Ragatz, *Fall of the Planter Class*, 47–8.

35 Ibid., 47; English, "Records of Montserrat," 180–4, 191. McCusker gives two figures for 1788, reflecting two slightly conflicting primary sources. McCusker, *Rum and the American Revolution*, 2: Table B-49, 638, and notes 745*n*330 and 745*n*331.

36 English, "Records of Montserrat," 186.

37 The Semper family had risen remarkably. In 1729, a Sarah Semper, presumably a widow, was a tavern keeper in Plymouth.

38 On the religious affiliations, compare Demets, *The Catholic Church in Montserrat*, 43–4, and English, "Records of Montserrat," 186, 215–16.

39 Derived from English, "Records of Montserrat," 191. Queely Shiell had reduced his stock of slaves to 370, probably a sell-off occasioned by the prospect of emancipation.
40 English, "Records of Montserrat," 182.
41 Ibid., 183.
42 Hamshere, *The British in the Caribbean*, 148.
43 English, "Records of Montserrat," 187.
44 Ibid., 215.
45 The full text is in ibid., 188–9.
46 Messenger, "Montserrat," 294. Messenger based this on information he was given by local church authorities, notably Bishop Antoine Demets.
47 Ibid.
48 Demets, *The Catholic Church in Montserrat*, 44; English, "Records of Montserrat," 186, 215.
49 Messenger, "Montserrat," 294.
50 Gwynn, "First Irish Priests," 225–6.
51 Demets, *The Catholic Church in Montserrat*, 45–6, and English, "Records of Montserrat," 215. In the mid-nineteenth century, Montserrat was a shared charge with St Christopher and Antigua.
52 Demets, *The Catholic Church in Montserrat*, 13; English, "Records of Montserrat," 215.
53 See Roger Anstey, "Religion and British Slave Emancipation," in Eltis and Walvin (eds.), *The Abolition of the Atlantic Slave Trade*, 37–61.
54 English, "Records of Montserrat," 214; Fergus, *Alliouagana*, 47.
55 The Established Church baptismal, marriage, and death records for the 1720s are found in PROL, CO 152/18.
56 Davy, *The West Indies*, 413.
57 Ibid., 415. I think (but am not certain) that the attorney referred to was one Francis Burke.
58 Ibid., 415.
59 English, "Records of Montserrat," 204–5.
60 Deerr, *History of Sugar*, 2: 384.
61 Hall, *Five of the Leewards*, Table 14, 150.
62 Davy, *The West Indies*, 412.
63 Ibid., 422.
64 Ibid., 426.
65 Burns, *British West Indies*, 655.
66 For a useful survey, see Sires, "Government in the British West Indies," 108–21.
67 See the production series in Deerr, *History of Sugar*, 2: 196.
68 Hall, *Five of the Leewards*, 129–30.
69 Fergus, *Alliouagana*, 30–1. The Sturge family continued active in the firm until 1961.

70 Davy, *The West Indies*, 420–1.
71 Hall, *Five of the Leewards*, 30–1.
72 Pulsipher, "Cultural Landscape," 83.
73 Sturge and Harvey, *The West Indies in 1837*, 81.
74 Ibid., 81–2.
75 Hall, *Five of the Leewards*, 31.
76 See English, "Records of Montserrat," 215–16.

CHAPTER SIX

1 *Laws* 1668: 11.
2 For example, Jeffrey (ed.), *"An Irish Empire?"* and Akenson, *The Irish Diaspora*, 141–51.
3 Pulsipher, "Cultural Landscape," 159.
4 An excellent scholarly work is Philpott, *West Indian Migration*. Data cited are from 36–7.
5 Ibid., 50.
6 Kurlansky, *A Continent of Islands*, 251.
7 Messenger, "St Patrick's Day." The letter was not published.
8 List compiled from Messenger, "The 'Black Irish' of Montserrat"; "The Influence of the Irish in Montserrat"; "Montserrat"; "African Retentions in Montserrat"; and "St Patrick's Day."
9 McGinn, "How Irish Is Montserrat?" 21. Fenton, though frequently English, is also a common County Cork surname.
10 Wells, "The Brogue that Isn't." See also Mervyn C. Alleyne, "A Linguistic Perspective on the Caribbean," in Mintz and Price (eds.), *Caribbean Contours*, 155–79.
11 See Parsons, *Folk-Lore of the Antilles*.
12 Fergus, "Montserrat, 'Colony of Ireland,'" 327.
13 Dobbin, *The Jombee Dance of Montserrat* and "Religion and Cultural Identity."
14 Messenger, "The 'Black Irish' of Montserrat," 37.
15 Sokolov, "History in a Stewpot." That Irish stew and the goat stew of Montserrat resemble each other is hardly surprising. There are, after all, only two basic ways of cooking a goat: roasting and boiling.
16 Messenger, "Montserrat," 296.
17 Metraux, "Montserrat, B.W.I." I think Metraux' observation about short historical memory is sound. Whenever I have been able to check local oral traditions (usually as cited in written works) that have anything to do with the period before the present century, the traditions usually are wildly inaccurate. This is true of secular tradition, and even more true of religious ones. The reason for this sort of memory-erasure is brilliantly caught by V.S. Naipaul in *A Way in the*

World, 79. There his protagonist talks about memory loss among Trinidadians, but it could be any West Indian island:

> The idea of a background – and what it contained: order and values and the possibility of striving: perfectibility – made sense only when people were more truly responsible for themselves. We weren't responsible in that way. Much had been taken out of our hands. We didn't have backgrounds. We didn't have a past. For most of us the past stopped with our grandparents; beyond that was a blank.

18 The classic discussion of these and a score of other invented traditions is found in Eric Hobsbawm and Terence Ranger's excellent collection, *The Invention of Tradition*.
19 Francis, "Franz Tieze (1842–1932)."
20 Colley, *Britons*.
21 Deer, "Disunited we stand," 9.
22 Ibid.
23 See, for example, Fergus, *Montserrat*, 14–17.
24 Fergus, *Alliouagana*, 49.
25 Demets, *The Catholic Church in Montserrat*, 52.
26 Ibid., 50–67.
27 The reader may think that here, and in chapter 5, I have been a bit hard on the Catholic church on Montserrat, so three points are in order. The first is simply that, although the pre-emancipation Catholic church was notably callous towards its potential black members (their souls were effectively ignored for the first 200 years of the colonial period), the Church of England did only marginally better. Only the Wesleyan Methodists showed a serious concern for the spiritual welfare of the African slaves, and they came to the game quite late, near the end of the era of slavery.

Second, there is a reason for emphasizing the indifference of the Catholic church towards the blacks, and for making it clear that the Catholic church was definitely not the natural church of the African-descended slaves (despite the spurious claims that 10,000 slaves were baptized Catholic at the time of emancipation). The reason is that the legend of black Catholicity (which is not a nasty, or morally dangerous legend, as far as I can see) ties into a legend that *is* quite dangerous. This is the myth of the Irish as nice slave holders, better, more decent, kinder than the rest.

Third, though I have no objection to the church creating a set of legends about itself, as an historian, one must at least note that on occasion these legends can be created only by a form of cultural imperialism – in this case a claiming of a past that, in the historian's sense, belongs to someone else. So, for the sake of historical clarity, one should note that the invented history of the Catholic church on Montserrat has been advanced in remarkable terms. There has been an attempt to capture the edifice of the Established Church built by Anthony Briskett in the 1630s, for Roman Catholic history. This seems to have begun as early as 1880, when an Irish-born prelate, Michael Naughton, visited Montserrat and announced that St Anthony's church in its then-extant form (which, actually, was the fourth Anglican church on the site, and dated from the 1730s), being cruciform, and being dedicated to St Anthony (who in Ireland and in the United States in the nineteenth century was considered to be a "Catholic saint"), could not have been Protestant (McGinn, "How Irish Is Montserrat?" 17). Somehow, this reasoning (wrong though both its premises were), served as a basis of a syllogism that pushed the origin of the original St Anthony's, of 1630, into Catholic history: that first building, it was claimed, was Roman Catholic. (Bishop Morris of Montserrat, author of the now-lost "History of the Catholic Church in Montserrat," made this claim; Demets, *The Catholic Church in Montserrat*, 26, 42). Although the Belgian-born Redemptorist, Bishop Antoine Demets did not endorse this opinion in his 1980 memorial of the Catholic church on Montserrat, in the 1960s, he informed the anthropologist John C. Messenger that St Anthony's originally was a Catholic church and that during the seventeenth century it had a contiguous monastery, attended by two Dominicans and two Franciscans (Messenger, "Montserrat," 292). Even more imaginative was Demets' showing Messenger, "a well-preserved building converted into a sugar mill, now forest and vine enclosed on Galway's Estate a mile about St. Patrick's Village." Messenger continues: "As regards the latter structure, Delores Somerville [a writer and local genealogist] informed me that she had seen, about 1960, 'St. Augustine's Church,' and a date incised on a stone at the left side of the doorway" (ibid., 292). Apparently, Ms Somerville did not remember the date incised, and, curiously, the stone has yet to be seen by other parties. Despite that, Howard Fergus, the island's most recent local historian, uses Messenger's account as the basis of the retelling of the hypothesis as absolute fact. (Fergus, *Alliouagana*, 26, and Fergus, "Montserrat, 'Colony of Ireland,'" 336 and 339 *n* 72). He backs away from this assertion in his 1994 study (*Montserrat*, 84). It is a major nuisance to these views concerning the hypothetical St Augustine's church that the site has been the focus of a major archaeological dig by competent outside specialists. Their findings are unequivocal. There is no physical evidence whatsoever that the building was ever used as a church. Further, it is best dated about 1750. And it was a sugar boiling house. (Goodwin, "Archeology," and Pulsipher and Goodwin, "A Sugar-

Boiling House.") Such appropriation of physical sites to join with invented traditions is not restricted either to the Catholic church or to the Irish: one of the archaeologists who worked on the Montserrat site referred to a comparable misconception that was held in Philadelphia, Pennsylvania, in the mid-1970s, namely that a local building which was really the meter house for the old Philadelphia Gas Works was actually a small church built by "Swedish monks" (Goodwin, "Archeology," 251).

28 E.A. Markham, "Ireland's Islands in the Caribbean: Poetry from Montserrat and St Caesare," in Mackey (ed.), *The Cultures of Europe*, 140–1.

29 For an interesting case of a reverse effect – namely the impact of the island of Montserrat on the Irish imagination, see Stewart Parker's *Kingdom Come*, wherein Montserrat is used as a site for a commentary on the politics of Ireland. It played at the King's Head Theatre Club, Islington, London, in 1978. The script is in the Linen Hall Library, Belfast. The performance is reviewed by Conor Cruise O'Brien in *The Observer*, 29 January 1978.

30 See chapter 5, note 13.

31 The Irish dominance in small shopkeeping and in drinkinghouses can be inferred from the late seventeenth century onward. Compare population distributions, with items cited in T. Savage English, "Records of Montserrat," 59, 81–4, 140.

32 Demets, *The Catholic Church in Montserrat*, 49.

33 English, "Records of Montserrat," 215–16.

34 Messenger, "St Patrick's Day," 15, 16.

35 "The participation in the abortive uprising registered in blood the slaves' love of freedom and unsettled the whites somewhat. It was not until 1985 that the slaves who were involved came to be regarded as national freedom-fighters for their attempt, and Montserratians began to celebrate St. Patrick's Day annually as a public holiday" (Fergus, *Montserrat*, 75).

36 Quoted in Messenger, "St Patrick's Day," 17.

37 Fergus, "St Patrick's Day," 4, quoted ibid., 17.

38 See Fergus, "St Patrick's Day," 6.

39 For a list of words, see Irish, *A Handbook on Montserrat*, 18.

40 Fergus, *Montserrat*, 57.

41 Ibid.

42 Irish, *A Handbook on Montserrat*, 18.

43 Fergus ("Montserrat, 'Colony of Ireland,'" 337) labels them "the brown people," in contrast to the majority blacks. Elsewhere (*Allioua-gana*, 9), he calls them "yellow-skinned people."

44 Messenger, "African Retentions in Montserrat," 56.

45 Messenger, *Montserrat*, 13.

46 I am not dismissing entirely the possibilities either that JPs performed such marriages or that the unions of whites and blacks were sanctified by the Established Church. The families involved were of a social level that might have made such unions unusual, but not scandalous. The 1729 census shows an Allen in St Peter's division (the north of the island) as a mason, and various Sweeneys as labourers, and one as a carpenter. On the other hand, a Sarah Gibbons, in St Anthony's parish, presumably a widow, held eight slaves.

Bibliography

SEVENTEENTH- AND EIGHTEENTH-CENTURY OFFICIAL DOCUMENTS

An abridgment of the Acts of Assembly passed in the Island of Montserrat: From 1668–1740, inclusive. London: King's Printer, 1790.

Acts of Assembly, passed in the Charibbee Leeward Islands from 1690 to 1730. London: Lords Commissioners of Trade and Plantations, 1734.

Acts of Assembly, passed in the Island of Montserrat: From 1668–1740, inclusive. London: King's Printer, 1790.

Calendar of State Papers, Colonial Series (various publishers) 1574–1735 covered in forty-two volumes published in the nineteenth and twentieth centuries.

Journals of the Commissioners for Trade and Plantations. 1704, London: HMSO, twentieth century.

BOOKS, ARTICLES, AND UNPUBLISHED MONOGRAPHS

Akenson, Donald Harman. "Why the Accepted Estimates of the Ethnicity of the American People, 1780, Are Unacceptable," *William and Mary Quarterly*, 3 ser., vol. 41 (Jan. 1984), 102–19, 125–9.

– *The Irish Diaspora. A Primer*. Belfast: Institute of Irish Studies, the Queen's University of Belfast; Toronto: P.D. Meany Co., 1993.

Alleyne, Mervyn C. "A Linguistic Perspective on the Caribbean," in Sidney W. Mintz and Sally Price (eds.), *Caribbean Contours*. Baltimore: Johns Hopkins University Press, 1985, 155–79.

Andrews, K.R., N.P. Canny, and P.E.H. Hair (eds.) *The Westward Enterprise: English Activities in Ireland, the Atlantic, and the Americas, 1480–1650*. Liverpool: Liverpool University Press, 1978.

Arens, William. *The Man-Eating Myth. Anthropology and Anthropophagy.* New York: Oxford University Press, 1979.

Bailyn, Bernard, and Philip D. Morgan. *Strangers within the Realm. Cultural Margins of the First British Empire*. Chapel Hill: University of North Carolina Press, 1991.

Bartlett, Thomas. *The Fall and Rise of the Irish Nation: The Catholic Question, 1690–1830*. Savage, Maryland: Barnes and Noble, 1992.

Beckles, Hilary. "'Black Men in White Skins': The Formation of a White Proletariat in West Indian Slave Society," *Journal of Imperial and Commonwealth History,* vol. 15 (Oct. 1986), 5–21.

– *White Servitude and Black Slavery in Barbados, 1627–1715*. Knoxville: University of Tennessee Press, 1989.

– "A 'Riotous and unruly lot': Irish Indentured Servants and Freemen in the English West Indies, 1644–1713," *William and Mary Quarterly,* vol. 47 (Oct. 1990), 503–22.

Bell, Jonathan. "Relations of Mutual Help between Ulster Farmers," *Ulster Folk Life*, vol. 24 (1978), 48–58.

Berleant-Schiller, Riva. "Free Labor and the Economy in Seventeenth-Century Montserrat," *William and Mary Quarterly,* 3 ser., vol. 46 (July 1989), 539–64.

– *Montserrat*. Oxford: Clio Press Ltd., and Santa Barbara: ABC-Clio, 1991.

Blake, Martin J. (ed.) *Blake Family Records, 1600 to 1700*. London: Elliot Stock, 1905.

[Bourchier, Henry]. *Advertisements for Ireland, being a description of the state of Ireland in the Reign of James I, contained in a monograph in the library of Trinity College, Dublin*. (ed. by George O'Brien). Dublin: Royal Society of Antiquaries, 1923.

Brady, Ciaran and Raymond Gillespie (eds.). *Natives and Newcomers. Essays on the Making of Irish Colonial Society, 1534–1641*. Dublin: Irish Academic Press, 1986.

Bridenbaugh, Carl and Roberta. *No Peace Beyond the Line. The English in the Caribbean, 1624–1690*. New York: Oxford University Press, 1972.

Bryan, Edward. *The History, Civil and Commercial, of the British Colonies in the West Indies*. London: Josef Miller, 5th ed., 1819.

Burns, Alan. *History of the British West Indies*. London: George Allan and Unwin, 1954.

Caball, Marc. "Providence and Exile in Early Seventeenth-Century Ireland," *Irish Historical Studies*, vol. 29 (Nov. 1994), 174–88.

Canny, Nicholas. *The Elizabethan Conquest of Ireland: A Pattern Established, 1565–76*. Hassocks, Sussex: Harvester Press, 1976.

– and Anthony Pagden (eds.). *Colonial Identity in the Atlantic World, 1500–1800*. Princeton: Princeton University Press, 1987.

– (ed.). *Europeans on the Move. Studies on European Migration, 1500–1800*. Oxford: Clarendon Press, 1994.

Caulfield, Richard (ed.). *The Council Book of the Corporation of Kinsale from 1652–1800, edited from the original, with annals and appendices compiled from public and private records*. Guildford, Surrey: J. Billing and Sons, 1879.

Cell, Gillian T. *Newfoundland Discovered. English Attempts at Colonization, 1610–1630*. London: Hakluyt Society, 1982.

Codignola, Luca. *The Coldest Harbour of the Land. Simon Stock and Lord Baltimore's Colony in the Land, 1621–1640*. Kingston and Montreal: McGill-Queen's University Press, 1988.

Coldham, Peter W. *Emigrants in Chains. A Social History of Forced Emigration to the Americas, 1667–1776*. Baltimore: Genealogical Publishing, 1992.

Colley, Linda. *Britons. Forging the Nation, 1707–1837*. New Haven: Yale University Press, 1993.

Connolly, Sean J. *Religion, Law and Power. The Making of Protestant Ireland, 1660–1760*. Oxford: Clarendon Press, 1992.

Crouse, Nellis M. *The French Struggle for the West Indies, 1665–1713*. New York: Columbia University Press, 1943.

Cullen, Louis M. *Anglo-Irish Trade, 1660–1800*. Manchester: Manchester University Press, 1968.

– *An Economic History of Ireland since 1660*. London: B.T. Batsford Ltd., 1972.

– *The Emergence of Modern Ireland, 1600–1900*. New York: Holmes and Meier, 1981.

Davies, Kenneth G. *The Royal African Company*. London: Longmans Green and Co., 1957.

Davis, David Brion. *The Problem of Slavery in Western Culture*. Ithaca: Cornell University Press, 1966.

– "The Slave Trade and the Jews," *New York Review of Books*, vol. 41 (22 Dec. 1994), 14–16.

Davy, John. *The West Indies before and since Slave Emancipation comprising the Windward and Leeward Islands' Military Command, founded on notes and observations collected during a three year residence*. London: W. and F.G. Cash, 1854.

Deer, Brian. "Disunited We Stand," *Sunday Times Magazine* (5 February 1995), 8–10.

Deerr, Noel. *The History of Sugar*. London: Chapman and Hall, 1949. 2 vols.

de Forest, Mrs. Robert W. *A Walloon Family in America … together with a Voyage to Guiana being the journal of Jesse de Forest and his colonists, 1623–1625*. New York: Houghton Mifflin Co., 1914.

Demets, Antoine. *The Catholic Church in Montserrat, West Indies, 1756–1980*. Plymouth, Montserrat: privately pub., 1980.

Dobbin, Jay D. "Religion and Cultural Identity: The Montserratian Case," *Caribbean Issues*, vol. 4 (1980), 71–84.

– *The Jombee Dance of Montserrat. A Study of Trance Ritual in the West Indies*. Columbus: Ohio State University Press, 1986.

Dunn, Richard S. "The English Sugar Islands and the Founding of South Carolina," *South Carolina Historical Magazine*, vol. 62 (1971), 81–93.

– *Sugar and Slaves. The Rise of the Planter Class in the English West Indies, 1624–1713*. Chapel Hill: University of North Carolina Press, 1972.

Ekirch, Roger. *Bound for America: The Transportation of British Convicts to the Colonies, 1718–1775*. Oxford: Clarendon Press, 1987.

Eltis, David. "Europeans and the Rise and Fall of African Slavery in the Americas: An Interpretation," *American Historical Review*, vol. 98 (Dec. 1993), 1399–1423.

– "Labour and Coercion in the English Atlantic World from the Seventeenth to the Early Twentieth Century," *Slavery and Abolition*, vol. 14 (April 1993), 207–26.

– "The Total Product of Barbados, 1664–1701," *Journal of Economic History*, vol. 55 (June 1995), 321–38.

– and James Walvin (eds.). *The Abolition of the Atlantic Slave Trade*. Madison: University of Wisconsin Press, 1981.

Emmer, P.C. *Colonialism and Migration: Indentured Labour before and after Slavery*. Dordrecht: Martinus Nijhoff Publishers, 1986.

English, T. Savage. "Records of Montserrat," typescript, 1930. Public Library, Plymouth, Montserrat, and Institute of Commonwealth Studies, London.

Fergus, Howard A. *History of Alliouagana. A Short History of Montserrat*. Plymouth, Montserrat: University Centre, 1975.

– "Montserrat, the Last English Colony? Prospects for Independence," *Bulletin of Eastern Caribbean Affairs*, vol. 4 Part I (July-Aug 1978), 15–24, and vol. 4, Part II (Sept-Oct 1978), 23–8.

– "Montserrat, 'Colony of Ireland': The Myth and the Reality," *Studies*, vol. 70 (winter 1981), 325–40.

– *Montserrat. Emerald Isle of the Caribbean*. London: MacMillan, 1983.

– *Rule Britannia. Politics in British Montserrat*. Montserrat: University Centre, University of the West Indies, 1985.

– *Montserrat. History of a Caribbean Colony*. London: MacMillan, 1994.

Fischer, David Hackett. *Albion's Seed. Four British Folkways in America*. New York: Oxford University Press, 1989.

Francis, Peter. "Franz Tieze (1842–1932) and the Re-invention of History on Glass," *The Burlington Magazine* (May 1994), 291–302.

Frederickson, George M. *White Supremacy: A Comparative Study in American and South African History*. New York: Oxford University Press, 1981.

– *The Arrogance of Race: Historical Perspectives on Slavery, Racism, and Social Inequality*. Middleton: Wesleyan University Press, 1988.

Galeano, Eduardo. *Memory of Fire. I. Genesis*, translated by Cedric Belfrage. New York: Pantheon Books, 1985.

Galenson, David W. *White Servitude in Colonial America. An Economic Analysis*. Cambridge: Cambridge University Press, 1981.

Gillespie, Raymond. *Colonial Ulster. The Settlement of East Ulster, 1600–1641*. Cork: Cork University Press, 1985.

– The *Transformation of the Irish Economy, 1550–1700*. Dundalk: Dundalgan Press, 1991.

– and Harold O'Sullivan (eds.). *The Borderlands. Essays on the history of the Ulster-Leinster border*. Belfast: Institute of Irish Studies, the Queen's University of Belfast, 1989.

Goodwin, Conrad M. "Archaeology on the Galways Plantation," *Florida Anthropologist*, vol. 34 (Dec. 1982), 251–7.

Gookin, F.W. *Daniel Gookin*. Chicago: Privately Printed, 1912.

Goveia, Elsa V. *A Study on the Historiography of the British West Indies to the end of the nineteenth century*. Mexico City: Instituto Panamericano de Geografia e Historia, 1956.

– *Slave Society in the British Leeward Islands at the End of the Eighteenth Century*. New Haven: Yale University Press, 1965.

Greene, Jack P. *Pursuits of Happiness. The Social Development of Early Modern British Colonies and the Formation of American Culture*. Chapel Hill: University of North Carolina Press, 1988.

Gwynn, Aubrey. "Early Irish Emigration to the West Indies (1612–1643)," *Studies*, vol. 18 (Sept 1929), 377–93.

– "Early Irish Emigration to the West Indies–Part II," *Studies*, vol. 18 (Dec. 1929), 648–63.

– "Indentured Servants and Negro Slaves in Barbadoes, 1642–1650," *Studies*, vol. 19 (June 1930), 279–94.

– "Cromwell's Policy of Transportation–Part I," *Studies*, vol. 19 (Dec. 1930), 607–23.

– "Cromwell's Policy of Transportation–Part II," *Studies*, vol. 20 (June 1931), 291–305.

– "The First Irish Priests in the New World," *Studies*, vol. 21 (June 1932), 213–28.

– "Documents relating to the Irish in the West Indies," *Analecta Hibernica*, no. 4 (Oct. 1932), 139–286.

– "An Irish Settlement on the Amazon, 1612–29," *Proceedings of the Royal Irish Academy*, sect. C, vol. 41 (1932), 1–54.

Hall, Douglas. *Five of the Leewards, 1834–1870. The Major Problems of the post-emancipation period in Antigua, Barbuda, Montserrat, Nevis and St. Kitts*. Mona: Caribbean Universities Press, 1971.

Hamshere, Cyril. *The British in the Caribbean*. London: Weidenfeld and Nicolson, 1972.

Haring, C.H. *The Buccaneers in the West Indies in the XVII Century.* London: Methuen and Co., 1910.

Harlow, Vincent T. (ed.). *Colonising Expeditions to the West Indies and Guiana, 1623–1667*. London: Hakluyt Society, 1925.

– *Christopher Codrington, 1688–1710*. Oxford: Clarendon Press, 1928.

Henry, Grainne. *The Irish Military Community in Spanish Flanders, 1586–1621*. Dublin: Irish Academic Press, 1992.

– "Women 'Wild Geese,' 1585–1625: Irish Women and Migration to European Armies in the Late Sixteenth and Early Seventeenth Centuries," in Patrick O' Sullivan (ed.), *The Irish Worldwide*, vol. 4, *Irish Women and Irish Migration*. Leicester and London: Leicester University Press, 1995, 23–40.

Higham, C.S.S. *The Development of the Leeward Islands under the Restoration, 1660–1688. A Study of the Foundations of the Old Colonial System*. Cambridge: Cambridge University Press, 1921.

– "The Accounts of a Colonial Governor's Agent," *American Historical Review*, vol. 28 (Jan. 1923), 263–85.

– "Some Treasurer's Accounts of Montserrat, 1672–81," *English Historical Review*, vol. 38 (1923), 87–90.

Hobsbawm, Eric, and Terence Ranger (eds.). *The Invention of Tradition*. Cambridge: Cambridge University Press, 1983.

Horn, James. *Adapting to a New World. English Society in the Seventeenth-Century Chesapeake*. Chapel Hill: University of North Carolina Press, 1994.

Horowitz, Michael M. (ed.). *Peoples and Cultures of the Caribbean*. Garden City: Natural History Press, 1971.

Hughes, Thomas. *History of the Society of Jesus in North America, Colonial and Federal.* vol. I. *From the First Colonization till 1645*. London: Longmans, Green and Co., 1908.

Ingram, K.H. *Manuscripts Relating to Commonwealth Caribbean Countries in United States and Canadian Repositories*. New York: Bowker Publishing Co., 1975.

Irish, J.A. George. *A Handbook of Montserrat*. Plymouth, Montserrat: n.p., 1973.

– *Life in a Colonial Crucible. Labor and Social Change in Montserrat, 1946-Present*. New York: Caribbean Research Center, 1991.

Jeaffreson, John C. (ed.). *A Young Squire of the seventeenth century from the papers (A.D. 1676–1686) of Christopher Jeaffreson, of Bullingham House, Cambridgeshire*. London: Hurst and Blackett, 1878, 2 vols.

Jeffrey, Keith (ed.). *"An Irish Empire?" Aspects of Ireland and the British Empire*. Manchester: Manchester University Press, 1996.

Johnston, J.R.V. "The Stapleton Sugar Plantations in the Leeward Islands," *Bulletin of the John Rylands Library*, vol. 48 (1965), 175–206.

Jordan, Alma, and Barbara Comissiong. *The English-Speaking Caribbean. A Bibliography of Bibliographies*. Boston: G.K. Hall and Co., 1984.

Keogh, Daire. *The French Disease. The Catholic Church and Irish Radicalism, 1790–1800*. Dublin: Four Courts Press, 1993.

Kingsbury, Susan M. (ed.). *The Records of the Virginia Company of London. The Court Book from the Manuscript in the Library of Congress*. Washington: Government Printing Office, 1906, vols. I and II.

Kirnon, Hodge. *Montserrat and the Montserratians*. New York: The author, 1925.

Kuczynski, R.R. *Demographic Survey of the British Colonial Empire. Vol. III. West Indian and American Territories*. London: for the Royal Institute of International Affairs, by Oxford University Press, 1953.

Kupperman, Karen O. *Providence Island, 1630–1641. The Other Puritan Colony.* Cambridge: Cambridge University Press, 1993.

Kurlansky, Mark. *A Continent of Islands. Searching for the Caribbean Destiny.* New York: Addison-Wesley Publishing Co. Inc., 1992.

Laws, William. *Distinction, Death, and Disgrace. Governorships of the Leeward Islands in the Early Eighteenth Century.* Kingston: Jamaican Historical Society, 1976.

Ligon, Richard. *A True and Exact History of the Island of Barbadoes*. London: Peter Parker, 2nd ed. 1673, reprint Frank Cass, 1970.

"List of Inhabitants, Whites and Blacks, of Montserrat in 1729, referred to in Col Mathews' Letter of 28th May 1730," in V.L. Oliver (ed.), *Caribbeana*, vol. IV (1915–16), 302–11.

Loeber, Rolf. *The Geography and Practice of English Colonisation in Ireland from 1534 to 1609*. Dublin: Group for the Study of Irish Historic Settlement, 1991.

Lorimer, Joyce (ed.). *English and Irish Settlements on the River Amazon, 1550–1646*. London: Hakluyt Society, 1989.

Lux, William. *Historical Dictionary of the British Caribbean*. Matuchen, N.J.: Scarecrow Press, 1975.

MacCarthy-Morrogh, Michael. *The Munster Plantation: English Migration to Southern Ireland, 1583–1641*. Oxford: Clarendon Press, 1986.

Macfarlane, Alan. *The Origins of English Individualism. The Family, Property, and Social Transition*. Oxford: Basil Blackwell, 1978.

MacLysaght, Edward. *A Guide to Irish Surnames*. Dublin: Helicon, 1964.

Markham, E.A. "Ireland's Islands in the Caribbean: Poetry from Montserrat and St Caesare," in J.P. Mackey (ed.), *The Cultures of Europe: Ireland's Contribution*. Belfast: Institute of Irish Studies, the Queen's University of Belfast, 1994, 136–53.

Matheson, Robert E. *Special Report on Surnames in Ireland*. Dublin: orig. pub. 1894, reprint, HMSO, 1909.

McCavitt, John. "The Flight of the Earls, 1608," *Irish Historical Studies*, vol. 29 (Nov. 1994), 159–73.

McCourt, Desmond, "The Decline of Rundale, 1750–1850," in Peter Roebuck (ed.), *Plantation to Partition. Essays in Ulster History in Honour of J.L. McCracken*. Belfast: Blackstaff Press, 1981, 119–39.

McCusker, John J. *Rum and the American Revolution. The Rum Trade and the Balance of Payments of the Thirteen Continental Colonies*. New York: Garland Publishing, 1989, 2 vols.

McGinn, Brian. "How Irish Is Montserrat?" Part 1, *Irish Roots*, no. 1 (1994), 20–3; Part 2, Ibid, no. 2 (1994), 15–17.

McGrath, Charles I. "Securing the Protestant Interest: The Origins and Purpose of the Penal Laws of 1695," *Irish Historical Studies*, vol. 30 (May 1996), 25–46.

Merrill, Gordon G. "The Historical Record of Man as an Ecological Dominant in the Lesser Antilles," *Canadian Geographer*, no. 11 (1958), 17–22.

Messenger, John C. "The 'Black Irish' of Montserrat," *Eire-Ireland*, vol. 2 (spring 1967), 27–40.

– "The Influence of the Irish in Montserrat," *Caribbean Quarterly*, vol. 13 (June 1967), 3–26.

– *Inis Beag: Isle of Ireland*. New York: Holt, Rinehart and Winston, 1969.

– "Sex and Repression in an Irish Folk Community," in Donald S. Marshall and Robert C. Suggs (eds.), *Human Sexual Behaviour. Variations in the Ethnographic Spectrum*. New York: Basic Books, 1971, 3–31.

– "African Retentions in Montserrat," *African Arts*, (summer 1973), 54–7, 95–6.

– "Montserrat: The Most Distinctively Irish Settlement in the New World," *Ethnicity*, vol. 2 (Sept. 1975), 281–303.

– "St Patrick's Day in the 'Other Emerald Isle,'" *Eire-Ireland*, vol. 29 (spring 1994), 12–23.

Metraux, Rhoda. "Montserrat, B.W.I.: Some Implications of Suspended Culture Change," *Transactions of the New York Academy of Sciences*, 2 ser., vol. 20 (1957), 205–11.

– and Theodora M. Abel, "Normal and Deviant Behavior in a Peasant Community: Montserrat, B.W.I.," *American Journal of Orthopsychiatry*, vol. 27 (1957), 167–84.

"Molineux of Montserrat," in V.L. Oliver (ed.), *Caribbeana*, vol. 3 (1913–14), 1–5.

"Montserrat 1677–78," in V.L. Oliver (ed.), *Caribbeana*, vol. 2 (1912), 316–20, 342–7.

Moody, T.W., F.X. Martin, and F.J. Byrne (eds.). *A New History of Ireland*, vol. III, *Early Modern Ireland, 1534–1691*. Oxford: Clarendon Press, 1976.

Moody, T.W., and W.E. Vaughn (eds.). *A New History of Ireland*, vol. IV, *Eighteenth-Century Ireland, 1691–1800*. Oxford: Clarendon Press, 1986.

Morgan, Edmund. *American Slavery, American Freedom: The Ordeal of Colonial Virginia*. New York: W.W. Norton Inc., 1975.

Naipaul, V.S. *A Way in the World. A Sequence*. London: orig. pub. 1994, Minerva edition, 1995.

Nash, R.C. "Irish Atlantic Trade in the Seventeenth and Eighteenth Centuries," *William and Mary Quarterly*, 3 ser., vol. 42 (July 1985), 329–56.

O'Brien, Conor Cruise. *The Great Melody. A Thematic Biography and Commented Anthology of Edmund Burke*. Chicago: University of Chicago Press, 1992.

O'Buachalla, Breandan. "The Making of a Cork Jacobite," in Patrick O'Flanagan and Cornelius G. Buttimer, *Cork History and Society. Interdisciplinary*

Essays on the History of an Irish County. Dublin: Geography Publications, 1993, 469–97.

O'Cuiv, Brian. "James Cotter, a Seventeenth-Century Agent of the Crown," *Journal of the Royal Society of Antiquaries of Ireland*, vol. 89 (1959), 135–59.

O'Danachair, Caoimhin. "A Timber-Frame House near Slane, County Meath," *Ulster Folklife*, vol. 14 (1968), 24–7.

Ohlmeyer, Jane H. (ed.). *Ireland from Independence to Occupation, 1641–1660.* Cambridge: Cambridge University Press, 1995.

Oliver, Vere Langford. *The History of the Island of Antigua, one of the Leeward Caribbees in the West Indies from the first settlement in 1635 to the present time.* London: Mitchell and Hughes, 1884. 2 vols.

O'Riordan, Michelle. *The Gaelic Mind and the Collapse of the Gaelic World.* Cork: Cork University Press, 1990.

Pactor, Howard S. (compiler). *Colonial British Caribbean Newspapers. A Bibliography and Directory.* New York: Greenwood Press, 1990.

Palmer, William. *The Problem of Ireland in Tudor Foreign Policy, 1485–1603.* Woodbridge, Suffolk: Boydell Press, 1994.

Pares, Richard. *A West-India Fortune.* London: Longmans, Green and Co., 1950.

Parry, J.H. and P.M. Sherlock. *A Short History of the West Indies.* London: MacMillan and Co., 1956.

Parsons, Elsie Clews. *Folk-Lore of the Antilles, French and English.* New York: American Folklore Society, Part I, 1936; Part III, 1943.

Patterson, George (ed.). *A Few Remains of the Rev. James MacGregor, D.D.* Edinburgh: William Oliphant and Co., 1859.

Patterson, Orlando. *Slavery and Social Death. A Comparative Study.* Cambridge: Harvard University Press, 1982.

Perceval-Maxwell, Michael. *The Scottish Migration to Ulster in the Reign of James I.* London: Routledge and Kegan Paul, 1973.

Philpott, Stuart B. *West Indian Migration: The Montserrat Case.* London: Athlone Press, 1973.

Pitman, Frank Wesley. *The Development of the British West Indies, 1700–1763.* New Haven: Yale University Press, 1917.

Plomer, Henry R., and Tom Peete Cross. *The Life and Correspondence of Lodowick Bryskett.* Chicago: University of Chicago Press, 1927.

Power, Thomas P. "Parliamentary Representation in County Kilkenny in the Eighteenth Century," in William Nolan and Kevin Whelan (eds.), *Kilkenny: History and Society. Interdisciplinary Essays on the History of an Irish County.* Dublin: Geography Publications, 1990, 305–32.

– *Land, Politics and Society in Eighteenth-Century Tipperary.* Oxford: Clarendon Press, 1993.

– and Kevin Whelan (eds.). *Endurance and Emergence. Catholics in Ireland in the Eighteenth Century.* Dublin: Irish Academic Press, 1990.

Prendergast, John P. *The Cromwellian Settlement of Ireland*. Dublin: McGlashan and Gill, second ed., 1875.

[Anon]. *The Present Posture and Condition of Ireland*. London: n.p., 1652.

Pulsipher, Lydia M. "The Cultural Landscape of Montserrat, West Indies, in the Seventeenth Century: Early Environmental Consequences of British Colonial Development." PH.D. dissertation, Southern Illinois University, 1977.

– "Ridged Fields in Montserrat, West Indies," *Proceedings of the Association of American Geographers, Middle States Division*, vol. 12 (1978), 77–80.

– "English, Irish and African Influences on the Landscape of Seventeenth Century Montserrat in the West Indies," *Proceedings of the Association of American Geographers, Middle States Division*, vol. 13 (1979), 5–13.

– "Resource Management Strategies on an Eighteenth-Century Caribbean Sugar Plantation: Interpreting the Archaeological and Archival Records," *Florida Anthropologist*, vol. 35 (Dec. 1982), 243–9.

– *Seventeenth Century Montserrat: An Environmental Impact Statement*. Norwich: Geo Books, 1986.

– "Assessing the Usefulness of a Cartographic Curiosity: The 1673 Map of a Sugar Island," *Annals of the Association of American Geographers*, vol. 77 (Sept. 1987), 408–22.

– and Conrad M. Goodwin, "A Sugar Boiling House at Galways. An Irish Sugar Plantation in Montserrat, West Indies," *Post-Medieval Archeology*, vol. 16 (1982), 21–7.

Quinn, David B. *England and the Discovery of North America, 1481–1620*. London: Allen and Unwin, 1974.

– *Ireland and America. Their Early Associations, 1500–1640*. Liverpool: Liverpool University Press, 1991.

Ragatz, Lowell J. *The Fall of the Planter Class in the British Caribbean, 1763–1833. A Study in Social and Economic History.* New York: orig. pub. 1928; reprinted Octagon Books, 1971.

Reaney, P.H. *A Dictionary of British Surnames*. London: Routledge and Kegan Paul, 1958.

Robinson, Philip. *The Plantation of Ulster. British Settlement in an Irish Landscape, 1600–1670*. Dublin: Gill and Macmillan, 1984.

Rooke, Patricia T. "Papists and Proselytizers: Non-denominational Education in the British Caribbean after Emancipation," *History of Education*, vol. 23 (1994), 257–73.

Sheppard, Jill. "A Historical Sketch of the Poor Whites of Barbados: From Indentured Servants to 'Redlegs,'" *Caribbean Studies*, vol. 14 (Oct. 1974), 71–94.

– *The "Redlegs" of Barbados. Their Origins and History.* Millwood, N.Y.: KTO Press, 1981.

Sheridan, Richard B. *Sugar and Slavery. An Economic History of the British West Indies, 1623–1775*. Baltimore: Johns Hopkins University Press, 1973.

Sires, Ronald V. "Government in the British West Indies: An Historical Outline," *Social and Economic Studies*, vol. 6 (June 1957), 108–21.

Smith, John. *The Generall Historie of Virginia, New England and The Summer Isles, together with The True Travels, Adventures, and Observations, and A Sea Grammar.* Glasgow: James MacLehose reprint ed., 1907. 2 vols.

– *True Travels, Adventures, and Observations*. London: n.p., 1630.

Smyth, William J. "The Western Isle of Ireland and the Eastern Seaboard of America -England's First Frontiers," *Irish Geography*, vol. 11 (1978), 1–22.

– and Kevin Whelan. *Common Ground*. Cork: Cork University Press, 1988.

Sokolov, Raymond. "History in a Stewpot. Irish and Yoruba Traditions Meet on the Island of Montserrat," *Natural History*, vol. 101 (Nov. 1992), 78–82.

Solow, Barbara L. *Slavery and the Rise of the Atlantic System*. Cambridge: Cambridge University Press, 1991.

– and Stanley I. Engerman (eds.). *British Capitalism and Caribbean Slavery: The Legacy of Eric Williams*. Cambridge: Cambridge University Press, 1987.

Sturge, Joseph, and Thomas Harvey. *The West Indies in 1837, being the journal of a visit to Antigua, Montserrat, Dominica, St. Lucia, Barbados and Jamaica, undertaken for the purpose of ascertaining the actual condition of the Negro population of those islands*. London: Hamilton, Adams and Co., 1838.

Thornton, Archibald P. *West-India Policy under the Restoration*. Oxford: Clarendon Press, 1956.

Travis, Carole (ed.). *A Guide to Latin American and Caribbean Census Material. A Bibliography and Union List*. London: The British Library, 1950.

Truxes, Thomas M. *Irish-American Trade 1660–1783*. Cambridge: Cambridge University Press, 1988.

Walne, Peter (ed.). *A Guide to Manuscript Sources for the History of Latin America and the Caribbean in the British Isles*. London: Oxford University Press, 1973.

Ward, J.R. *British West Indian Slavery, 1750–1834. The Process of Amelioration*. Oxford: Clarendon Press, 1988.

Watson, James L. (ed.). *Asian and African Systems of Slavery*. Berkeley: University of California Press, 1980.

Waugh, Alec. *Love and the Caribbean. Tales, Characters, and Scenes of the West Indies*. New York: Farrar, Straus and Cudahy, 1958.

Wells, J.H. "The Brogue that Isn't," *Journal of the International Phonetics Association*, vol. 10 (1980), 74–9.

Wells, Robert V. *The Population of the British Colonies in America before 1776*. Princeton: Princeton University Press, 1975.

Whelan, Kevin, and William Nolan (eds.). *Wexford: History and Society*. Dublin: Geography Publications, 1987.

White, Laurie C. *Montserrat. A Bibliography*. Plymouth: The Public Library, 1977.

Williams, Eric. *British Historians and the West Indies*. Trinidad: P.N.M. Publishing, 1964.

– *Capitalism and Slavery*. Chapel Hill: University of North Carolina Press, 1944.

Williamson, James A. *The Caribbee Islands under the Proprietary Patents*. London: Oxford University Press, 1926.

– *English Colonies in Guiana and on the Amazon, 1604–1668*. Oxford: Clarendon Press, 1923.

Wilson, David. *The Irish in Canada*. Ottawa: Canadian Historical Association, 1987.

Winchester, Simon. *Outposts*. London: Hodder and Stoughton, 1985.

Woulfe, Patrick. *Sloinnte Gaedheal is Gall*. Dublin: M.H. Gill and Son, 1923.

Index